IBM's Official Guide to Building a Better Web Site

by
Deborah Morrison

An IBM Press Book

IDG Books Worldwide, Inc.
An International Data Group Company

Foster City, CA ✦ Chicago, IL ✦ Indianapolis, IN ✦ Braintree, MA ✦ Dallas, TX

IBM's Official Guide to Building a Better Web Site
An IBM Press Book

Published by
IDG Books Worldwide, Inc.
An International Data Group Company
919 E. Hillsdale Blvd.
Suite 400
Foster City, CA 94404

Library of Congress Catalog Card No.: 95-79926

ISBN: 1-56884-599-5

Printed in the United States of America

10 9 8 7 6 5 4 3 2 1

1B/RT/RR/ZV

Distributed in the United States by IDG Books Worldwide, Inc.

Distributed by Macmillan Canada for Canada; by Computer and Technical Books for the Caribbean Basin; by Contemporanea de Ediciones for Venezuela; by Distribuidora Cuspide for Argentina; by CITEC for Brazil; by Ediciones ZETA S.C.R. Ltda. for Peru; by Editorial Limusa SA for Mexico; by Transworld Publishers Limited in the United Kingdom and Europe; by Al-Maiman Publishers & Distributors for Saudi Arabia; by Simron Pty. Ltd. for South Africa; by IDG Communications (HK) Ltd. for Hong Kong; by Toppan Company Ltd. for Japan; by Addison Wesley Publishing Company for Korea; by Longman Singapore Publishers Ltd. for Singapore, Malaysia, Thailand, and Indonesia; by Unalis Corporation for Taiwan; by WS Computer Publishing Company, Inc. for the Philippines; by WoodsLane Pty. Ltd. for Australia; by WoodsLane Enterprises Ltd. for New Zealand.

For general information on IDG Books Worldwide's books in the U.S., please call our Consumer Customer Service department at 800-762-2974. For reseller information, including discounts and premium sales, please call our Reseller Customer Service department at 800-434-3422.

For information on where to purchase IDG Books Worldwide's books outside the U.S., contact IDG Books Worldwide at 415-655-3021 or fax 415-655-3295.

For information on translations, contact Marc Jeffrey Mikulich, Director, Foreign & Subsidiary Rights, at IDG Books Worldwide, 415-655-3018 or fax 415-655-3295.

For sales inquiries and special prices for bulk quantities, write to the address above or call IDG Books Worldwide at 415-655-3200.

For information on using IDG Books Worldwide's books in the classroom, or ordering examination copies, contact Jim Kelly at 800-434-2086.

For authorization to photocopy items for corporate, personal, or educational use, please contact Copyright Clearance Center, 222 Rosewood Drive, Danvers, MA 01923, or fax 508-750-4470.

About the author

Deborah Morrison is an award-winning author who has received corporate recognition for her work on TCP/IP. She works for the Networking Software division of IBM located in Research Triangle Park, North Carolina, and is the editor-in-chief of IBM's Internet Connections magazine. She is also the author of another IBM Press book, *OS/2 Warp Internet Connection: Your Key to Cruising the Internet and the World Wide Web.*

About IBM Press

IBM Press is committed to bringing you high-quality books about IBM products and technologies. You can count on IBM Press to provide books that are of interest to all computer users—home and office users, network and systems administrators, and application developers and programmers.

It is our pleasure to present another in the series of IBM Press books — *IBM's Official Guide to Building a Better Web Site.* We are especially pleased to introduce this book because it is the first guide for the World Wide Web that is authorized by IBM.

Inside these pages, readers will learn about the benefits of the Web and how they can join in. Written in plain English, this guide provides complete instructions for creating information for the Web, setting up your own Web server, and notifying the world of your presence on the Web.

We hope you'll enjoy this guide and that you find it to be the perfect blueprint for building the best Web site.

Beth Tripi

Imprint Manager

International Business Machines Corporation

Welcome to the world of IDG Books Worldwide.

IDG Books Worldwide, Inc., is a subsidiary of International Data Group, the world's largest publisher of computer-related information and the leading global provider of information services on information technology. IDG was founded more than 25 years ago and now employs more than 7,700 people worldwide. IDG publishes more than 250 computer publications in 67 countries (see listing below). More than 70 million people read one or more IDG publications each month.

Launched in 1990, IDG Books Worldwide is today the #1 publisher of best-selling computer books in the United States. We are proud to have received 8 awards from the Computer Press Association in recognition of editorial excellence and three from Computer Currents' First Annual Readers' Choice Awards, and our best-selling ...*For Dummies*® series has more than 19 million copies in print with translations in 28 languages. IDG Books Worldwide, through a joint venture with IDG's Hi-Tech Beijing, became the first U.S. publisher to publish a computer book in the People's Republic of China. In record time, IDG Books Worldwide has become the first choice for millions of readers around the world who want to learn how to better manage their businesses.

Our mission is simple: Every IDG and IBM Press book is designed to bring extra value and skill-building instructions to the reader. Our books are written by experts who understand and care about our readers. The knowledge base of our editorial staff comes from years of experience in publishing, education, and journalism — experience which we use to produce books for the '90s. In short, we care about books, so we attract the best people. We devote special attention to details such as audience, interior design, use of icons, and illustrations. And because we use an efficient process of authoring, editing, and desktop publishing our books electronically, we can spend more time ensuring superior content and spend less time on the technicalities of making books.

You can count on our commitment to deliver high-quality books at competitive prices on topics you want to read about. At IDG Books Worldwide, we continue in the IDG tradition of delivering quality for more than 25 years. You'll find no better book on a subject than one from IDG Books Worldwide.

John J. Kilcullen

John Kilcullen
President and CEO
IDG Books Worldwide, Inc.

IDG Books Worldwide, Inc., is a subsidiary of International Data Group, the world's largest publisher of computer-related information and the leading global provider of information services on information technology. International Data Group publishes over 250 computer publications in 67 countries. Seventy million people read one or more International Data Group publications each month. International Data Group's publications include: **ARGENTINA:** Computerworld Argentina, GamePro, Infoworld, PC World Argentina; **AUSTRALIA:** Australian Macworld, Client/Server Journal, Computer Living, Computerworld, Digital News, Network World, PC World, Publishing Essentials, Reseller; **AUSTRIA:** Computerwelt, PC TEST; **BELARUS:** PC World Belarus; **BELGIUM:** Data News; **BRAZIL:** Annuário de Informática, Computerworld Brazil, Connections, Super Game Power, Macworld, PC World Brazil, Publish Brazil, SUPERGAME; **BULGARIA:** Computerworld Bulgaria, Networkworld/Bulgaria, PC & MacWorld Bulgaria; **CANADA:** CIO Canada, ComputerWorld Canada, InfoCanada, Network World Canada, Reseller World; **CHILE:** Computerworld Chile, GamePro, PC World Chile; **COLUMBIA:** Computerworld Colombia, GamePro, PC World Colombia; **COSTA RICA:** PC World Costa Rica/Nicaragua; **THE CZECH AND SLOVAK REPUBLICS:** Computerworld Czechoslovakia, Elektronika Czechoslovakia, PC World Czechoslovakia; **DENMARK:** Communications World, Computerworld Danmark, Macworld Danmark, PC World Danmark, PC World Danmark Supplements, TECH World; **DOMINICAN REPUBLIC:** PC World Republica Dominicana; **ECUADOR:** PC World Ecuador, GamePro; **EGYPT:** Computerworld Middle East, PC World Middle East; **EL SALVADOR:** PC World Centro America; **FINLAND:** MikroPC, Tietoverkko, Tietoviikko; **FRANCE:** Distribitique, Golden, Info PC, Le Guide du Monde Informatique, Le Monde Informatique, Reseaux & Telecoms; **GERMANY:** Computer Business, Computerwoche, Computerwoche Extra, Computerwoche Focus, Electronic Entertainment, GamePro, I/M Information Management, Macwelt, PC Welt; **GREECE:** GamePro, Macworld & Publish; **GUATEMALA:** PC World Centro America; **HONDURAS:** PC World Centro America; **HONG KONG:** Computerworld Hong Kong, PCWorld Hong Kong, Publish in Asia; **HUNGARY:** ABCD CD-ROM, Computerworld Szamitastechnika, PC & Mac World Hungary, PC-X Magazine; **INDIA:** Computerworld India, PC World India, Publish in Asia; **INDONESIA:** InfoKomputer PC World, Komputek Computerworld, Publish in Asia; **IRELAND:** ComputerScope, PC Live!; **ISRAEL:** PC World 32 BIT, People & Computers; **ITALY:** Computerworld Italia, Computerworld Italia Special Editions, Lotus Italia, Macworld Italia, Networking Italia, PC Shopping, PC World Italia, PC World/Walt Disney; **JAPAN:** Macworld Japan, Nikkei Personal Computing, SunWorld Japan, Windows World Japan; **KENYA:** East African Computer News; **KOREA:** Hi-Tech Information/Computerworld, Macworld Korea, PC World Korea; **MACEDONIA:** PC World Macedonia; **MALAYSIA:** Computerworld Malaysia, PC World Malaysia, Publish in Asia; **MEXICO:** Computerworld Mexico, GamePro, Macworld, PC World Mexico; **MYANMAR:** PC World Myanmar; **NETHERLANDS:** Computable, Computer! Totaal, LAN Magazine, Macworld, Net Magazine; **NEW ZEALAND:** Computer Buyer, Computerworld New Zealand, MTB, Network World, PC World New Zealand; **NICARAGUA:** PC World Costa Rica/Nicaragua; **NIGERIA:** PC World Africa; **NORWAY:** Computerworld Norge, Computerworld Privat, CW Rapport Klient/Tjener, CW Rapport Nettverk & Telecom, CW Rapport Offentlig Sektor, IDG's KURSGUIDE, Macworld Norge, Multimedia World, PC World Ekspress, PC World Nettverk, PC World Norge, PC World's Produktguide, Windows Spesial; **PAKISTAN:** Computerworld Pakistan, PC World Pakistan; **PANAMA:** GamePro, PC World Panama; **PARAGUAY:** PC World Paraguay; **P. R. OF CHINA:** China Computerworld, China Infoworld, Computer & Communication, Electronic Product World, Electronics Today, Game Camp, PC World China, Popular Computer Week, Software World, Telecom Product World; **PERU:** Computerworld Peru, GamePro, PC World Profesional Peru, PC World Peru; **POLAND:** Computerworld Poland, Computerworld Special Report, Macworld, Networld, PC World Komputer; **PHILIPPINES:** Computerworld Philippines, PC Digest, Publish in Asia; **PORTUGAL:** Cerebro/PC World, Correio Informático/Computerworld, Mac•In/PC•In Portugal; **PUERTO RICO:** PC World Puerto Rico; **ROMANIA:** Computerworld Romania, PC World Romania, Telecom Romania; **RUSSIA:** Computerworld Rossiya, Network World Russia, PC World Russia; **SINGAPORE:** Computerworld Singapore, PC World Singapore, Publish in Asia; **SLOVENIA:** MONITOR; **SOUTH AFRICA:** Computing S.A., Network World S.A., Software World; **SPAIN:** Computerworld España, COMUNICACIONES WORLD, Dealer World, Macworld España, PC World España; **SWEDEN:** CAP&Design, Computer Sweden, Corporate Computing, MacWorld, Maxi Data, MikroDatorn, Nätverk & Kommunikation, PC/Aktiv, PC World, Windows World; **SWITZERLAND:** Computerworld Schweiz, Macworld Schweiz, PCtip; **TAIWAN:** Computerworld Taiwan, Macworld Taiwan, Publish Taiwan, Windows World; **THAILAND:** Thai Computerworld, Publish in Asia; **TURKEY:** Computerworld Monitör, MACWORLD Turkiye, PC WORLD Turkiye; **UKRAINE:** Computerworld Kiev, Computers & Software Magazine, PC World Ukraine; **UNITED KINGDOM:** Acorn User, Amiga Action, Amiga Computing, Amiga, Appletalk, CD Powerplay, CD-ROM Now, Computing, Connexion, GamePro, Lotus Magazine, Macaction, Macworld, Open Computing, Parents and Computers, PC Home, PC Works, The WEB; **UNITED STATES:** Cable in the Classroom, CD Review, CIO Magazine, Computerworld, Computerworld Client/Server Journal, Digital Video Magazine, DOS World, Electronic, InfoWorld, I-Way, Macworld, Maximize, MULTIMEDIA WORLD, Network World, PC World, PUBLISH, SWATPro Magazine, Video Event, WebMaster; **URUGUAY:** PC World Uruguay; **VENEZUELA:** Computerworld Venezuela, GamePro, PC World Venezuela; and **VIETNAM:** PC World Vietnam   10/17/95

Acknowledgments

The author wishes to thank her husband, Tony Morrison, for his endless patience and constant encouragement.

In addition, she would like extend a special thanks to:

Diane Figueroa for her tireless support throughout the creation of this book.

Gretchen Moore for her excellent editing and infinite patience.

Thanks to the following people for their contributions:

David Bradford	Marla Martin
Terry Foster	Dan Nagy
John Holtman	Ravi Narasimhan Raj

Thanks to the following people for their assistance:

Gavin Bell	Rick Jansen
Thomas Boutell	Leonid Kitainik
Mike Callahan	Chini Krishnan
John Christy	Paula Lupriore
Drew Clark	Paul Luther
Dr. Grahame Cooper	Peter Moree
Dave Dalva	David Nessl
Jim Diefendorff	Julian Perry
Carl Forde	Igor Plotnikov
Jeanette Fucella	Paul Schmidt
Dave Garaffa	Linas Vepstas
Chris Hector	Norma Wolcott
Natasha Hyndman	David Wood
John Irwin	

The author would also like to acknowledge the following companies and organizations for their programs, products, and services mentioned in this book:

Adobe Systems Incorporated
Aldus Corporation
Alias Research Incorporated
Apple Computer, Incorporated
Asymetrix Corporation
AutoDesk, Incorporated
BBS One Online Service
BC Systems
CompuServe, Incorporated
Conseil Europeen pour la Recherche Nucleaire (CERN)
Corel Systems Corporation
Dataplace B. V.
Digital Equipment Corporation (DEC)
Enterprise Integration Technologies Corporation (EIT)
Freemont Avenue Software
Hewlett-Packard Company
Information Warehouse, Incorporated
Inset Systems
Intel Corporation
Interleaf, Incorporated
International Business Machines (IBM)
Intervista Software, Incorporated
Limitless Technical Dimensions
Livermore Software Laboratories, Incorporated
Lotus Development Corporation
Matterform Media
Micrografx Incorporated
Microsoft Corporation
National Center for Supercomputing Applications (NCSA)
NaviSoft Incorporated
Netscape Communications Corporation
Novell Incorporated
Pacifica Blue Corporation
Paragraph International

Photodex Corporation
Radiance Software International
RSA Data Security, Incorporated (RSA)
Silicon Graphics, Incorporated (SGI)
SoftQuad Incorporated
Spyglass, Incorporated
Sun Microsystems, Incorporated (Sun)
Trusted Information System, Incorporated (TIS)
UniPress Software, Incorporated
Unisys Corporation
Wavefront Technologies, Incorporated
The Web Factory
Web Towers
W3 Consortium
Yahoo

Shortened forms of these company names are used in this book. All trademarks are owned by their respective companies.

Credits

IBM PRESS STAFF

Imprint Manager
Beth Tripi

Acquisitions Manager
Diane Walewski

RTP Manager
Diane Figueroa

Managing Editor
Gretchen Moore

Cover Designer
Jeffery Lewis

Designers
Dan Nagy
Margie Stewart

Production Manager
Ginny Black

Production Specialist
John Mangrum

IDG BOOKS WORLDWIDE STAFF

Vice President and Publisher
Brenda McLaughlin

Publishing Director
John Osborne

Brand Manager
Pradeepa Siva

Associate Developmental Editor
Amy Marks

Editor
Anne Marie Walker

Production Director
Beth Jenkins

Supervisor of Project Coordination
Cindy L. Phipps

Supervisor of Page Layout
Kathie S. Schnorr

Associate Project Coordinator
Sherry Gomoll

Pre-Press Coordination
Tony Augsburger
Patricia Reynolds
Theresa Sánchez-Baker

Production Staff
Maridee Ennis
Laura Puranen

Proofreaders
Betty Kish
Gwenette Gaddis
Dwight Ramsey
Carl Saff
Robert Springer

Table of Contents

Welcome

To the reader

Welcome to the most comprehensive, step-by-step guide for establishing a presence on the World Wide Web!

The World Wide Web is one of the fastest growing means of communication in history. Using the Web, more people have faster access to a greater amount of information than ever before. Whether you are a company trying to reach your customers and potential customers, an organization looking for a better way to spread your message, or an individual wanting to make a statement to the world—you should be on the Web.

This self-contained book gives you the total picture and all the information you need to establish a presence on the Web. No other source is needed. Written with the novice *and* the expert in mind, this book removes the mystery of the Web while providing tips and techniques useful to even the most experienced Webmaster. This book is for *anyone* who wants to take advantage of the power of the Web.

Organization of this book

Part One is written to the person who creates the information for the Web.

Part Two is written to the person who sets up and maintains the Web server.

Part Three is a handy reference. It describes each of the HTML 2.0 tags, explains how to decipher URLs (Web addresses), provides a list of useful Web resources, and includes several coding examples.

Conventions used in this book

To make the book easier to read and use, we have established some conventions for this book:

The URLs of Web documents (or other resources) are **bold**.

New words defined in text are ***bold italic***.

Variables, or placeholders in code, are *italic*.

Caveats

In an effort to make this book more useful, we include many references to additional information on the Web. We have made every effort to ensure that the Web addresses (URLs) are listed correctly. However, because the Web is a dynamic entity, changes may occur that cause the URL we list to be inaccurate. If this should occur, we apologize for any inconvenience and ask that you send an e-mail message to TCPIPNEWS@VNET.IBM.COM and make us aware of the change.

Also, in this book, we describe many programs, products, and services. We want to provide you with as much information as possible to assist you in your tasks. However, mention of a program, product, or service in this book does not constitute any endorsement by the author, the publisher, or IBM.

ile   **O**ptions   **C**onfigure   **N**avigate   **Q**uickList   **H**elp

http://www.austin.ibm.com/ibmpress/

PART ONE

WRITING FOR THE WEB

IDG BOOKS
WORLDWIDE

his part of the book is written to the Web editor and explains how to create HTML documents for the World Wide Web. There are eight chapters that make up this part of the book.

Chapter 1, "Introduction to the Web," discusses what the Web is, how it got started, and how it works.

Chapter 2, "A tour of Web browsers," discusses what a Web browser is and how one works. It also provides brief descriptions of several of the more popular browsers.

Chapter 3, "Designing information for the Web," discusses the opportunities and challenges inherent in writing on-line information, particularly Web information. The majority of the chapter provides tips for writing Web information.

Chapter 4, "Creating an HTML document," discusses the steps involved in creating an HTML document. It also provides brief descriptions of some of the tools that you can use to create and edit HTML documents, including conversion tools.

Chapter 5, "Including images in your document," discusses the types of images that can be used in Web documents, how you can create them, and how you can use them to improve the usefulness of your document.

Chapter 6, "Including forms in your document," discusses the types of forms and the purpose of each, as well as how they work and how you can use them in your document.

Chapter 7, "Including multimedia in your document," discusses how you can use multimedia in your document. It describes four types of multimedia: animation, audio clips, video clips, and virtual reality. It also discusses the requirements for creating multimedia, as well as the requirements for playback of each type.

Chapter 8, "Testing and maintaining your document," discusses the steps you should take to ensure the quality of your document. It also provides some tips about creating documents in such a dynamic medium.

Introduction to the Web

omputers and computer technology have been around for decades. And personal computers have been accessible to the public for many years. But it seems that it took the introduction of the Internet, and specifically the World Wide Web, to capture the public's attention and make computers a common household item. Now, people who had never before touched a computer are spending hours "surfing" the World Wide Web, catching up on the latest news and sports, trying out free programs and games, exchanging opinions on countless topics, ordering items from their favorite catalogue, and more. It is a phenomenon that is sweeping the world.

Where did the Web come from? How does it work? And who created it? Is it as new as it seems, or has it just now been made available to the general public? This chapter answers these and many other questions. It describes the sequence of events that led up to the first implementation of the Web and provides an overview of the technologies involved. It also offers some thoughts on how the Web can be useful to you, as a user or a provider.

Chapter 1. Introduction to the Web

What the World Wide Web is

The *World Wide Web* (the Web, for short) is the fastest growing communication medium in history, providing access to information on a wide (and ever increasing) variety of topics, as well as access to services that allow you to order merchandise on-line, obtain software on-line, and more. Superimposed over the Internet, the Web is a network of servers that contain hypertext documents. It started as a simplified means of sharing scientific data, but it has blossomed into far more.

Background information on the Web, including a copy of the initial proposal that started the Web, can be found at the following URL:
http://www.w3.org/hypertext/WWW/Project/Background/Overview.html.

Also, there is a multimedia overview of the Web that was developed by Xerox at **http://pubweb.parc.xerox.com/hypertext/wwwvideo/wwwvideo.html**.

If you are unfamiliar with URLs, see the explanation on page 11.

What makes the Web possible

The Web is based on three key inventions: client/server technology, the Internet, and hypertext.

Client/server technology

Over the years the size and complexity of software programs have grown. Although the capacity of computers and the skill of users have also increased, the computer industry recognized the need to reduce the space requirements of the programs and to centralize the management of databases used by the programs. With the advent of networking came the concept of *client/server technology*.

In client/server technology, the functions of a program are divided into two or more separate processes that are distributed between the client and the server. The *client* provides the user with the interface, while the *server* provides centralized data management, security, and information sharing. The clients (which are numerous) request services (access to information and additional functions) from the servers (which are fewer in number). In the Web, the client is called a *Web browser*, which is a program located on a user's computer. The Web browser can access information and functions on Web servers.

The Internet

The *Internet* is a computer network that spans the globe and links more than 20 million users. Users of the Internet include: universities, corporations, nonprofit organizations, and individuals who want to acquire, distribute, and share information.

When the Internet was first introduced, it was managed by a branch of the Department of Defense (DOD) called the Advanced Research Projects Agency (ARPA) and was known as the ARPANet. The ARPANet then became so popular (with numerous nonmilitary participants) that it was divided into two parts: the original ARPANet, for the nonmilitary participants, and the MILNet, for the military participants. Soon, members of the National Science Foundation research facilities (some of whom were already interconnected) joined with the ARPANet and formed the NSFNet.

Today's Internet is composed of these and other networks in the U.S. and almost every other country in the world. It links together thousands of organizations and millions of users in a global communications network, providing services such as electronic bulletin boards, electronic mail, and the World Wide Web.

The basis for the Internet is an ever-evolving set of *protocols* called *Transmission Control Protocol/Internet Protocol* (TCP/IP). A protocol is a set of rules for governing the exchange of data. The TCP/IP protocols are described in documents called Request For Comments (RFCs), which are developed through a process that is overseen by the Internet Architecture Board (IAB).

There is a helpful list of documents about the Internet provided by Joann Miller at **http://info.er.usgs.gov/network/resources.html**.

There is also a brief chronology of the Internet at **http://tig.com/IBC/Timeline.html**.

Hypertext

Hypertext is the concept (and practice) of linking *nodes* of related on-line information. Nodes are discrete "chunks" of information. At first, nodes were limited to documents or sections of documents. However, with the development of enhanced image support and audio and video cards, the possibilities have dramatically increased. In fact, today many people still use the term hypertext to describe inter-connected information, but *hypermedia* would be a more accurate description.

In some implementations of hypertext, all the nodes of information reside in a single physical location. In the Web, however, nodes may be in the same or different locations. For example, a document describing great authors of the 19th century that is located on a Web server in North Carolina may contain a link to a document describing

Charles Dickens' life that is located on a Web server in England, which may contain links to on-line versions of his works located on a Web server in New York. However, because the links appear only as highlighted words or framed images, the fact that the information is scattered across several locations is not apparent to the reader.

In contrast to printed information, which is linear, hypertext neither assumes nor presents a single path for the reader. Readers can arrive at a node from numerous places and are free to select their next node from the available links. While this opens up numerous possibilities for both the writer and the reader, it also makes navigation more complex. But writers can counter the complexity with careful writing and the judicious use of navigation cues.

There is a helpful list of such design considerations provided by Michael Herrick of Matterform Media at
http://www.matterform.com/mf/hypermedia/hypermediahome2.html.

How the Web evolved

There are a number of events that have taken place over the years that have made the World Wide Web possible. Most of them have occurred rather recently, while others occurred more than 50 years ago. The following table provides a snapshot of the evolution of the Web.

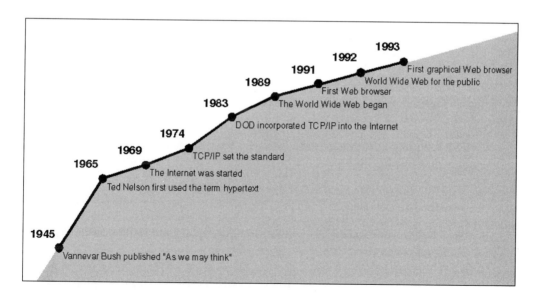

Figure 1-1. Evolution of the Web

1945	Vannevar Bush published an article, "As we may think," which proposed the idea of interconnecting on-line information.
1965	Ted Nelson first used the term hypertext to describe the concept of interconnected information.
1969	The Internet was initiated by the United States Department of Defense (DOD) as a means of connecting companies and universities that were working on military-related projects.
1974	Transmission Control Protocol/Internet Protocol (TCP/IP), the standard set of protocols used on the Internet, was developed by Robert Kahn and Vinton G. Cerf.
1983	The DOD completed the incorporation of TCP/IP into the Internet, resulting in the rebirth of the Internet as we know it today.
1989	The World Wide Web began at CERN (the European Laboratory for Particle Physics in Geneva, Switzerland) with a proposal written by Tim Berners-Lee, who sought to give researchers a better way to share information.
1991	The first line-mode Web browser was released to a limited audience at CERN.
1992	CERN completed work on its first browser and made the Web available to the public.
1993	The first graphical Web browsers were made available to the public, including Mosaic, a very popular browser created by Chris Wilson and Jon Mittelhauser at the National Center for Supercomputing Applications (NCSA) at the University of Illinois.

How the Web works

Although finding your way around the Web may be difficult (mainly due to the vast amount of accessible information), the principles of the Web are quite simple.

- The Web consists of a network of thousands of Web servers running the Hypertext Transfer Protocol daemon (HTTPD), physically connected via the Internet.

- Each Web server contains one or more documents that are written in the Hypertext Markup Language (HTML).

- Web browsers request the documents using a standard format called a Uniform Resource Locator (URL). This same format is used to establish links between hypertext documents.

- Requests and responses are exchanged between Web browsers and Web servers using the Hypertext Transfer Protocol (HTTP).

As part of the Internet, the Web is governed by the Internet Architecture Board (IAB). However, there is another organization, the W3 Consortium, which also lends a hand in overseeing the Web. The W3 Consortium is run by the Massachusetts Institute of Technology (MIT) in collaboration with CERN.

Information about the W3 Consortium can be found at **http://www.w3.org/hypertext/WWW/Consortium**.

Web browsers

A *Web browser* is a client program that provides an interface to the World Wide Web. It establishes the connection to the specified Web server, interprets and formats the information found on the server, and displays the formatted information. And, despite the name, a browser can do much more than browse. Most browsers, for example, also allow you to obtain copies of files from FTP servers, correspond with other users, participate in on-line forums, and log into remote computers.

The first Web browsers were strictly line-mode. It wasn't long, however, before the full-screen, graphical browsers appeared. Today, numerous browsers are available for a variety of environments, including Windows, OS/2, UNIX, NeXT, VM, VMS, and Macintosh.

Web browsers are discussed in more detail in Chapter 2, "A tour of Web browsers."

There is information about several browsers (including instructions for downloading many) at **http://www.w3.org/hypertext/WWW/Clients**.

HTML

Hypertext Markup Language (HTML) is a set of markup tags that you include in a file to govern the formatting of the information and the behavior of selectable elements.

- Formatting tags govern the font, size, and placement of information. For example, heading tags placed around a string of text cause the text to be displayed on a separate line in a larger, bold font.

- Behavior tags govern the interaction between the reader and the Web. For example, anchor tags placed around a string of text cause the Web browser to link to the specified information when the reader selects the text.

HTML is based on Standard Generalized Markup Language (SGML), a developing standard for word-processing programs. SGML will allow disparate word-processing programs to import (receive) source files from one another and to export (produce) numerous types of formatted output, such as PostScript and various on-line help file formats. Unlike an SGML document, however, HTML documents exist on the Web servers in an unformatted state. The Web browser interprets the HTML coding in the file and formats the information.

HTML is discussed in more detail starting with Chapter 4, "Creating an HTML document."

The current specifications for HTML can be found at **http://www.w3.org/hypertext/WWW/MarkUp/HTML.html**.

HTTP

The *Hypertext Transfer Protocol* (HTTP) is the protocol that governs communication on the Web. It is a fast, *stateless*, application-level protocol. Stateless means that the connection between the client (the browser) and the server is maintained only as long as is necessary to process a request. HTTP defines how:

- The Web browser establishes a connection to the Web server

- The Web browser requests information from the Web server

- The Web server responds to the browser's request

- The Web server or browser closes the connection

HTTP is similar to the Multipurpose Internet Mail Exchange (MIME) protocol in the way it allows for transmission of multimedia files. However, there are some significant differences, such as the default character type for text files (MIME uses US-ASCII, and HTTP uses ISO88591), that prevent HTTP from being MIME-compliant.

Conducting business on the Internet has become very popular recently. You can order goods and services from companies that have a Web server. You simply fill out an on-line form, which may include your credit card number, and press the submission push button. As designed, HTTP does not provide any protection for such information, which has resulted in more than one case of credit card fraud. To address the security issue, an extension to HTTP, Secure HTTP, has been developed. S-HTTP provides a means of protecting the contents of the transaction and verifying the origin of the transaction.

The current specifications for HTTP can be found at **http://www.w3.org/hypertext/WWW/Protocols/HTTP/HTTP2.html**.

HTTPD

The *Hypertext Transfer Protocol daemon* (HTTPD) is the program that runs on the Web server and communicates with the Web browser. It controls the connection and processes the browser's requests.

Web servers are discussed in more detail in Chapter 10, "A tour of Web servers."

Information about CERN's implementation of HTTPD can be found at **http://www.w3.org/hypertext/WWW/Daemon/User/Guide.html**.

URL

Uniform Resource Locator (URL) is the standard identifier used to locate information on the Web. A URL is a form of a Universal Resource Identifier (URI), which is the standard syntax for encoding the names and addresses of entities on the Internet. URLs are used in HTML documents to specify the end point of a hypertext link. Also, most Web browsers allow you to directly enter a URL to request a specific document (or other information, such as a program).

A URL consists of two parts. The first part specifies the protocol that should be used to access the information. This is often **http**, but can be another protocol such as: ftp, gopher, telnet, or news. The second part specifies the location of information to be accessed. The syntax of this second part varies by protocol. For example, to access an HTML document on a Web server, the URL would consist of the protocol (http), the name of the Web server, and possibly the path and file name of the document. For example:

---

http://www.w3.org/hypertext/WWW/Status.html

To access a file on an FTP server, the URL would consist of the protocol (FTP), possibly the login information (password and userID), and the path of the file. For example:

---

ftp://ftp01.ny.us.ibm.net/pub/WebExplorer

If no login information is specified, "anonymous" is assumed for the userID.

For more information about URLs, see Appendix B, "Understanding URL formats." Additional information about URIs and URLs can be found at **http://www.w3.org/hypertext/WWW/Addressing/Addressing.html**.

WIT

WWW Interactive Talk (WIT) is a new (and experimental) method of communication on the Web. It is similar to a newsgroup in that it is a forum for exchange of ideas and information. But the format is different. WIT was created by Tim Berners-Lee and Ari Luotonen after the WWW Conference '94 as a means of communicating (and debating) technical proposals.

The WIT database contains a list of topics. Some topics are of a serious nature, such as the topic of security on the Web; others are more whimsical, such as a poll to gather a list of good movies. Within each topic is a list of proposed answers. Readers can join in the discussion by agreeing or disagreeing with a proposal or by proposing a new answer of their own.

Additional information about WIT can be found at **http://www.w3.org/hypertext/WWW/WIT/User/Overview.html**.

Benefits of the Web

The Web is beneficial to users and providers alike. The benefits can be grouped into three categories: reduced cost, reduced time, and increased scope.

Reduced cost

From a user's perspective, the Web can save you money in many ways. For example, it provides access to free software and information (such as the freeware on **www.cdrom.com** and the information on **www.loc.gov**). It also provides access to information about cost-saving programs, such as travel promotions and discounted on-line books and encyclopedias.

From a provider's perspective, the Web can also save your company or organization money in many ways. For example, if your company produces software, you can use the Web as a mechanism for on-line advertising, order management, and distribution, thereby saving your company the cost of traditional advertising, of toll-free order phone lines, and of manufacturing and distribution. If yours is an educational organization, you can use the Web to distribute information about upcoming courses and seminars and obtain registration information on-line, thereby saving your organization the cost of producing printed course catalogues and mailing registration forms to students.

Reduced time

From a user's perspective, having easy access to information, such as research data, up-to-the minute financial reports, and upgraded software, can save you a great deal of time. No need to drive to the community library to search for the reference material you need for tomorrow's report. No need to wait for the six o'clock news to find out the latest stock prices. And no need to wait for weeks while the software vendor sends you the latest upgrade for their programs.

From a provider's perspective, the ability to distribute information and files via the Web will save hours, even days of work. For example, if your company sells clothing, there is a continuous push to get the next season's catalogue out before the season begins. Usually, this means you must have everything (photos, descriptions, and prices) ready months in advance, because the catalogue has to be printed, and then mailed to your customers. If you publish your catalogue on the Web, there is no lag time for printing or for sending your catalogue across the country by trucks. The moment you complete your HTML catalogue, it is ready for distribution, and the moment it is stored on your Web server, it is available to your customers.

Increased scope

From a user's perspective, you can access information from resources around the world. If, for example, you want to plan a vacation to Paris but need more information before you go, you needn't contact your travel agent and wait for brochures sent by mail. Instead, you can go to the on-line tour of Paris and have the information, including pictures, right at your finger tips.

From a provider's perspective, you can reach colleagues, competitors, customers (and potential customers), and other interested parties all over the world immediately, simultaneously, and without having to spend a penny on phone calls or postage.

If, for example, you just started a small mail-order company, your catalogue mailing list would be limited to the names and addresses of people you know (or those on a mailing list that you purchase from another company). And the distribution of your first catalogue might also be limited by your budget. By placing your first catalogue on the World Wide Web, you can reach tens of thousands of potential customers and never waste a penny sending copies of your catalogue to uninterested customers.

A tour of Web browsers

browser is to the Web as your monitor is to your computer. A monitor allows you to access and work with the information stored in your computer; it provides an interface to the contents of your computer. A browser provides an interface to the contents of the Web. By definition, a Web browser is client software that establishes a connection to a Web server, requests information, and displays the returned information.

New browsers are entering the market at an astounding rate. And updates to existing browsers are popping up weekly. With so much to choose from, the choice should be easy, but it's not. This explosion of Web client offerings has made it difficult to keep up with who provides what in which environments and at what cost. In recognition of this problem, some people have begun maintaining repositories of browsers and information on browsers. Yahoo provides links to articles on Web browsers, including a review of Web browsers by PC Magazine. You can find this information at **http://www.yahoo.com/Computers/World_Wide_Web/Browsers/Articles/**. Dave Garaffa maintains a helpful repository of announcements, evaluations, and general information on browsers and related software. This repository, called BrowserWatch, can be found at **http://www.ski.mskcc.org/browserwatch/**.

As a user, you should "try out" several of the browsers in order to choose the one that is best for you. If you are building a Web site, you should access your Web site using a sampling of browsers to understand how the various browsers will handle the information you provide. This section provides an overview of browsers and describes some of the browsers available for different environments.

Chapter 2. A tour of Web browsers

The (short) history of Web browsers

As with the Web itself, the first Web browsers were developed at CERN. Nicola Pellow wrote the original line-mode browser, which was first demonstrated in December of 1990. In March of 1991, line-mode browsers for Vax, RS/6000, and Sun systems were made available to a limited audience. A little less than a year later, CERN made their line-mode browser available to the general public.

The line-mode browser continued to be the only Web client software until September of 1993 when the National Center for Supercomputing Applications (NCSA) at the University of Illinois released NCSA Mosaic. NCSA Mosaic, the first graphical browser, launched a new era in the Web's brief history. With NCSA Mosaic, the interface to the Web became friendlier, allowing novice users to access the vast repositories of information on the Web. NCSA Mosaic runs on UNIX, Windows, and Macintosh systems. In the brief time since the introduction of NCSA Mosaic, numerous other graphical browsers have been released, but NCSA Mosaic continues to be the favorite of many and the yardstick against which all other browsers are measured.

Browsers in general

Browsers are the interface to the Web. They all are designed with one purpose: to communicate with Web servers and display the information on those servers. To that end, there are some commonalties among browsers, regardless of the operating system and regardless of whether they are graphical or text-based browsers. In general, all browsers provide these basics:

- Highlight words and phrases that are links to other information

- Dynamically format text to fit the screen size

- Support the basic HTML tags, such as paragraphs and headings

- Allow users to set a default home page

- Provide a *hot list* function, which allows users to keep a list of interesting or frequently visited sites

- Allow users to view and save the HTML source of a document

- Allow users to retrace their path by allowing them to move backward and forward between previously viewed documents

There are numerous differences, though. For example, some browsers support more advanced HTML tags, such as tables. There are also differences in support for graphics (or images). Some browsers can display in-line JPEG images. And, last, but not least, there are certainly differences in the features provided by the browser. Some browsers support the use of proxies and various navigational aids.

The following sections describe a few of the numerous browsers available, highlighting the less common features that make each unique. However, because browsers are changing so rapidly, we encourage you to also test these and others for yourself. Lists of many of the most current browsers are available from **http://www.yahoo.com/Computers/World_Wide_Web/Browsers/** and from **http://www.w3.org/hypertext/WWW/Clients.html**.

NCSA Mosaic

NCSA Mosaic was the first graphical Web browser. It was created by Marc Andreessen at the National Center for Supercomputing Applications (NCSA) at the University of Illinois Urbana-Champaign. NCSA Mosaic is offered as a stand-alone application; NCSA does not provide any connection software.

Mosaic allows you to configure a broad range of parameters, including *proxy gateways*, which allow users within the confines of a secured network to access Web servers outside the network. Mosaic also supports *caching* and *presentation mode*. Using caching, the browser stores the documents and images you view in memory for easy, faster repeat access. In presentation mode, the browser hides the window frame (including the title bar, menu bar, and tool bar), allowing increased space for displaying documents.

In addition to the basics, NCSA Mosaic provides:

- An *annotation* function, which allows you to record and save your own comments about a document.

- A *cloning* function, which opens a duplicate of the current window. This is useful if, for example, you want to keep a copy of the current document visible as you move through linked documents.

- A *history list*, which is a document that contains hypertext links to all the Web sites you have visited since you started the browser.

- Built-in menu choices that link you to useful Web resources.

- Support for caching, including the option of clearing, or flushing, the cache in order to free up memory.

Figure 2-1. NCSA Mosaic for X Windows

The on-line help is in HTML format and is accessed from a central Web server. While this means the people at NCSA can provide updated help in a more timely fashion, it also means that the help is available to you only if you have established a connection to the Internet.

NCSA Mosaic is available for Windows, Macintosh, and X Window systems. You can obtain copies of Mosaic from
http://www.ncsa.uiuc.edu/SDG/Software/Mosaic/.

IBM WebExplorer Mosaic

IBM WebExplorer Mosaic is included in the IBM Internet Connection for Windows. It is a third-generation version of NCSA Mosaic: IBM used Spyglass's Enhanced Mosaic and added enhancements of their own to produce WebExplorer Mosaic.

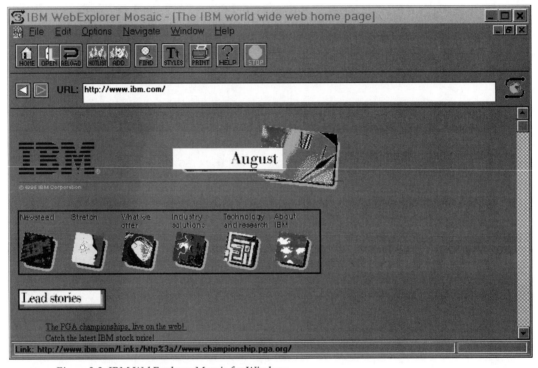

Figure 2-2. IBM WebExplorer Mosaic for Windows

In addition to the basics, IBM WebExplorer Mosaic provides:

- *Persistent caching*, which saves cached documents and images even after you exit WebExplorer

- *Document and image streaming*, which allows you to move through a document even before the entire document is displayed

- Built-in viewers for in-line GIF, TIFF, JPEG, BMP, and XBM images, and easy configuration for external viewers

- Support for dragging and dropping documents and images to your desktop

- Presentation mode for full-screen document viewing

For more information about IBM WebExplorer Mosaic, see
http://www.raleigh.ibm.com/icw/icwprod.html.

SPRY Mosaic

SPRY Mosaic (previously known as AIR Mosaic) was created by SPRY (CompuServe's Internet Division), the people who brought you Internet in a Box, Mosaic in a Box, and more recently, Internet Office. Mosaic in a Box is a combination of SPRY Mosaic and the dial-up software necessary to connect to the Internet. Internet Office provides a suite of applications, including a version of SPRY Mosaic that includes integrated security, as well as LAN support and dial-up programs to enable Internet communication.

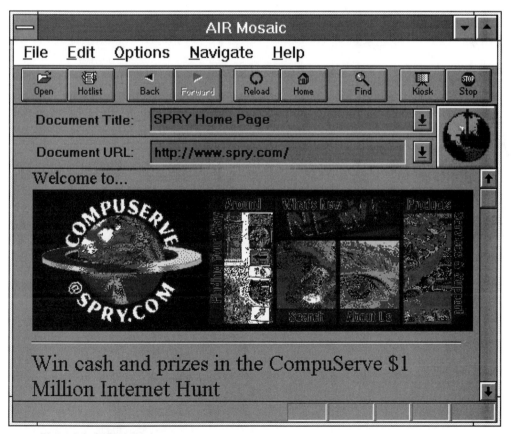

Figure 2-3. SPRY Mosaic

In addition to the standard Mosaic functions, SPRY Mosaic provides:

- Enhanced hot list support, including support for multiple hot lists and grouping of hot list items

- A full-screen viewing mode, which they call *Kiosk mode*

- Support for dragging and dropping documents and images to your desktop

- A configurable interface, including easy customization of the toolbar and external viewers

Like most browsers, SPRY Mosaic provides a chronological history list. However, SPRY Mosaic also provides:

- A drop-down list of previously-visited sites (listed by URLs and document title)

- Support for caching

- Support for proxy servers for FTP and Gopher requests, as well as HTTP (Web) requests

Currently, SPRY Mosaic runs under Windows only. You can get a demonstration copy of SPRY Mosaic from **http://www.spry.com/sp_prod/airmos/airmos.html**.

IBM WebExplorer for OS/2

WebExplorer is a Web browser that comes with OS/2 Warp. Unlike many other browsers, WebExplorer is not Mosaic reincarnate. WebExplorer was built from scratch by four folks at IBM. To browse documents on the Web, you will need to establish a connection to the Internet. OS/2 Warp provides LAN support and dial-up software that you can use to access the Internet.

WebExplorer provides a fully-customizable interface allowing you to specify preferences for fonts, colors, and more. You can also specify a proxy gateway or socks server, for access outside a secured network, as well as the maximum number of documents and images to be held in cache.

WebExplorer also provides:

- Built-in viewers for in-line GIF, TIFF, JPEG, BMP, and XBM images, and easy configuration for external viewers

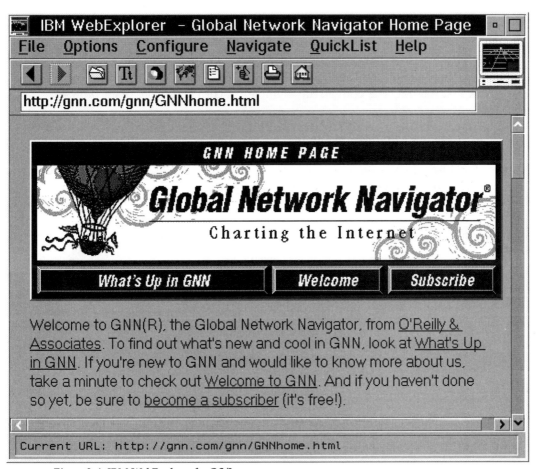

Figure 2-4. IBM WebExplorer for OS/2

- Support for *interlaced images*, which takes advantage of the interlaced format by displaying each line of the image as it is received. This produces a "fade in" effect and significantly improves perceived browser performance. For more information about interlaced images, see Chapter 5 "Including images in your document."

- Support for dragging and dropping documents and images to your desktop

- Presentation mode for full-screen document viewing

- A history list, or WebMap, that lists documents in relative order (the order in which they relate to one another) rather than in chronological order

- Document and image streaming, which allows you to work with a document even before all text and images have been received

The latest release of WebExplorer for OS/2 provides support for two common types of transaction security: SSL and S-HTTP. Another nice thing about WebExplorer is that, because it uses OS/2, you can run multiple, concurrent sessions of the browser.

You can download a copy of WebExplorer from **ftp://ftp.ibm.net/pub/WebExplorer/**. WebExplorer Version 1.01 and earlier can run on OS/2 2.11. However, due to some changes in the program to take advantage of Workplace Shell, versions of WebExplorer after 1.01 require OS/2 Warp. The secure version of WebExplorer for OS/2 is not available on-line.

Netscape Navigator

Netscape Navigator was created by Netscape Communications, one of the fastest growing companies in the Internet community. Netscape Communications was formed in April of 1994 by Marc Andreessen, creator of NCSA Mosaic, and Dr. James H. Clark, founder of Silicon Graphics, Inc. Netscape Navigator Personal Edition combines a Web browser, Netscape Navigator, with LAN support and dial-up software that you can use to establish a connection to the Internet.

In addition to the standard functions, Netscape Navigator provides:

- Support for interlaced images, which takes advantage of the interlaced format by displaying each line of the image as it is received.

- Simultaneous loading of images and text.

- Persistent caching, which means documents and images are saved in cache even after you exit the browser.

- Built-in viewers for in-line GIF and JPEG images, and easy customization of external viewers.

- Security and encryption techniques for communication with secure Web servers.

As with NCSA Mosaic, the on-line help is accessed via the Internet from a central Web server. While this means the people at Netscape can provide updated help in a more timely fashion, it also means that the help is available to you only if you have established a connection to the Internet.

Figure 2-5. Netscape Navigator for X Windows

In the short time since its founding, Netscape has become a recognized leader in Web technology. While most browser manufacturers are working to ensure that their browsers support the latest in images and HTML, Netscape is helping to define the "latest." Working with the W3 Consortium, Netscape has developed a number of enhancements to HTML. For more information about the proposed HTML extensions, see
http://www.netscape.com/assist/net_sites/html_extensions.html.

Versions of Netscape Navigator are available for Windows, Macintosh, and X Window systems. For information about how to obtain a copy of Netscape Navigator, see **http://www.netscape.com/info/how-to-get-it.html**.

Albert

Albert is a text-based browser for mainframes running IBM's VM/CMS operating system. Albert was created by David Nessl at the University of Florida (UFL). Navigating through the screens presented by Albert is a matter of using your keyboard to move your cursor to a highlighted phrase and pressing Enter. This seems a bit primitive by comparison to clients that make full use of the "point and click" technology of a mouse, but it works quite well once you become accustomed to it. To browse documents on the Web, your VM system must, of course, be set up to access the Internet.

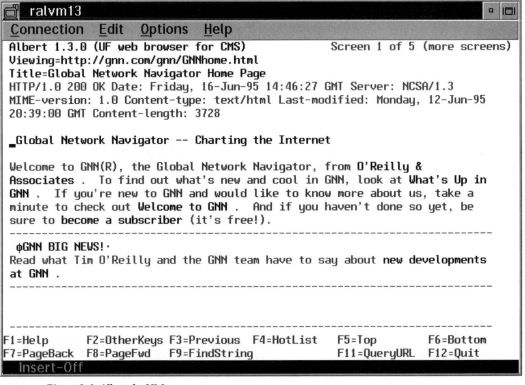

Figure 2-6. Albert for VM

As with many VM programs, Albert provides a group, actually three groups, of function keys to allow you to perform numerous tasks, such as moving forward and backward in a document and searching within a document. Although Albert does not maintain a history list as many browsers do, it does allow you to:

- Maintain a hot list of URLs

- Save, print, or mail the text of a document

- Save a local copy of the HTML source of a document

Preferences such as font and screen color are left up to the emulator.

For more information about Albert, see **ftp://ftp.nerdc.ufl.edu/pub/vm/www/README**.

Charlotte

There is another Web client for VM named Charlotte. Charlotte was created by the people at BC Systems in British Columbia, Canada. Charlotte provides functions similar to Albert. It is written in REXX (a simple programming language from IBM) and uses CMS Pipelines and REXX Sockets. Version 1.2 supports forms, proxy servers, and basic authentication. Charlotte will run on any version of CMS from Version 5 to 11 without change. If you have a non-ESA version of CMS, you must install the Pipeline programming request for price quotation (PRPQ) from IBM. According to the author of Charlotte, Carl Forde, Charlotte should be easily portable to TSO (but no one has attempted to port it yet).

For more information about Charlotte, see **gopher://p370.bcsc.gov.bc.ca/11/vmtools**.

Chapter 3

Designing Information for the Web

Although there are many printable documents available on the Web, the primary purpose of the Web is to provide information in an on-line format. This section assumes that you know something about creating printed information. It therefore begins with a discussion of the movement from printed to on-line information.

Whether you are producing printed or on-line information, there are three aspects to consider: the style, the content, and the mechanics. This section provides some style guidelines and tips to help you produce "good" Web information. Although you are responsible for the content of your Web information, this section provides some etiquette guidelines that you may find helpful. The mechanics of creating Web information are discussed in later chapters.

Chapter 3. Designing Information for the Web

Moving from printed to on-line information

The movement from printed information to on-line information has been in progress since the invention of the first computer monitors.

At first, on-line information was very similar to printed information, linear in form and hierarchical in structure. In 1945, Vannevar Bush published an article, entitled "As we may think," in which he proposed a new approach to on-line information, one that would make use of the retention and retrieval capabilities of computers. The concept was exciting: a non-linear approach to information that would allow the user to choose his or her own path through a database of interconnected information. However, the technology to implement such a proposal was not yet perfected and the proposal was therefore not implemented.

A copy of Bush's article, "As we may think," is available on-line (in hypertext format) at **http://www.csi.uottawa.ca/~dduchier/misc/vbush/as-we-may-think.html**.

But all was not lost. Despite the lack of implementation, the concept behind the proposal lived on. In the mid-1960s, technology had advanced to the point that it could support a nonlinear network of information. Experiments in information networking took on new interest. It was then that Ted Nelson, a pioneer in on-line information systems, gave the concept a name, "hypertext."

Advances in technology continued, and in May of 1983, MIT, in collaboration with Digital Equipment Corporation and IBM, embarked on a project to develop the optimal educational system. This project, named Athena, resulted in the development of state-of-the-art hardware, software, and networking technologies that forged the way for many of today's multimedia on-line information systems.

However, while the technology to create and display hypertext has advanced rapidly since the 1960s, the skills required to write it have not. Skills often come with an understanding of rules and, in many respects, there are no rules for hypertext. Because this is a relatively young medium for information, the rules are largely recommendations from those who have discovered what works and what doesn't.

There are a number of very good books that attempt to spell out these recommendations, such as *Text, Context, and HyperText* by Edward Barrett, and *The Society of Text*, also by Barrett. And there are many techniques, such as Robert Horn's Information Mapping, which attempt to translate empirical data gathered through research into rules for organizing information. These and other sources of information on hypertext are listed in the Bibliography.

Whether printed on a page or displayed on a screen, all good documentation starts with good writing. Beyond that, there are two levels of additional considerations for writers of hypertext: how to create effective on-line information, and when to link information.

Creating effective on-line information

Considerations for writing effective on-line information fall into two categories: form and content.

Form

With form, remember that information is often displayed in sizable windows. You do not have control over the size of the window as you would with a printed book. Therefore, you should steer away from complex formats, such as multiple columns and large amounts of information in tabular format. Simplicity is the key to good form.

In many cases, the form can reinforce the content. If the information describes a procedure, place the steps in an ordered (numbered) list. If the information contains a set of choices, benefits, or considerations, use an unordered (bulleted) list. Lists can enhance the appearance of information as well as aid in user comprehension.

Content

With content, keep in mind that if a document is longer than a single window, the user will have to scroll to read the additional information. Most users are willing to scroll through two or three windows of information. After that, however, your audience retention decreases with each additional scroll. So keep your information brief and try to place crucial information within the first three windows.

It is also a good idea to "chunk" your information. *Chunking* information means grouping information into discrete parts, based on content, and labeling each chunk. For example. if you are describing how to play a game, you might have the following chunks:

- Origin of the game

- Description of the game board and pieces

- Instructions for setting up the game

- Instructions for playing the game

- Criteria for winning the game

Chunking is a good practice because it helps provide structure to your information. It will also help you when you begin designing your linking scheme.

Deciding when to link

In some cases, despite attempts to keep it simple and concise, a topic cannot be covered in a few pages of information. This situation calls for linking. Consistency is one of the most important guidelines of linking. It is important that you adopt a well-defined criteria for deciding when to include information in-line in an on-line document and when to separate it out as a separate entity to which you link. Users become accustomed to "how" information is presented. For example, we are all accustomed to finding the index in the back of the book. Because on-line information is a relatively young medium, the rules of consistency are still being developed.

In general, you should design the initial page of information for the high-level user: the user who needs the least amount of information. Then, provide links to additional information, such as definitions of terms that a novice user might not understand, technical information that an experienced user might want, or information about related topics. This will help reduce the amount of information on the initial page.

In on-line information, the term *page* is used to mean discrete blocks of information. This block may be more than a single window's worth of information. It may also contain links to (and be linked to by) other pages.

Take the example previously mentioned, describing how to play a game. The initial page might read something like this:

Welcome to Success!

Success is an exciting game of strategy and intrigue designed for two to four players. It is played with carved game pieces, called Quins, placed on a three-dimension gameboard, called a Strategy Grid.

Players start by choosing their Quins and placing them at one of the designated markings on the gameboard. As you move from one grid location to another and from one level to another, you gain points. The goal of the game is to reach the top of the Success Grid with enough points to acquire independence. Beware, though, the Strategy Grid contains traps, called pitfalls and setbacks, that can cause you to lose all your points.

In this example, the hypertext links are shown as underscored words or phrases.

- <u>Success</u> would link to an overview of the origin of the game.

- <u>Quins</u> and <u>Strategy</u> <u>Grid</u> would link to a description of the game pieces and board.

- <u>Players</u> <u>start</u> would link to a description of how to set up the game.

- <u>As</u> <u>you</u> <u>move</u> would link to a description of the rules of the game.

- <u>The</u> <u>goal</u> <u>of</u> <u>the</u> <u>game</u> would link to an overview of the criteria for winning the game.

If you are blazing new trails and have no precedent to follow, then be consistent within your own information. However, if you are adding to a database of hyper-text, such as the Web, try to follow the same criteria as the existing information.

Rules of thumb for Web information

In the field of information presentation, the Web is a relatively young technology. And, as such, it does not yet have the definitive set of rules and regulations for producing "good" information that have been established for more mature technologies. Even so, there are some guidelines or "rules of thumb" that could be helpful to you as you create information for the Web.

Be brief

The acceptable length of a Web document varies. First, as we said before, try to limit the number of times a reader has to scroll through a document. Three times is a good limit. However, keep in mind that the acceptable length of a document should also depend on the topic. On the whole, high-level documents such as overviews, should be kept short. The reader expects this type of information to be brief. In-depth documents are expected to be longer. Remember, you can separate out and link to related information. But don't try to break up a document unnaturally just to make it shorter.

Another element to consider is time. The information a reader is accessing is likely to reside on a computer hundreds or thousands of miles away. The amount of time it takes a browser to access and display a document will depend on the speed of the reader's connection. We accessed a certain document using a computer that is attached to our company network, which is connected to the Internet via a dedicated line. It took 12 seconds to display the entire document. We then accessed the same document using a computer with a 9600 baud dial-in connection to the Internet. It took 23 seconds. Individually, these access times may seem acceptable. But when you consider that readers may be waiting several seconds for each document, they may not be willing to wait for your document to be displayed if it takes even a few seconds longer than expected.

Consider the impaired reader

There are many things to consider when you create information for the Web, not the least of which is the audience. You must make certain assumptions about the reader, such as the language they are likely to speak and the terms they are likely to understand. You also take into consideration their visual and auditory abilities.

Computer technology has made numerous advances in the support for visually- or hearing-impaired users. Although many programs are available to assist the impaired, few provide the functions necessary to assist users with information on the Web.

NCSA sponsors a project, called the NCSA Mosaic Access Project, to assist in identifying the barriers an impaired Web user may encounter and to help identify solutions. Their home page provides many useful tips and techniques. It is located at **http://bucky.aa.uic.edu/**.

In addition, there are specific ways you can assist your impaired readers.

For the visually impaired

IBM offers a line of products called the Special Needs Solutions. One of these products, Screen Reader, converts text to speech, enabling users to hear rather than read the words displayed on their screen. And because it can recognize changes in font, it can even help users navigate through hypertext links. Screen Reader cannot, however, process images. But you can help. To assist the visually impaired:

- Provide labels for images included in your document. In fact, some Web sites that contain documents relying heavily on images provide separate text-only versions of the documents. Though this is done primarily to compensate for nongraphical browsers, it aids the visually impaired as well.

- If you include image maps (images with defined areas that link to other information) in your document, include a text-only equivalent.

For more information about Screen Reader, see **http://www.austin.ibm.com/pspinfo/snssrd.html**.

For the hearing impaired

Although there are several voice recognition programs available, none is able to take audio clips as input. To assist the hearing impaired, if you include an audio clip in your Web document, you should provide a text file that describes the contents of the clip.

Provide navigation aids

It is not unusual for a reader to get lost perusing the thousands of interconnected documents on the Web. In addition to any links that you may have in your document, it will be helpful to your readers if you provide push buttons or icons at the bottom of your document that link back to the parent document or forward to another related topic. If yours is an exceptionally long document, you might consider providing a link at the bottom to the top.

Clearly identify the document

When you send out a memo, write a letter to a friend, or provide a report for others to read, it is important that you include the date and your name. This helps those who receive the document know where it came from and when. Considering the increased distribution that your document may experience on the Web, this identification is even more important.

For example, we were looking for the latest HTTP specifications. We located a document called "HTTP specs" on one server. Then we found another document by the same name on another server. Fortunately, the documents contained the date they were written, so it was easy for us to determine which was the most current.

Despite the fact that HTML allows you to easily link to documents on other servers, sometimes people prefer to copy a document to their own server. Therefore it is a good idea to always clearly identify your document at the beginning of your document. You should include the date, the status (such as "Draft" or "First revision"), and your name (including your e-mail address). Including your e-mail address will allow others to contact you if they have comments or notify you if they plan to link to your document.

Construct links appropriately

The intent of hypertext coding is to allow you to highlight phrases that, when selected, lead the reader to additional information. However, the content of a document should read well without the links. Consider, for example, if someone wanted to print a document. The links would no longer be functional, but the sentences should read coherently regardless.

The following sentence demonstrates good use of linking.

If you want more information about any of these products, contact your <u>IBM Marketing</u> <u>Representative.</u>

In this case, the words <u>IBM</u> <u>Marketing</u> <u>Representative</u> provide a link to information about how to contact IBM via phone or e-mail. However, if you remove the link, the sentence still makes sense.

The following sentence does not demonstrate a good use of linking.

If you want more information about any of these products, <u>click</u> <u>here</u>.

If the link is not operational, the sentence no longer contains useful information.

Use complete headings

Although you control the links within your document, you do not control other documents that may link to yours. Consequently, there is no way to know where readers may be coming from. Therefore, when you are creating headings for your document, be as complete as possible.

For example, if you created a document about manatees, you might break it up into smaller documents with the following headings:

- Origins

- Characteristics

- Living environment

- Diet

- Population: current status

If a reader begins with your initial page, these headings may make sense. However, if someone links from another document, for example, a listing of endangered species, to the section of your document named "Characteristics," the title doesn't clearly identify the information. And the reader may wonder, "Characteristics of what?" One solution would be to add the word Manatee before each heading. "Characteristics" then becomes "Manatee Characteristics." Because most Web browsers maintain a listing, by heading, of URLs that a reader has visited, complete headings will also help the reader recognize this document in that list.

Be consistent

It is generally helpful to the reader if the format of your Web information is consistent with other Web information, or at least with other related Web information. Indeed, one of the reasons for the limited number of formatting controls available with HTML is that it forces some level of consistency in the documents. Human nature being what it is, many people have found ways to coerce HTML to produce a variety of formats, which can make it difficult, if not impossible, for you to be consistent with all the information you might link to.

If nothing else, however, you should be consistent with yourself. If you are producing several documents, it is a good idea to create an HTML template that you can follow. The template can help ensure consistency in your documents as well as save some coding time.

Avoid copying documents

As the old saying goes, there's "no need to reinvent the wheel." If you look long enough, you will find information on the Web on just about everything. And when you find information that you want to include in your document, don't copy it, link to it. A good deal of the documents on the Web are living documents, which means that they are likely to evolve and change. If you copy a document to your server, the author may update the original document, making your copy obsolete. If you link to the document, your readers will always be linking to the latest information.

Once you begin to maintain your own Web server, you will be surprised at how quickly you can run out of space if you don't plan and manage your information well. In addition to saving time (with change management), linking to a document rather than copying one will also save space.

The W3 Consortium maintains a list of many Web resources organized by topic. This is a good place to start when you are trying to locate information or determine if information on a certain topic already exists. The URL for this list is:
http://www.w3.org/hypertext/DataSources/bySubject/Overview.html.

If, for whatever reason, you cannot link to the original document and must make a copy on your local server, add a warning at the top of the copied document, identifying it as a copy and indicating where the original can be found. This will not only help those who may link to your information but will also help you remember where to find the original when you want to see if the document has been updated.

Also, when you link to a document, send a note to the document's owner. Some document owners keep lists of those who have linked to their document and send an e-mail if the document is updated, moved, or removed. Likewise, you should do the same for those who notify you that they have linked to one of your documents.

Costs and considerations

Hypertext documents on the World Wide Web represent a significant achievement in documentation. More information is available to more people, and the retrievability of the information is relatively easy. With the introduction of images and multimedia, these documents can be more effective than their printed predecessors. But nothing is free. This section discusses some of the trade-offs to consider when including images and multimedia in your Web document. It also gives a brief overview of some of the security issues to be considered.

Images

Images can enhance a document. An illustration of a concept is sometimes more meaningful than words. In most cases, an image can convey a message without using words. The image is therefore language-independent, making your document more useful to those who may not speak your language. Images can also add flair to a document, making it more interesting to your reader.

However, using images in a Web document is not without its problems. Some browsers do not support in-line images. Therefore, if your image contains important information, such as links to other information, you will need to supply a text equivalent for the image.

Also, because images are transferred separately from the text of a Web document, they require additional transfer time. For a reader with a dial-in connection, the additional time can seem like an eternity, causing the reader to lose interest and cancel the request for the document. This is particularly true for readers who have a browser that does not display Web documents until all associated images have been transferred.

We will discuss using images in Web documents in further detail in Chapter 5, "Including images in your document."

Multimedia

Multimedia (video and audio clips) can also enhance the appeal and usefulness of a document. Video clips can bring a concept to life. For example, without multimedia, an overview of heart functions would take paragraphs of text and include numerous medical terms that require further explanation. Chances are, many readers would abandon the document after they hit the second or third paragraph. By including a video clip, the action of the heart comes to life! The video clip captures the attention of the reader while providing the information in a format that can be understood by readers of various knowledge levels. Add to that an audio clip that narrates the action portrayed in the video, and it is like having a biology class in your computer.

It is quite easy to include video and audio clips in your Web document. Once you have created your video or audio file, it is simply a matter of linking to that file. The server and browser take care of the rest.

However, be careful of relying too heavily on multimedia to convey your message. Not all browsers are capable of audio and video playback. Also remember, that for most browsers, the playback of these files is provided through a separate program. Therefore, the entire audio or video file must be transferred to the reader's computer before it can be played back. This will require additional wait time, additional disk space, and additional memory. This may prevent some of your readers with more modest equipment from viewing or hearing your message.

We will discuss using multimedia in Web documents in further detail in Chapter 7, "Including multimedia in your document."

Security

The Web is built on a set of "open" protocols. This fact has allowed numerous individuals and companies to develop information and programs for the Web, which accounts for its rapid growth over the past few years. However, this openness has also made the Web vulnerable to a number of security problems. These problems can be grouped into three categories: client corruption, server infiltration, and compromised data integrity.

Web browsers are client programs that issue requests to servers and display the returned data. They do not perform any type of data checking. Therefore viruses may be hidden in the data and pass undetected to a client. Once received by the client, the viruses, often termed "Trojan horses," can spread to other code on the client computer.

Although there are mechanisms for protecting data on a server, they are often not sophisticated enough to block attempts by users who wish to bypass them. The lack of user authentication creates a hole through which users can access (what should be) protected information. Also, the lack of data checking could allow corrupted data to be stored using accepted access methods, such as the PUT method used in some forms.

Another area of concern is data integrity. This area is receiving increasing focus given the rise in commercial activity on the Web. The main issue is that certain information passed back and forth on the Web needs to be encrypted to prevent would-be interceptors from extracting the data. For example, consider one of the on-line shopping services: a florist. Rather than calling a florist and ordering a floral arrangement sight unseen, you can access one of many on-line shopping services, view images of various floral arrangements, select one, and fill out an on-line form to place your order. Along with your name and the name and address of the recipient, you will need to include your credit card number and its expiration date. If this information is intercepted by a dishonest person and it is not encrypted, you could end up spending a lot more money than you intended.

We will discuss security on the Web in further detail in Chapter 11 "Security on the Web."

Creating an HTML document

ypertext Markup Language (HTML) is the basis for all Web documents. A **markup language** is a set of tags, or codes, included in a document that indicate how a document is to be formatted. A markup language, for example, identifies headings, paragraphs, and lists. HTML is based on the Standard Generalized Markup Language (SGML), which is a set of codes used for printed documents. The importance of SGML is that it is designed to be platform-independent, meaning that you can take a file coded in SGML and process and print it on any platform (UNIX, Windows, OS/2, MVS, etc.). Similarly, HTML files can be interpreted and displayed by browsers on any platform.

This chapter briefly describes the history of HTML and includes tips for creating HTML documents as well as an overview of some of the HTML editors that are available. The syntax of the individual HTML tags is described in more depth in Appendix A, "HTML tagging reference."

Chapter 4. Creating an HTML document

Evolution of HTML

HTML was developed by Tim Berners-Lee in 1990 as the basis for all information published on the Web. It was further refined by Dan Connolly. And, in 1993, the first HTML specification was released as an Internet Draft.

Rather than create an entirely new markup language, Tim used an existing (though still evolving) platform-independent language, SGML, as the basis for the markup language for the Web. Because formatting options for on-line information are more limited than those for printed, only a small subset of the SGML tags were included in the first version of HTML, HTML 1.0. In addition to formatting tags, HTML 1.0 included tags for linking on-line documents.

In July of 1994, Dan Connolly presented the HTML 2.0 specification at a meeting of the Internet Engineering Task Force (IETF) in Toronto. After some revisions and refinement, the HTML 2.0 specification was released as an Internet Draft in November of 1994. This second version of HTML added tags to create on-line forms and an extended list of symbols. HTML 2.0 is currently supported by most Web browsers.

In March of 1995, HTML 3.0 was proposed. This version of HTML proposes tags that allow you to create tables, format mathematical formulas, and wrap text around images. It also proposes support for style sheets, which give you more control over the appearance of a document.

The tags discussed in this section are included in the HTML 2.0 specification. For more information on HTML 3.0, see
http://www.w3.org/hypertext/WWW/MarkUp/html3/CoverPage.html.

Creating an HTML document

Basically, an HTML document is a text file that includes markup tags. As a markup language, HTML consists of fewer tags than others. Though some people may find this constraining, most find this makes creating an HTML document a simple task. The capitalization of a tag is not important, but each tag must be surrounded by a less-than, <, and greater-than, >, symbol. Also, the values of some attributes must be surrounded by quotes. You can use either single quotes,
' ', or double quotes, " ", but they must match.

There are some basic steps for creating an HTML document:

1. Identify the file as an HTML document.
2. Include general document information in the head of the document.

3. Include the content of the document in the body of the document.
4. Create the hypertext links.
5. For lengthy documents, include a table of contents.
6. Use comments to help organize your HTML source file.
7. Identify the end of the document.

Once you have created your document, you will need to place it in a directory on the Web server. This is usually done by the administrator of the server. In some cases, the administrator may give you access to place documents on the server yourself. For more information about placing documents on a Web server, see Chapter 10, "A tour of Web servers."

Identifying a file as an HTML document

Web browsers are designed to display HTML documents. So, the first thing you must do is identify the file as an HTML document. To do this, start the document with the <HTML> tag, and end it with the </HTML> tag.

Including general document information

The beginning of an HTML document should contain some general document information, which must be surrounded by <Head> and </Head> tags.

- Although it is not required, you should give the document a title. To do this, use the <Title> and </Title>. Most browsers display the title of the current document across the top of the browser window. Therefore, you should keep the title concise. Also, the title is often used to identify documents in a hot list, so you should make the title meaningful. For example, "Course Catalogue" is not as meaningful as "UNC Course Catalogue 1996."

- It is a good idea to also specify the *root URL* of the document. The root URL is the protocol and server name of the document. To specify a root URL, use the <Base> tag with an HREF attribute.

The beginning of your HTML document should look similar to the following:

```
<HTML>
<HEAD>
<TITLE>Yahoo</TITLE>
<base href="http://www.yahoo.com/">
</HEAD>
```

Figure 4-1. Example of the beginning of an HTML document (from the Yahoo home page)

Creating the document content

As we mentioned earlier, the presentation (or format) of on-line documents should be kept simple. Designed with that thought in mind, HTML provides only a subset of the SGML formatting tag. Basic tags, such as those that identify paragraphs, lists, highlighting, and headings, are included. But more advanced or complex tags, such as those that support multiple columns and rotated text, are not. In most cases, however, the basic tags will suffice.

Beginning the body of the document

To begin the body of your document, use the <Body> tag. This tag indicates that the information that follows constitutes the content of the document (as opposed to the identifying information contained within the <Head> and</Head> tags).

Including a main heading

Next, give your document a main heading. The main heading is similar to a chapter title in a book. Depending on the length and content of the document, the main heading may be the same as the document title (though it can be longer). The main heading is displayed at the top of the document (not at the top of the window like the title). To create a main heading, use the <H1> and </H1> tags.

Using subheadings

Use subheadings to identify subordinate sections of a document. HTML provides six levels of headings: <H1>, <H2>, <H3>, <H4>, <H5>, and <H6>. You should not skip head levels in a document. For example, subordinate headings within a main heading should use <H2>, and subordinate headings within a secondary heading should use <H3>.

If you plan to refer (link to) a heading from other places in a document, such as from the table of contents, use the anchor tag <A> within the heading tags, and give each heading a unique identifier or name. For more information about the anchor tag, see "Creating hypertext links" on page 54.

Creating paragraphs and line breaks

Identify each new paragraph with a paragraph tag, <P>. The paragraph tag causes a line break and an extra line of space. You can place this tag at the end of a paragraph, or at the beginning of the next paragraph. The important thing is to be consistent in placement.

Certain HTML tags automatically generate space, so you do not need to include additional paragraph tags. A space is automatically generated after <H1>, so you do not need to begin your first paragraph with a <P>. List tags, block quote tags, and address tags automatically generate a space prior to the element, so you do not need to include a <P> prior to those tags.

If you want to cause a line break (force the text to the next line) but do not want an extra space, use the line break tag <BR>. For example, you may want to use line break tags to ensure the proper format of a poem.

```
<P>The time has come, the Walrus said, to talk of many things<br>
of ships and shoes and sealing wax<br>
of cabbages and kings.<br>
```

Figure 4-2. Example of the line break tag

Including symbols

In HTML, certain characters are reserved for use in tags. These characters are <, >, &, and ". When a browser encounters one of these characters, it assumes the character is part of an HTML tag and tries to process it as such. If you need to use one of these characters in your HTML document, you can use an HTML symbol.

For...	Use...
<	&lt;
>	&gt;
&	&amp;
"	&quot;

HTML symbols are preceded by an ampersand, &, and followed by a semicolon (;). HTML also provides symbols for many characters that may not be available on your keyboard, such as Á. For a list of these symbols, see Appendix A, "HTML tagging reference."

Highlighting words and phrases

HTML provides several tags that you can use to highlight words or phrases. The highlighting tags provided with HTML can be grouped into two categories: explicit and interpreted. *Explicit highlighting* tags instruct the browser to display the surrounded text in a specific manner, such as bold or italic. *Interpreted highlighting* tags give the browser some leeway. They allow the browser to determine the specific type of highlighting. Because treatment of interpreted highlighting varies from browser to browser, you might want to view your document using several browsers before making it publicly available.

Explicit highlighting

The following lists the explicit highlighting available with HTML.

To display text in...	Surround the text with...
Bold font	<B> and </B>
Italic font	<I> and </I>
Monospaced font	<TT> and </TT>
Underscored font	<U> and </U>

Interpreted highlighting

The following lists the interpreted highlighting available with HTML.

To identify the text in...	Surround the text with...
Requiring emphasis	<EM> and </EM>
Requiring strong emphasis	<Strong> and </Strong>
A programming sample	<Code> and </Code>
A variable	<VAR> and </VAR>
A new term	<DFN> and </DFN>
A citation, such as a book title	<CITE> and </CITE>

Highlighting blocks of text

In addition to tags for highlighting, HTML provides tags for special handling of these types of information: addresses, long quotes, and examples.

Addresses

You may want to include your address in your document, either for correspondence or for identification purposes. To help distinguish an address from other types of information, HTML provides an <Address> tag. The <Address> tag is similar to an interpreted highlighting tag; it indicates that the information requires special handling, but allows the browser to determine how the information is displayed. If you want to stack your address, as you would on an envelope, you must specify where the lines should break using the <BR> tag. For example:

```
<Address>
Debbie Morrison<br>
IBM Networking Software<br>
4205 South Miami Blvd<br>
RTP, NC 27709
</Address>
```

Figure 4-3. Example of an address

Long quotes

Typically, when you quote a source in a document, you surround the information with quotation marks. However, if it is a long, multiple-line quote, you might want to give it more emphasis. To do this, use the <Blockquote> tag. Like the <Address> tag, this is an interpreted highlighting tag. Typically, however, the information is indented and displayed in an italic font.

Examples

If you want to include preformatted information (information that you do not want the browser to format), such as an example of the source code for a program, use the <PRE> tag. This tag indicates that the information is to be displayed as is. <PRE> causes line breaks to be preserved and the information to be displayed in a monospaced font.

HTML tags included within preformatted text will still be processed. However, if you want to use a less-than symbol or greater-than symbol in your example (for instance, to show an example of HTML source code), you must use the < and > symbols to represent < and >.

```
If you want to link to this site, include the following in your
document:<P>
<PRE>
&lt;A HREF=&quot;http://www.acme.com/&quot;&gt;Acme Products&lt;/A&gt;
(a wholly owned subsidiary of Coyote, Inc.)
</PRE>
```

Figure 4-4. Example of preformatted text

When viewed with a browser, the preformatted text looks similar to this:

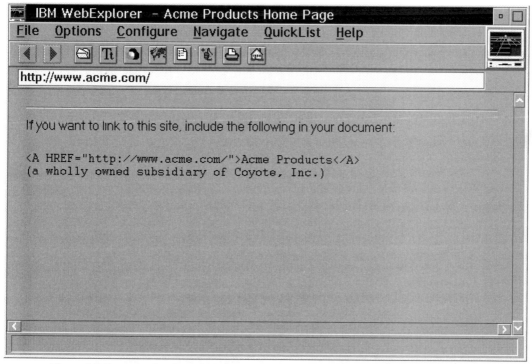

Figure 4-5. Example of preformatted text

Creating lists

Whether printed or on-line, information in a simpler format is easier to comprehend. Lists are an effective way to simplify the format of information. HTML provides tags for creating several types of lists:

- If sequence is important, such as the steps to install a program, use the ordered list tag, <OL>. Items in an ordered list can be several lines long.

- If sequence is unimportant, such as a list of services offered, use an unordered list tag, <UL>. Items in a unordered list can be several lines long.

- If sequence is unimportant and each item is brief, such as an ingredient list, use a menu tag, <MENU>. Items in a menu should not require more than a single line.

For any of these lists, identify each item with a list item tag, <LI>, and end the list with the appropriate tag, </OL>, </UL>, or </MENU>.

At times, you may need to create a multilevel list, for example, if a list of items needs to be associated with a particular step in a procedure. To create a multilevel list, you can nest the list tags. Nesting means including a list within a list. With most browsers, the nested list is indented from its parent list.

You can nest different types of lists, such as an unordered list within an ordered list or a menu within an unordered list. Be sure, however, to end the lists in proper order, ending the most recently started list first.

```
<OL>
<LI>Make sure you have the following:
<Menu>
<LI>A 12" clay pot
<LI>Potting soil
<LI>Peat moss
<LI>Medium-sized gravel
<LI>A small trowel
<LI>Newspaper
</Menu>
<LI>Place the gravel in the clay pot, approximately 1" deep.
<LI>Place a single layer of newspaper over the gravel, trim to fit.
<LI>Using the trowel, mix 2 parts potting soil to 1 part peat moss and
add to clay pot, approximately 8" deep.
<LI>Place seedlings in soil mixture 3" deep.
```

```
<LI> Water thoroughly.
</OL>
```

Figure 4-6. Example of nested lists

When viewed with a browser, the nested list looks similar to this:

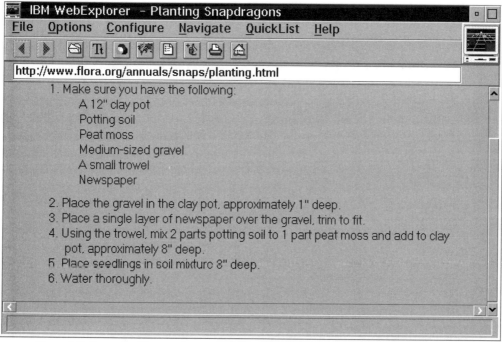

Figure 4-7. Example of formatted nested lists

HTML also provides tags to create a definition list. Definition lists are useful if you need to list and describe items, such as in a glossary. In general, each item or term is displayed on a separate line and the description is indented on the next line. To start a definition list, use the <DL> tag. Precede each item or term with <DT> (definition term) and each description with <DD> (definition description). For example:

```
<DT><EM>retained earnings</EM>
<DD>The excess of a company's post-tax income over all dividends distrib-
uted to stockholders.
```

```
<DT><EM>return on investment (ROI)</EM>
<DD>A measure of the yield or return on invested capital.
<DT><EM>revaluation</EM>
<DD>The upward or downward change in a currency's value relative to gold
or other currencies.
```

Figure 4-8. Example of a definition list

Definition tags do not produce any highlighting. In this example, <EM> has been used to give emphasis to the terms.

Using horizontal rules

To give your document more structure, you can use a horizontal rule to add a visual separation between sections of information. To include a horizontal rule, use the <HR> tag. The <HR> tag causes a line break and a vertical space (similar to a paragraph tag) followed by a rule that extends the width of the page and another vertical space.

Creating hypertext links

The whole purpose of hypertext documents is, of course, to provide cross-reference links. A reader need only click on the highlighted word or phrase to access related information. Each link has a point of origin, or launch point, and a destination. The destination can be within the same document or outside, to another HTML document, another file, or another resource on the Internet.

Linking within a document

Linking within a document is particularly useful with a lengthy document. One of the best examples is a table of contents that allows readers to skip to the topic they want.

To create a link within a document, you must first identify the destination. The destination can be any element of a document: a word, a phrase, an in-line image, or a heading (as with the table of contents). To identify an element as a destination point, use the anchor tag <A> with the NAME attribute. You must use the NAME attribute to assign an identifier to the element.

To create a table of contents, each heading should be identified as a destination and assigned an identifier. (It is best to include the anchor tags within the heading tags.) For example:

```
<H2><A NAME="install">Installation Instructions</A></H2>
```

Then, you can identify the launch point. Like the destination, the launch point can be any element of a document. To identify an element as a launch point, use the anchor tag <A> with the HREF attribute. You must use the HREF attribute to point to the destination. If you are linking within a document, the value of the HREF attribute is the assigned name preceded by a pound sign.

Continuing with the table of contents as our example, the heading would appear as a list item and be tagged as follows:

```
<LI><A HREF="#install">Installation Instructions</A>
```

Linking outside a document

If you want to link from your document to another document, file, or resource on the Web, you only need to identify the launch point. To identify an element as a launch point, use the anchor tag <A> with the HREF attribute. The value of the HREF attribute is simply the URL of the destination. For example, if you want to link to another HTML document, the HTML tagging will look similar to this:

```
<P>Many helpful tips are also listed in the
<A HREF="http://www.acme.com/news/tips.html">Acme Tips and Techniques</A>.
```

If you want to link to another file, such as a text file, the HTML tagging will look similar to this:

```
<P>The latest <A HREF="http://www.acme.com/admin/usage.txt">usage
statistics</A> show that our Web site is becoming more popular than our
FTP site.
```

Note: Although capitalization of HTML tags is not important, the capitalization of a URL might be. The file systems of some operating systems are case-sensitive. For example, the UNIX file system distinguishes between a file called Overview.html and one called overview.html. Therefore, to be on the safe side, when you find a resource that you want to access or link to, take care to make note of the exact URL, including capitalization.

Absolute vs. relative linking

The HREF attribute of the anchor tag can take two types of URLs, depending on whether or not the document or file you are linking to is on the same server as the document you are linking from.

If the document or file you want to link to is on a different server, you must use an *absolute URL* to establish the link. An absolute URL includes the protocol, server name, location, and file name of the document or file. For example, this is an absolute link:

```
<P>Many helpful tips are also listed in the
<A HREF="http://www.acme.com/news/tips.html">Acme Tips and
Techniques</A>.
```

If the document (or file) you want to link to is on the same server as the document you are linking from, you can use an absolute URL, or you can use a shortened form of the URL, called a *relative URL*. With relative URLs, the root URL (the protocol and server name) is assumed and you need only specify the name of the document, and perhaps the directory.

For example, to link to a document in the same directory on the same server, you can simply specify the file name. The HTML tagging would look similar to this:

```
<P>We also offer a wide range of <A HREF="jetveh.html">
jet-propelled vehicles</A>.
```

To link to a document in a different directory on the same server (regardless of the current directory), you can specify the directory, preceded by a slash, and the file name. The HTML tagging would look similar to this:

```
<P><A HREF="/orders/orderfrm.html">Order</A> yours today.
```

To link to a document in a subdirectory of the current directory, you can specify the subdirectory (without the leading slash) and the file name. The HTML tagging would look similar to this:

```
<P>While you are here, take a look at our assortment of
<A HREF="TOOLS/pwrtools.html">power tools</A>.
```

To link to a document in a parent directory of the current directory, you can specify ..
(two dots, which indicates the parent directory) and the file name. The HTML tagging
would look similar to this:

```
<P>We also offer an assortment of <A HREF="../choc.html"> chocolates
and candies</A>.
```

Relative URLs are easier to use than absolute URLs, because they require less information (less room for error). And if you move the base document (and all its relative
documents), you don't have to change all the URLs used in links. However, if you
move the base document but do not move the relative documents, the browser will not
be able to find the linked documents using the relative URLs. For this reason, you can
use the <Base> tag to override the current root URL. If specified, the value of the HREF
attribute of the <Base> tag is appended to any relative URLs.

Linking to other types of servers

You can also link to other resources on the Internet, such as FTP servers, Usenet
newsgroups, and Gopher servers. To link to another resource, simply include the URL
as the HREF. For example:

```
<P>The latest usage statistics show that our Web site is
becoming more popular than our
<A HREF="ftp://ftp.acme.com/pub/">FTP site</A>.
```

When linking to other types of servers, it is important to use the proper URL format for
each type of server. If you are unsure about the URL format, see Appendix B, "Understanding URL formats."

Including comments

There will be times when you want to include information in a document that you do
not want to display, such as the date the document was created. This type of information is called a comment. You can also use comments to help visually organize the
source of a document. For example, you might want to include a line of asterisks
between blocks of information. In HTML, a comment must begin with <! and end with
>. Each comment is limited to a single line, but you can stack lines of comments.
Although browsers do not display the content of a comment, the comment is part of
the source, which readers can easily access. Therefore, do not include sensitive or
confidential information as a comment.

```
<! This document was created on 10/24/94 by Gene Myers.  >
<! It was reviewed by Tom Smith and Karen Taylor. It was >
<! revised on 2/15/95 to include information about our    >
<! new products.                                          >
<H1>Welcome to Acme Products</H1>
<P>Acme products has a long-standing reputation for quality prod-
ucts and reliable service. In the past, our products have been
available only to a select group of customers. We are pleased to
be able to now offer our full product line to the general public.
<!*******************************************************>
<H2>Acme Catalogue<H2>
```

Figure 4-9. Example of an HTML document with comments

Including a table of contents

For lengthy documents or documents with many parts, it is a good idea to include a table of contents near the beginning of the document. Unfortunately, HTML does not provide any tags to allow you to automatically create a table of contents. You must create one manually. In general, it is beneficial to the reader if the format of the table of contents represents the hierarchy of the document (with subheadings being indented under their parent heading). To do this, you can use *nested lists*. A nested list is a list within a list.

It is also a good idea to make each entry in the table of contents a hypertext link using anchor tags.

```
<UL>
<LI><A NAME="SEC1" HREF="html-spec_1.html#SEC1"
REL=SUBDOCUMENT>Introduction</A>
<UL>
<LI><A NAME="SEC2" HREF="html-spec_1.html#SEC2">Scope</A>
<LI><A NAME="SEC3" HREF="html-spec_1.html#SEC3">Conformance</A>
<UL>
<LI><A NAME="SEC4" HREF="html-spec_1.html#SEC4">Documents</A>
<LI><A NAME="SEC5" HREF="html-spec_1.html#SEC5">Feature Test Entities</A>
<LI><A NAME="SEC6" HREF="html-spec_1.html#SEC6">User Agents</A>
</UL>
</UL>
```

```
<LI><A NAME="SEC7" HREF="html-spec_2.html#SEC7">Terms</A>
<LI><A NAME="SEC8" HREF="html-spec_3.html#SEC8">HTML as an Application
of SGML</A>
<UL>
<LI><A NAME="SEC9" HREF="html-spec_3.html#SEC9">SGML
Documents</A>
<LI><A NAME="SEC10" HREF="html-spec_3.html#SEC10">HTML Lexical Syntax</
A>
<UL>
<LI><A  NAME="SEC11"  HREF="html-spec_3.html#SEC11">Data
Characters</A>
<LI><A NAME="SEC12" HREF="html-spec_3.html#SEC12">Tags</A>
<LI><A NAME="SEC13" HREF="html-spec_3.html#SEC13">Names</A>
<LI><A NAME="SEC14" HREF="html-spec_3.html#SEC14">Attributes</A>
```

Figure 4-10. Example of table of contents

When viewed with a browser, the table of contents looks like this:

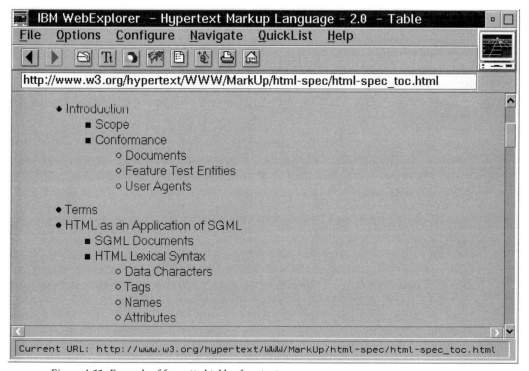

Figure 4-11. Example of formatted table of contents

Ending an HTML document

To end an HTML document, first end the body using the </Body> tag, and then end the document using the </HTML> tag.

HTML tools

Because the source for an HTML document is an ASCII text file, you can create your document using any text editor. However, if you need help remembering the tags, or if you simply want to conserve key strokes, there are a number of tools you can use to help you create your document. In general, these tools can be grouped into two categories: HTML editors and HTML converters.

HTML editors

HTML editors provide an interface to help you create HTML documents. Most work as word processors do, allowing you to enter text or import a text file, select elements in the text, and assign a format to the selected text. With the continuous evolution of HTML, it is difficult for the makers of these editors to keep up, but most do a good job of making updates available in a timely fashion.

The W3 Consortium maintains a good list of HTML editors at **http://www.w3.org/hypertext/WWW/Tools/Overview.html**. Many of the editors are freeware or shareware programs that you can download. Some are licensed programs that you must purchase. In many cases, there is a demonstration version of the licensed program that you can try out.

We chose two of the editors to describe in this section: HoTMetaL and NaviPress. That is not to imply that the others do not warrant consideration, but we couldn't describe them all in this book. We chose these because they are likely to be maintained and updated for new versions of HTML and because they are available for several operating systems.

HoTMetaL

HoTMetaL (note the capitalization) by SoftQuad is available for Windows, Macintosh, and Sun systems. There are actually two versions of HoTMetaL: HoTMetaL Free, which is freeware, and HoTMetaL Pro, which is a licensed program.

HoTMetaL Free provides a point and click interface that allows you to create and edit:

- An HTML document without having to know the syntax of the HTML tags

- Hypertext links to other documents

- Image maps

- HTML forms

The latest edition of HoTMetaL Free allows you to include in-line images.

To help you get started, HoTMetaL Free provides several HTML templates. It also provides a built-in tag-checking feature that prevents you from using the wrong tag or inserting a tag in the wrong place. This feature, however, can cause problems if you want to use HoTMetaL to edit an existing HTML document that does not strictly

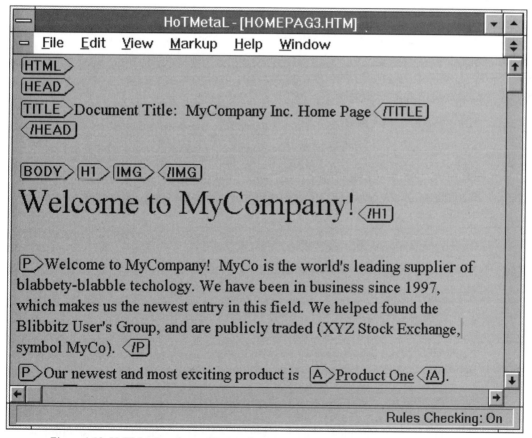

Figure 4-12. HoTMetaL and one of its templates

adhere to the rules of HTML tagging or that contains tags not yet supported by HoTMetaL. As a WYSIWYG editor, HoTMetaL attempts to render the contents of a document as they would look with a Web browser.

HoTMetaL Free is available for downloading from several FTP sites in the U.S., Canada, and Europe. For a list of these sites, see **http://www.sq.com/products/hotmetal/hm-ftp.htm**. HoTMetaL Free is unsupported and not to be used for commercial use.

HoTMetaL Pro provides all the features of HoTMetaL Free plus several add-ons to make it a more complete editing tool. With HoTMetaL Pro, you get:

- An on-line dictionary, on-line thesaurus, and a spelling-check program

- An editor for creating and editing HTML tables

- Filters for importing documents from other word processing programs

- Improved tolerance of HTML coding for editing existing documents

For more information about HoTMetaL Free and HoTMetaL Pro, see **http://www.sq.com/**.

NaviPress

NaviPress by NaviSoft is available for Windows, Macintosh, and SunOS systems. NaviPress provides an easy-to-use interface for creating and editing HTML documents. As a stand-alone product, NaviPress provides many of the same functions as HoTMetaL or any other HTML editor. It provides a point and click interface that allows you to create and edit:

- An HTML document without having to know the syntax of the HTML tags

- Hypertext links to other documents

- In-line images

- HTML forms

Unlike HoTMetaL, NaviPress allows you to view the HTML source of your document. In addition, NaviPress can display a visual representation of the relationships between your HTML documents, called a *MiniWeb*. In a MiniWeb, documents and images are represented as icons and the relationships between the documents and icons are represented with arrows. This allows you to see the overall hierarchy of your interconnected documents. While in the MiniWeb view, you can edit any of the documents shown, import existing documents, or add new documents to your MiniWeb.

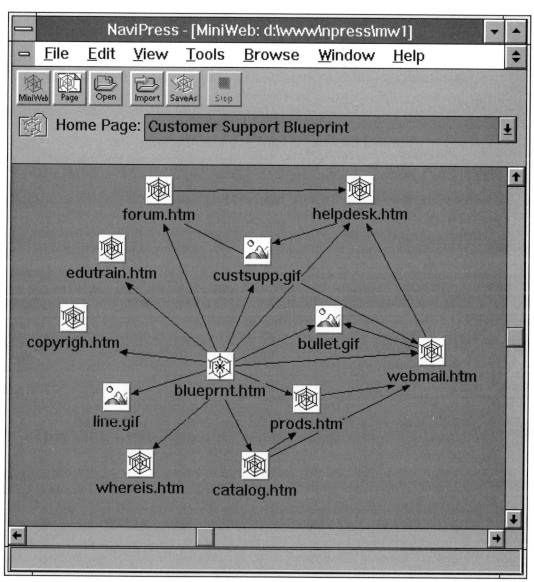

Figure 4-13. NaviPress' MiniWeb view

As part of its on-line help, NaviPress offers MiniWeb templates, called blueprints, that provide you with a series of linked HTML templates designed for various purposes, such as customer support. Unfortunately, to obtain the blueprints (or any of the on-line help information), you must have access to the NaviSoft homepage. Therefore, you cannot use the templates or the on-line help unless you are connected to the World Wide Web.

Although NaviPress can be used alone as an HTML editor, it is most useful when used with NaviSoft's NaviServer. When used with NaviServer, NaviPress allows you to:

- Place HTML documents on the Web server without having to go through a system administrator

- Create simple processing scripts for handling data from HTML forms without having to understand the programming language

- Automatically scan a document and turn plain text into hypertext links

For more information about NaviPress and NaviServer, see
http://www.navisoft.com/.

HTML converters

HTML converters allow you to take documents in various formats and convert them to HTML documents. Many of these programs convert files from word processors to HTML. Some convert information from other Internet programs to HTML. And others can be used to extract information from the source code of programs and convert it to HTML documents.

Yahoo maintains an extensive list of HTML converters at
http://www.yahoo.com/Computers/World_Wide_Web/HTML_Converters/.

Conversion programs for word processors

The following list is a sampling of the word processor-to-HTML conversion tools available on the Web.

WordPerfect

Internet Publisher, developed by Novell, is an add-on for WordPerfect 6.1 for Windows. It allows you to convert a WordPerfect 6.1 document to HTML or to create an HTML document using familiar WordPerfect tools. Internet Publisher incorporates Netscape Navigator, which allows you to interactively browse and test your document. For more information about Internet Publisher, see
http://wp.novell.com/elecpub/intpub.htm.

WPtoHTML, developed by Hunter Monroe, converts WordPerfect documents to HTML format. It runs on DOS and will not convert documents created with WordPerfect for OS/2, Windows, or UNIX. For more information, see
ftp://oak.oakland.edu/SimTel/msdos/wordperf/ and look for wpt51d10.zip (for

converting WordPerfect 5.1 documents) or wpt60d10.zip (for converting WordPerfect 6.0 documents).

WP2X, originally developed by Raymond Chen, converts WordPerfect documents to many formats including HTML. You can compile the source code to run on UNIX or DOS. For more information, see
http://www.milkyway.com/People/Michael_Richardson/wp2x.html.

Word

Internet Assistant, developed by Microsoft, is an add-on for Word for Windows. It allows you to convert a Word document to HTML format or to create an HTML document using familiar Word tools. Internet Assistant adds push buttons to the Word toolbar for functions such as adding an image or hypertext link to your document. With a built-in browser, Internet Assistant allows you to toggle between editing mode and browsing mode and to test your hypertext links. For more information about Internet Assistant, see
http://www.microsoft.com/MSOffice/Word/ia/default.htm.

HTML Author, developed by Dr. Grahamme Cooper, is another add-on for Word for Windows. Like Internet Assistant, it allows you to convert a Word document to HTML or to create an HTML document using Word. HTML Author adds a pull-down menu with options for inserting images and hypertext links, as well as an option to generate a table of contents. It also adds push buttons to the Word toolbar for easy access to the highlighting options of HTML. For more information about HTML Author, see
http://www.salford.ac.uk/docs/depts/iti/staff/gsc/htmlauth/summary.html.

Interleaf

Cyberleaf, developed by Interleaf, is an add-on for Interleaf that converts Interleaf documents to HTML format. It simultaneously converts text to HTML and images to GIF. Cyberleaf can also convert FrameMaker, Word, and WordPerfect documents to HTML. For more information, see **http://www.ileaf.com/ip.html**.

FrameMaker

FMtoHTML, developed by Jon Stephenson von Tetzchner, converts documents in FrameMaker document format or FrameMaker Interchange Format (MIF) to HTML format. The program will convert figures and tables. It can also create links for phrases that have been identified in FrameMaker with a marker of "hypertext." For more information, see
http://www.w3.org/hypertext/WWW/Tools/fm2html.html.

PageMaker

PM2HTML (author unknown) converts PC-PageMaker documents to HTML format. For more information, see **ftp://ftp.gate.net/pub/users/edco**.

Dave, developed by Jeff Boulter, converts Mac-PageMaker documents to HTML format. It runs on the Macintosh and requires AppleScript. For more information about Dave, see **http://www.bucknell.edu/bucknellian/dave/**.

Quark

QT2WWW, developed by Jeremy Hylton, converts QuarkXpress documents to HTML format. It runs on UNIX, Macintosh, and DOS. It uses a map file to convert Quark tags to HTML tags. For more information, see **http://the-tech.mit.edu/~jeremy/qt2www.html**.

RTF

RTFtoHTML, developed by Chris Hector, converts documents in Rich Text Format (RTF) to HTML format. It runs on UNIX and Macintosh, but can also convert RTF documents that were created on Windows or DOS. For more information, see **ftp://ftp.cray.com/src/WWWstuff/RTF/rtftohtml_overview.html**.

PostScript

PS2HTML, developed by Alessandro Agostini and Stefano Cerreti, converts PostScript files (PS 3.0 and EPS 2.0) to HTML documents. It generates the appropriate tags to include small images in-line and to link to large images (for external viewing). For more information, see **ftp://ftp.area.fi.cnr.it/pub/dos/misc/ps2html/**.

Conversion programs for Internet information

The following list is a sampling of the Internet information-to-HTML conversion tools available on the Web.

Mail

Hypermail, developed by Tom Gruber and refined by Kevin Hughes, converts a file of e-mail messages to HTML format. Each message is converted to a separate document. References to messages are converted to hypertext links. Hypermail is a UNIX program. The original version was written in Lisp and is still available. The latest version is written in C. For more information, see **http://gummo.stanford.edu/html/hypermail/hypermail.html**.

MHonArc, developed by Earl Hood, converts a file of e-mail messages to HTML format. As with Hypermail, each message is converted to a separate document, and references are converted to hypertext links. However, MHonArc also provides full support for Multipurpose Internet Mail Extensions (MIME) encoded messages. MIME messages can have multiple parts, which can include images and binary attachments. MHonArc can run on UNIX or MS-DOS. For more information, see **http:// www.oac.uci.edu/indiv/ehood/mhonarc.doc.html**.

News

Hyperactive, developed by Mike Brudenell, converts a user-defined list of Usenet newsgroups to a hierarchical listing in HTML format. For more information, see **http://www.york.ac.uk/ftparchive/WWW/utils/hyperactive/**.

Newslist, developed by Quentin Stafford-Fraser, converts all Usenet newsgroups available on a specified server to a hierarchical listing in HTML format. For more information, see **http://pelican.cl.cam.ac.uk/people/qs101/newslist/**.

Conversion programs for program source code

The following list is a sampling of the source code-to-HTML conversion tools available on the Web.

Cxx2HTML, developed by Darrell Schiebel, extracts the header information from C++ files and converts it to an HTML document. There are several special tags developed for use with Cxx2HTML that you can include in your source code to enhance the HTML output (such as tags to produce hypertext links between related classes). Depending on how well the source code is documented, Cxx2HTML can be used to produce a reference manual for the program (in HTML format). For more information, see **http://info.cv.nrao.edu/aips++/RELEASED/cxx2html/**.

C++2HTML, developed by Stefan Schwarz, also extracts header information from C++ files and converts it to an HTML document. Unlike Cxx2HTML, it neither requires nor recognizes any special tags in the source code, yet it still converts class cross-references to hypertext links. For more information, see **http://www.bauv.unibw-muenchen.de/graphics/projects/c++2html.html**.

Including images in your document

n old but valid saying is: "A picture is worth a thousand words." And when you are working with limited space, as we often are with on-line documents, the economical use of words becomes very important. Images included in HTML documents can not only save space, but they can also make the document more appealing. Also, if used correctly, they can make the document language-independent; universal images require no translation.

However, as we discussed in Chapter 3, these benefits are not without a price. The price is reduced response time and possible incompatibility with some browsers.

Despite the possible drawbacks, images are widely used in HTML documents. This chapter describes many of the types of images that can be included and how you can use them to enhance your document.

Chapter 5. Including images in your document

Types of images

If you look around at enough Web sites, you will find just about every type of image that you can imagine. There are maps, cartoons, photographs, backgrounds, diagrams, screen images, and a wide variety of high-resolution computer-generated images. Basically, these all fall into three categories: created images, imported images, and captured images. There is also a fourth category, which may include images from the other three. This fourth category is borrowed images.

Created images

Created images are produced on a computer using one of a variety of image programs. These programs are capable of producing images of varying complexity and resolution. To some of us, the idea of using a computer to create a picture may sound intimidating. But fear not! Programs are available for a wide range of artistic expertise.

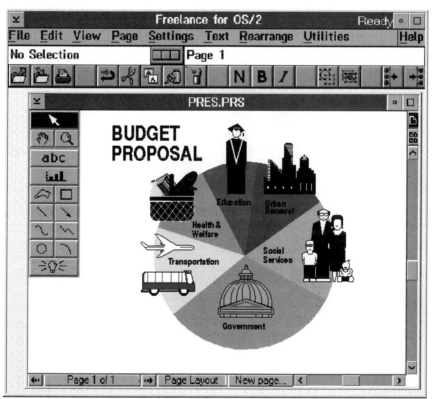

Figure 5-1. Example of a simple image

For the novice artist, programs such as Lotus Freelance, Microsoft's Paintbrush, and xpaint (which is available from **ftp://ftp.x.org/R5contrib**) are easy to learn and easy to use to produce simple images consisting of basic shapes. Programs such as these are useful for creating charts and graphs, and for creating images for document headings or navigational push buttons.

For the more experienced artist, programs such as CorelDraw and Micrografx Designer provide a variety of tools and functions to create high-quality, 2-dimensional images. Programs such as these are useful for creating many types of images including complex diagrams and logos.

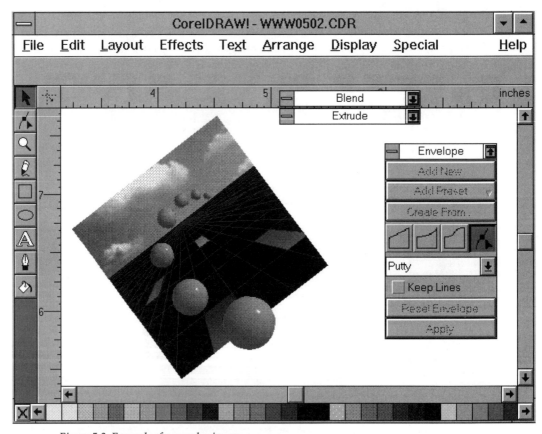

Figure 5-2. Example of a complex image

For the expert, state-of-the-art programs such as AutoDesk's 3D Studio and Adobe's Dimensions provide an artist with the tools necessary to produce high-quality, 3-dimensional images, some of which are hard to distinguish from photographs.

Another program is Persistence of Vision Raytracer. This is a 3-D package that you can use on many types of systems, including DOS, Windows, OS/2, and UNIX. Persistence of Vision Raytracer is available at **ftp://alfred.ccs.carleton.ca/pub/pov-ray/**.

Currently, viewer support for 3-D images on the Web is limited. However, there are a number of programs in the works, including Silicon Graphics' WebSpace. For more information about 3-D images, see Chapter 7, "Including multimedia in your document."

Most programs can produce (or export) images in a variety of file formats. Often they are capable of producing files in one or more of the formats used on the Web. However, if your program cannot produce files in one of the popular Web formats, there are a number of conversion programs that you can use to bridge the gap. See "Changing image formats" on page 82.

Imported images

Imported images are created using methods other than a traditional image program. If necessary, they are then converted to a format that can be read by the computer. A scanned photograph or data from a spectroscopic or thermal analysis program are examples of imported images.

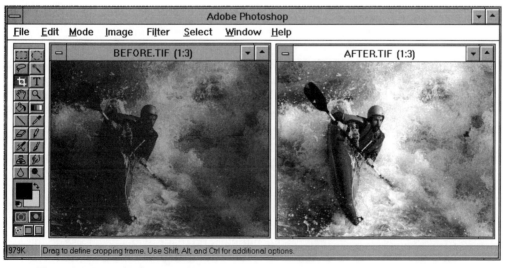

Figure 5-3. Example of a scanned image

For scanned images, many scanner driver programs can now produce files in formats that can be used on the Web. However, if yours does not, you can use a conversion program. (See "Changing image formats" on page 82.) Also, there are programs such as Adobe's Photoshop that allow you to import and manipulate scanned images.

For visual representation of scientific data, you can use a program such as IBM's Visualization Data Explorer. Data Explorer is an easy-to-use program for interactive visualization of scientific data. It provides a full set of tools for creating and manipulating the data. The data can come from models, simulations, observations, experiments, and commercial applications and can be converted to two- or three-dimensional images. Data manipulation is easy using the graphical user interface or the application programming interface (API). For more information about IBM's Visualization Data Explorer, see **http://www.ibm.com/dx/**. For information about other visualization programs, see the repository at Yahoo, **http://www.yahoo.com/ Computers_and_Internet/Software/Visualization_Software/**.

Captured images

Captured images are created by taking a computer snapshot of information displayed on a computer screen. There are numerous screen capture programs available on a range of operating systems. Most allow you to capture images in color and many allow you to capture the entire screen or part of it.

There are many screen capture programs available, such as PM Camera (for OS/2) and HiJaak Pro (for Windows). There are also many programs available on the Internet. Many are offered free of charge (freeware). Others are free for evaluation. SimTel maintains a repository of Windows capture programs at **http://www.acs.oakland.edu/oak/SimTel/win3/capture.html**. There are a few OS/2 capture programs available from Walnut Creek at **http://www.cdrom.com/pub/os2/graphics/**. There are a couple of UNIX capture programs available from the X Consortium at **ftp://ftp.x.org/contrib/applications**.

Screen capture tools typically produce .bmp files. This file format is widely used on the Web. However, as with created and imported images, you can use a conversion program to produce other formats. (See "Changing image formats" on page 82.)

Borrowed images

Borrowed images are created by someone else and made available for use on the Internet. Several Web sites contain a repository of images in different formats. Some images are simple, such as small images that can be used as bullets in an unordered list. Some are quite complex, such as illustrations from the Star Trek series. Some images may be copyrighted and require a notation of credit. It is not always apparent whether an image is copyrighted or not. So, if you use someone else's image in your document, it is proper to acknowledge its origin.

A good selection of images and icons that you can borrow can be found at **http://WWW.Stars.com/Vlib/Providers/Images_and_Icons.html** and at **http://www.cis.ohio-state.edu/hypertext/faq/usenet/graphics/fileformats-faq/faq-doc-23.html**.

Image file formats

For the text of an article, HTML is the accepted standard. For images, however, there is no standard. For images, you are limited only by what the browser can display, either in-line or through an external viewer. There are numerous image file formats that are supported by various Web servers and browsers. In this section, we discuss the more common formats.

GIF

The *Graphic Interchange Format (GIF)* is the most widely-used image format on the Web. Many browsers support in-line GIF images. And, of those that do not, most support viewing of GIF images through an external viewer. GIF is a *raster-based* file format that supports transparent backgrounds (GIF89a) and a maximum of 256 colors. Raster images consist entirely of dots, or pixels. For example, a line in a raster image is actually a string of pixels that appear to form a line. Although raster images may appear to contain text, because the text is stored as a series of pixels rather than a complete object, it cannot be edited.

GIF is a proprietary file format belonging to CompuServe. It uses a compression method called LZW (Lempel-Zev-Welch), which is patented by Unisys. In December of 1994, Unisys stated that they would begin enforcing their patent rights, requiring "all of the major commercial on-line information services companies employing the LZW patent to license the technology from Unisys at a reasonable rate."[1] For a while, several alternative formats were suggested and it appeared that the GIF file format would no longer be the image format of choice on the Web. Recently, due to challenges by numerous members of the Web community, the controversy seems to have subsided and the use of GIF files seems unchanged.

---

[1]Excerpt from Unisys's January 6, 1995, Press Release.

For more information about the GIF format, see
http://www.w3.org/hypertext/WWW/Graphics/GIF/spec-gif87.txt and
http://www.w3.org/hypertext/WWW/Graphics/GIF/spec-gif89a.txt.

For more information about the LZW patent and Unisys's position, see
http://www.xmission.com/~mgm/gif.

Interlaced GIFs

There is a variation of the GIF file format, called *interlaced GIF*, which can improve
browser performance. With interlaced GIFs, the image is saved in a series of layers. For
browsers that support interlaced GIFs (such as IBM WebExplorer for OS/2 and
Netscape Navigator), layering the file makes it quicker to display. With standard GIFs,
the browser must wait until the entire image file is received before it is displayed. With
interlaced GIFs, the layers are displayed as they are received, causing a "fade in"
effect. For browsers that do not support interlaced GIFs, the image is treated as a
standard GIF.

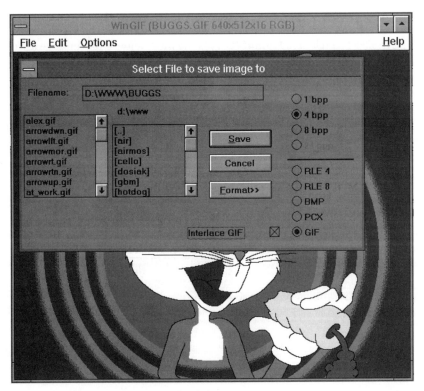

Figure 5-4. Example of creating an interlaced GIF

One program that you can use to convert your image to an interlaced GIF is WinGIF. WinGIF, created by Kyle Powell, is an easy-to-use Windows program. Simply start WinGIF, open the image (which can be a format other than GIF), and then save the file as an interlaced GIF.

WinGIF is a shareware program. You can try it out for free, but if you decide to continue to use it, you are asked to pay a nominal registration fee. You can find a copy of WinGIF at **ftp://ftp.best.com/pub/craig/windows_apps/wingif14.zip**.

There are several other programs that you can use. The Transparent/Interlaced GIF Resource Page, maintained by Adam Bernstein, lists many of them (grouped by platform). You can find this page at **http://dragon.jpl.nasa.gov/~adam/transparent.html**.

Transparent GIFs

Many aspects of Web browsers can be configured by the user. One of these aspects is the background of the window. Images, too, generally have a background, often w h i t e . Consider what it might look like if you create a green bullet on a white background that is then displayed using a Web browser that has a grey background.

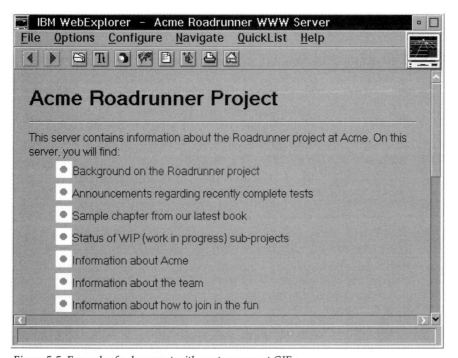

Figure 5-5. Example of a document with nontransparent GIFs

You could make the background of your bullet grey, but then you would have a problem with Web browsers that have a white background. To solve this problem, you can use a *transparent GIF*. In transparent GIFs, the pixels in the image that are designated as transparent (usually the background) will take on the color of the browser background.

One of the programs that you can use to create transparent GIFs is GIFtrans. GIFtrans, created by Andreas Ley, is a program that allows you to translate a specified color in a GIF to a "transparent" color. There are a few preliminary steps before you can convert your image.

1. Ensure that the background color in your GIF is unique; that it is not used anywhere else in your image.
2. Determine the RGB (red, green, blue) value of the background color. GIFtrans can take either the hexadecimal equivalent or the index equivalent of the RGB value as input.

    To determine the RGB (red, green, blue) value of the background color, you can use an image editing program such as xv or Adobe Photoshop. These programs provide the RGB value in decimal format; for example, white is 255 255 255.

    *   **Determining the hexadecimal equivalent**

        For the *hexadecimal equivalent*, each of the numbers in the RGB value is converted to hexadecimal, and then the three numbers are concatenated. For example, the hexadecimal equivalent of the decimal number 255 is FF. Therefore, an RGB value of 255 255 255 translated to hexadecimal is FFFFFF. To convert the three decimal values to hexadecimal, you can use a tool such as BEACH RaT (Background Electronically Automated Converter for HTML to RGB Translations). BEACH RaT is a fast and easy-to-use on-line service. Simply enter the decimal values for red, green, and blue, and BEACH RaT returns the hexadecimal equivalent. To use BEACH RaT, go to **http://www.novalink.com/pei/hex/hex.html**. You can also use the -l option of GIFtrans to determine the hexadecimal value (as described below).

    *   **Determining the index equivalent**

        For the *index equivalent*, the three values of red, green, and blue are converted to a single decimal number. To determine the index equivalent of the RGB value, you can use the -l option of GIFtrans. This option generates a list of the RGB values and corresponding index and hexadecimal values of the colors used in the file. For example, when we entered:

```
giftrans -l greenb.gif
```

GIFtrans returned:

```
Color 246: Red 255, Green 251, Blue 240, #fffbf0
Color 247: Red 160, Green 160, Blue 164, #a0a0a4
Color 248: Red 128, Green 128, Blue 128, #808080
Color 249: Red 255, Green 0, Blue 0, #ff0000
Color 250: Red 0, Green 255, Blue 0, #00ff00
Color 251: Red 255, Green 255, Blue 0, #ffff00
Color 252: Red 0, Green 0, Blue 255, #0000ff
Color 253: Red 255, Green 0, Blue 255, #ff00ff
Color 254: Red 0, Green 255, Blue 255, #00ffff
Color 255: Red 255, Green 255, Blue 255, #ffffff
```

Based on this information, the index equivalent of 255 255 255 is 255.

Now that you have determined the value of the color to be translated, you are ready to convert the image. Enter the GIFtrans command with:

1. -t followed by the hexadecimal or index value of the color to be translated. If you use the hexadecimal value, precede it with a # and do not include spaces in the value, for example #FFFFFF.
2. -o followed by the name of the file to be created, for example greenb1.gif.
3. The name of the file to convert, for example greenb.gif.

Using our example, the complete command to create the transparent GIF is:

```
giftrans -t 255 -o greenb1.gif greenb.gif
```

Once the transparent GIF is created, the background of the image will take on the color of the background of the browser.

For a copy of GIFtrans, see **http://melmac.corp.harris.com/files/giftrans.exe**.

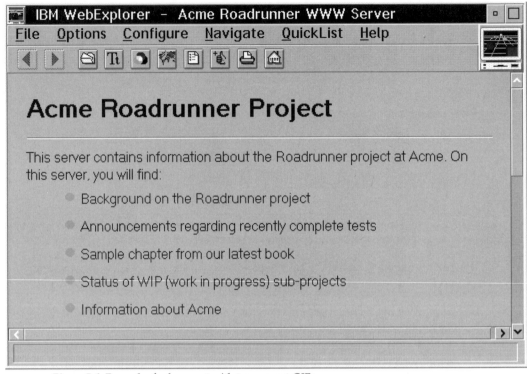

Figure 5-6. Example of a document with transparent GIFs

There are several other programs that you can use. The Transparent/Interlaced GIF Resource Page, maintained by Adam Bernstein, lists many of them (grouped by platform). You can find this page at **http://dragon.jpl.nasa.gov/~adam/transparent.html**.

JPEG

The *Joint Photographic Experts Group (JPEG)* format is another popular file format for Web images. Some browsers now have built-in JPEG viewing capabilities, and many let you use external viewers to view JPEGs.

JPEG is best suited for "true color" images such as scanned photographs. It does not work as well as GIF for computer-generated images with few colors. For this reason, it is seen as a complement to the GIF format, not a replacement. JPEG is a raster-based file format that supports 16 million colors. At this time, most of the display equipment on the market supports a maximum of 256 colors. However, as higher-resolution equipment becomes more prevalent (and less expensive), the true value of the JPEG format will be realized.

A key advantage of the JPEG compression algorithm is that it produces a file that is much smaller than that of a GIF, nearly half the size in most cases. However, there is a trade-off. The compression algorithm results in a *lossy* file. Lossy means that image is not of the same quality after it has been compressed and decompressed. Depending on the purpose of the image, this may or may not be a problem. Also, there are ways to alter the compression parameters to produce a larger compressed file that retains more of the quality of the original.

Another advantage of the JPEG format is that there are no patents on the basic file format. There are, however, patents on some of the extensions.

For more information about JPEG, see **http://www.cis.ohio-state.edu/hypertext/faq/usenet/jpeg-faq/faq.html**.

TIFF

The *Tag Image File Format (TIFF)* was developed by Aldus Corporation. It is designed to store raster-based images from scanners, screen capture programs, and photo-enhancement programs. Aldus worked with several manufacturers of scanners and imaging hardware to produce an extensible file format. This extensibility is one of the benefits of TIFF; the numerous extensions allow for greater flexibility. However, it is also one of the drawbacks; the variety of extensions makes it difficult for viewers to anticipate and handle the various flavors of TIFF.

Initially, TIFF images were not compressed, requiring more space than many other image file formats. With Revision 5, LZW compression was added, making TIFF a more usable file format. With Revision 6, Aldus added JPEG compression. However, numerous problems were discovered in the design, and on March 17, 1995, Aldus withdrew Revision 6.

For more information about TIFF 5, see **http://www.dcs.ed.ac.uk/students/cs4/iat/index.html**. For more information about TIFF 6, including the withdrawl statement, see **ftp://sgi.com/graphics/tiff/**.

BMP

The *Bitmap (BMP)* file format is another common file format. It was created by Microsoft to store raster-based images. It is a fairly simple, device-independent file format. There are four variations of BMP files: monochrome, 16-color, 256-color, and 24-bit (which contains 2^{24} colors). The BMP format is often used for screen captures and icons.

For more information about BMP, see **http://www.dcs.ed.ac.uk/students/cs4/iat/index.html**.

CGM

The *Computer Graphics Metafile (CGM)* format was developed by the American National Standard for Information Systems (ANSI). It is best suited for *vector-based* information, but as a metafile, it can also include raster-based information. As opposed to raster images, which consist of thousands of dots, a vector image can contain complete objects, such as lines and circles. Vector images can also contain text in a form that can be edited and changed.

For more information about CGM, see **http://www.dcs.ed.ac.uk/students/cs4/iat/index.html**.

Changing image formats

Most of the methods and programs mentioned in "Types of images" produce files in formats that can be used on the Web. However, if the method or program you use does not, you can use another program to convert your image to an acceptable file format.

Most of these programs are very simple to use. It is a matter of importing a file of one format and exporting the same file in a different format. One such tool is Inset System's HiJaak Pro. It will convert:

- From one raster format to another raster format, such as BMP to GIF

- From one vector format to another vector format, such as MET (an OS/2 Metafile) to CGM

- From vector format to raster format, such as CGM to GIF

HiJaak Pro cannot, however, convert raster format files to vector format. Currently, this program is only available for Windows.

Other tools are available (some free for use, others free for evaluation) on the Internet. Here is just a sampling:

- For Windows, Picture Man, which is a shareware program, is available from **ftp://oak.oakland.edu/pub/mdos/windows3/pman155.zip**. This program, written by Igor Plotnikov, allows you to create new images, view and modify existing images, and convert images between various formats, including: GIF, JPEG, TIFF, and BMP. Picture Man provides a workspace window, a handy tool pallet, and an assortment of options that allow you to manipulate elements of an image.

- For UNIX, ImageMagick is available from **ftp://ftp.x.org/contrib/applications/ImageMagick/**. This program, written by John Cristy, is an X11 package that allows you to create, view, modify, and convert images of various formats, including: JPEG, TIFF, BMP, MPEG, XBM, and Targa. In addition, ImageMagick also allows you to string images together (animation) and create composite images (montage).

- For DOS, Graphics Display System (GDS) is available from **ftp://oak.oakland.edu/SimTel/msdos/graphics**. This program, developed by Photodex, allows you to modify and convert images of various formats.

- For OS/2, Generalised Bitmap Module (GBM) is available from **ftp://ftp.cdrom.com/pub/os2/graphics/gbm.zip**. This program, written by Andy Key, allows you to create, view, modify, and convert files of various formats, including: GIF, JPEG, BMP, TIFF, XBM, and MET. In addition, GBM can also be used to capture OS/2 windows.

Including in-line images

It is simple to include an in-line image in your HTML document. First, ensure that the image is in one of the commonly supported file formats for in-line images, such as GIF or BMP. Then use the image tag to include the image in your document. As part of the image tag, you must specify the name (and location) of the image file. You should also provide a text string that describes the image as an alternative for viewers that do not support in-line images.

For example, to include a scanned photograph of yourself (mypic.gif) in your document, the HTML tag would be as follows:

```
<IMG src=mypic.gif alt='Picture of me'>
```

For more information about the image tag and its attributes, see Appendix A, "HTML tagging reference."

Linking to and from images

There are two types of image links. In one case, the image is the destination of the link. In the other, the image is the launch point of the link.

The image as the destination

When the Web was first developed, most of the browsers did not support in-line images. If you wanted an image to accompany your document, you had to link to it. Today, many browsers support in-line images, so linking is no longer as much of a necessity. However, many browsers do not display a document until all the text and in-line images have been transferred. So, if the image is large, it is still a good idea to link to it.

It is quite easy to link to an image. Linking to an image is similar to linking to another HTML document. Simply use the HTML anchor tag to create a link. When the reader clicks on the link, the browser requests a copy of the image, determines its file format (based on its extension), and launches the appropriate viewing program. For example, to link from a document that discusses the use of your Web server to a graph that shows the increase in users, you might include the following:

```
In the past six months, our Web site has seen <a href="growth.bmp">a
substantial increase in usage.</a>
```

growth.bmp is a Bitmap that shows the progress over the past six months. For more information about the anchor tag and its attributes, see Appendix A, "HTML tagging reference."

The image as the launch point

In addition to linking *to* an image, you can also link *from* an image. In this case, you are using an image as a launch point for a link. For example, let's assume that your document contains pictures of the members of your support staff, and you want to create a link from each picture to a listing of the person's e-mail address, phone number, working hours, and areas of expertise. To do so, you could include the following anchor tag:

```
<a href="johninfo.html"><img src=john.gif align=middle alt="John
Wilder"></a>
```

When the reader selects the image of John, the browser gets and displays the HTML document that contains the information about John. For more information about the anchor tag and its attributes, see Appendix A, "HTML tagging reference."

There is also a way to link from different points in an image to different HTML documents. This is called image mapping and is discussed in the next section.

Using image maps

An *image map* is an image that contains defined areas that link to different documents; the document displayed depends on where in the image you click. For example, consider a campus map. You could create an image map to link each building on the campus map to an HTML document that describes the departments housed in that building.

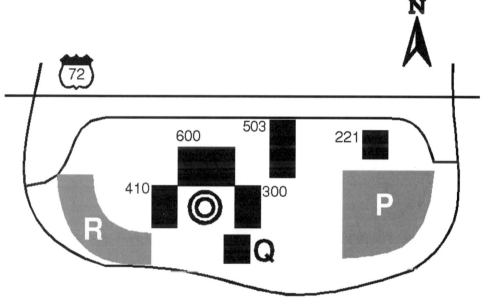

Figure 5-7. Map of a campus

Image maps are often used for *button bars*, such as the one you see below. A button bar is a single image that contains selectable objects or push buttons.

Figure 5-8. Button bar from the IBM home page

How image maps work

Image maps are not as complicated as they might seem.

An image map is a combination of an in-line image and a map file. It is included in a document in much the same way as any other linked image. The *map file* contains a table that associates each area in an image with the URL of the linked information. These areas can be circles, rectangles, or polygons.

When the reader clicks on an area of the image, the coordinates of the click are sent to the server along with the name of the map file. The server searches through the map file and initiates a link to the URL associated with those coordinates.

Creating an image map

To use an image map, your Web server must support image mapping. Both the NCSA and the CERN servers support image mapping. However, there are some differences, so you need to determine which one you are using before you begin. If you are unsure, ask the administrator of your Web server.

Step 1. Make sure you have what you need

You need a program that can process image maps. The **htimage** program is available with CERN servers. The **imagemap** program is available with NCSA servers. You can use either of these programs. But you may find the **imagemap** program is more restrictive, because it requires all map files to be registered in a central configuration file (**imagemap.conf**).

Figure 5-9. Sample image for mapping

Step 2. Create your image

Your image can be a created, imported, or captured image. But it should be in GIF format. Because the map file allows you to define linked areas in terms of circles, rectangles, and polygons, the image should ideally contain distinct regions in these shapes. Figure 5-9 shows a simple example that we named **tpmusic.gif**.

Step 3. Determine the location of your link areas

Link areas are defined by coordinates, and coordinates are defined in *pixels*. A pixel is the smallest unit that makes up an image. When determining the coordinates of the link areas, remember that the image mapping programs assume that the upper left corner of the image is the origin (0,0). There are several tools that you can use to determine the coordinates (in pixels) of an area, such as Paintbrush, which comes with Windows, or XV for UNIX, which you can get from **ftp://ftp.x.org/contrib**. Both of these use the upper left corner as the origin.

- For polygons, you need the coordinates of each vertex.

- For rectangles, you need the coordinates of two opposite corners, such as the lower left and upper right corners. In our example, the lower left corner of the Video Tapes rectangle is 139,190 and the upper right corner is 187,262.

- For circles, it depends on the type of server you are using. If you are using the imagemap program, you need the coordinates of the center and the coordinates of any spot on the circumference. If you are using the **htimage** program, you need the coordinates of the center and the radius (in pixels). In our example, the center of the CDs circle is 444,97 and a point on the circumference is 444,134, which means the radius is 37.

Step 4. Determine the destination for your links

You need the URL of the destination document for each linked area. You should also have a default URL, which specifies the information to be displayed if the reader clicks on an undefined area of the image. The URL can be absolute or relative. Absolute URLs specify the protocol, the hostname, and location (path and filename) of the linked file. Relative URLs specify only the location (path and filename) of the linked file and must begin with a slash /.

Step 5. Create your map file

The map file is an ASCII file that contains a table of information that maps a location in the image to a destination URL. The name and extension of the map file are up to you. For our example, we chose **tpmusic.map**. The format of the map file depends on the image mapping program you are using. In either file format, comments are preceded by a pound sign #.

If you are using the **imagemap** program, the format of each line is:

shape   *url*   *coordinates*

Possible entries are as follows:

```
default    url
rect       url     x1,y1     x2,y2
circle     url     x1,y1     x2,y2
poly       url     x1,y1     x2,y2     x3,y3     ...
```

Using our imagemap example, the map file (which we named **tpmusic.map**) looks like this:

```
default  http://www.tpm.com/
#Record selections
circle   http://www.tmp.com/vinyl.html   137,105 150,156
#Compact Disc selections
circle   http://www.tpm.com/cd.html 444,97 444,134
#Video Tape selections
rect     http://www.tpm.com/video.html   139,190 187,262
#Cassette Tape selections
rect     http://www.tpm.com/audio.html   386,207 464,248
```

If you are using the **htimage** program, the format of each line is:

shape   *(coordinates)*   *url*

Possible entries are as follows:

```
default    url
rect       (x1,y1)     (x2,y2)     url
circle     (x1,y1)     radius      url
poly       (x1,y1)     (x2,y2)     (x3,y3)     ...     url
```

Using our **htimage** example, the map file (which we named **tpmusic.map**) looks like this:

```
default   http://www.tpm.com/
#Record selections
circle (137,105) 53   http://www.tpm.com/vinyl.html
#Compact Disc selections
```

```
circle (444,97) 37   http://www.tpm.com/cd.html
#Video Tape selections
rect (139,190) (187,262)   http://www.tpm.com/video.html
#Cassette Tape selections
rect (386,207) (464,248)   http://www.tpm.com/cass.html
```

Step 6. Place the image and map file on your server

The image and the map file must be stored on the Web server. They should be placed in a subdirectory of the server root directory. If you are using the imagemap program, you must also update the **imagemap.conf** file to include the location of your new map file. The format of the imagemap.conf file is:

symbolic_name : *map_file*

symbolic_name is a name you assign to your map file, such as **music**. *map_file* is the actual path and name of the file, such as **/images/tpmusic.map**. For our example, the new line in our **imagemap.conf** would be:

```
music : /images/tpmusic.map
```

Step 7. Include the image map in your HTML document

Including an image map is similar to using an image as a launch point for a link. The HTML coding is a combination of an anchor and an image tag. However, instead of pointing to a destination document, your anchor tag will point to the image map file (for **htimage**) or to the symbolic name for your image map file (for **imagemap**). The format of the tags is:

<a href="/*image_map_program*/*map_file*"><img src=*image* ISMAP></a>

image_map_program is the location and name of the program you are using, such as /cgi-bin/htimage or /cgi-bin/imagemap. *map_file* is either the location and name of the map file (if you are using htimage) or the symbolic name you assigned to the map file (if you are using imagemap). *image* is the location and name of the image. ISMAP indicates that the image is an image map.

In our example, we named the image **tpmusic.gif** and the map file **tpmusic.map**. If we were using htimage, we would include the following:

```
<a href="/cgi-bin/htimage/images/tpmusic.map">
<img src=tpmusic.gif ISMAP></a>
```

If we were using imagemap, we would include the following:

```
<a href="/cgi-bin/imagemap/music">
<img src=tpmusic.gif ISMAP></a>
```

Step 8. Test your links

It is always a good idea to test the links in any HTML document, and image maps are no exception. You should verify that each defined link area links to the appropriate document. You should also verify that areas outside the defined link areas link to the default URL.

The entries in a map file are read in order from top to bottom. When you click on a particular area of an image map, the mapping program reads the map file and links to the first URL defined for that area. If you find that your links are not working as expected, check your map file to ensure that there are no overlaps in the coordinates used to define link areas.

Another way to create map files

There are some tools available that are helpful in creating image maps. One is MapEdit. With MapEdit, creating a map file is easy:

1. Specify the name of the image and the map file that you want to use.
2. Specify whether you are using **htimage** (CERN) or **imagemap** (NCSA) as your image mapping program.
3. Select a shape and use your mouse to mark the link area.
4. Specify the URL of the link destination.
5. Repeat steps 3 and 4 for all link areas.
6. Save the map file. MapEdit creates a map file in the format you have chosen (**htimage** or **imagemap**).

MapEdit was written by Tom Boutell and is available from **http://sunsite.unc.edu/boutell/mapedit/mapedit.html**. Both the Windows and UNIX versions of the program are included in the MapEdit zip file. Make note, though, this is not a freeware program. Unless you are a nonprofit or educational institution, you must pay a small fee to use the program.

Chapter 6

Including forms in your document

eb browsers, as the term implies, allow users to peruse the information on the Web, much the same as they might browse through the information at a library or book store. But, because the Web is a dynamic, on-line resource (as opposed to a static, printed book), users can also interact with the Web. Using HTML forms, you can allow users to exchange information with you and your company or organization.

There are two aspects to using HTML forms. One is creating the form; the other is processing the form. This chapter discusses how to create a form. Processing is discussed in Chapter 12, "Using the Common Gateway Interface."

Chapter 6. Including forms in your document

Types of forms

If you want to allow users to make on-line purchases, send inquiries, or exchange information with you or your company, an HTML form is the answer. For example, you can create forms that allow users to:

- Request information on a specific topic

- Purchase goods and services

- Submit comments and suggestions

- Register for on-line services

- Configure a server from a remote location

Let's look at some examples.

Search forms

The most common type of form on the Web is the *search form*. A search form allows a user to submit a request for information on a specific topic. Carnegie

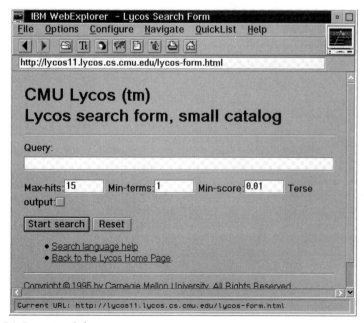

Figure 6-1. Lycos search form

Mellon University maintains a popular search facility called Lycos. Using the Lycos search form, users can locate resources on the Internet that contain information that meets their specified criteria.

Order forms

With the advent of transaction security, the Web is becoming a more viable channel for commerce. Many companies who have a presence on the Web have implemented on-line ordering systems using HTML forms. One example is Pacifica Blue, which has a system for ordering Gund stuffed animals from their Bear St. on-line store. The Pacifica Blue ordering form (Bear St. Adoption Form) is interesting in the way it conserves space. It uses "place holders" in the fields rather than labels beside the fields.

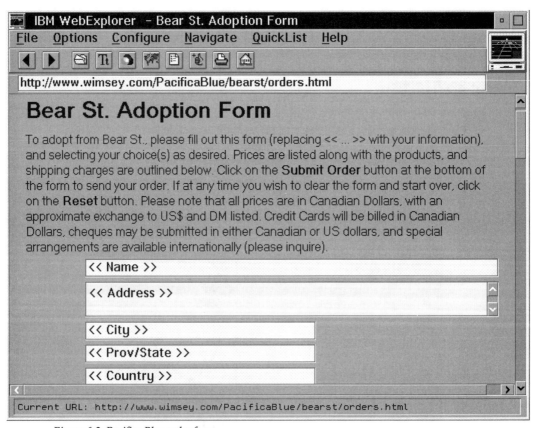

Figure 6-2. Pacifica Blue order form

Another example is Cheryl's Cheesecakes. Cheryl, with the help of BBS One Online Service, offers a variety of cheesecakes available for on-line ordering.

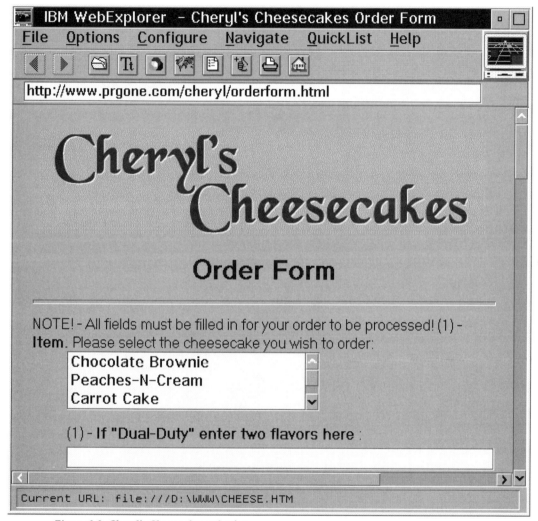

Figure 6-3. Cheryl's Cheesecakes order form

Comment, survey, and suggestion forms

Because the Web is a new means of distributing information, many of us are still learning how to use it effectively. There is often a lot of trial and error in developing a good Web site. And one of the best ways to find out what works and what doesn't is to ask your users. Many companies and organizations are starting to use comment forms to solicit input from users. One example is the IBM Networking Home Page Evaluation form.

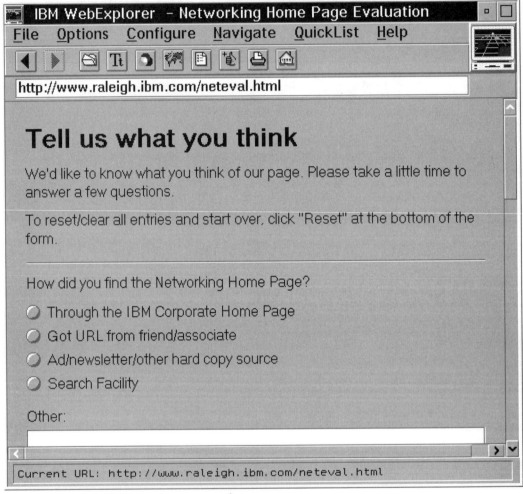

Figure 6-4. IBM Networking comment form

Registration and subscription forms

Many of the providers of fee-based services on the Web require users to fill out a registration form before using their service. Even some of the providers of free services now require users to fill out a registration form. This allows the providers of services to keep track of who is accessing their information and to gather information for future communication. Requiring users to register also helps limit the number of users (and therefore conserves valuable server resources). Only users who have more than a casual interest in the service are likely to take the time to register.

For example, the Global Network Navigator (GNN) is a free service that provides access to a wide range of information, including travel tips, financial information, sports and business news, as well as an on-line ordering system. GNN asks you to register before using their service.

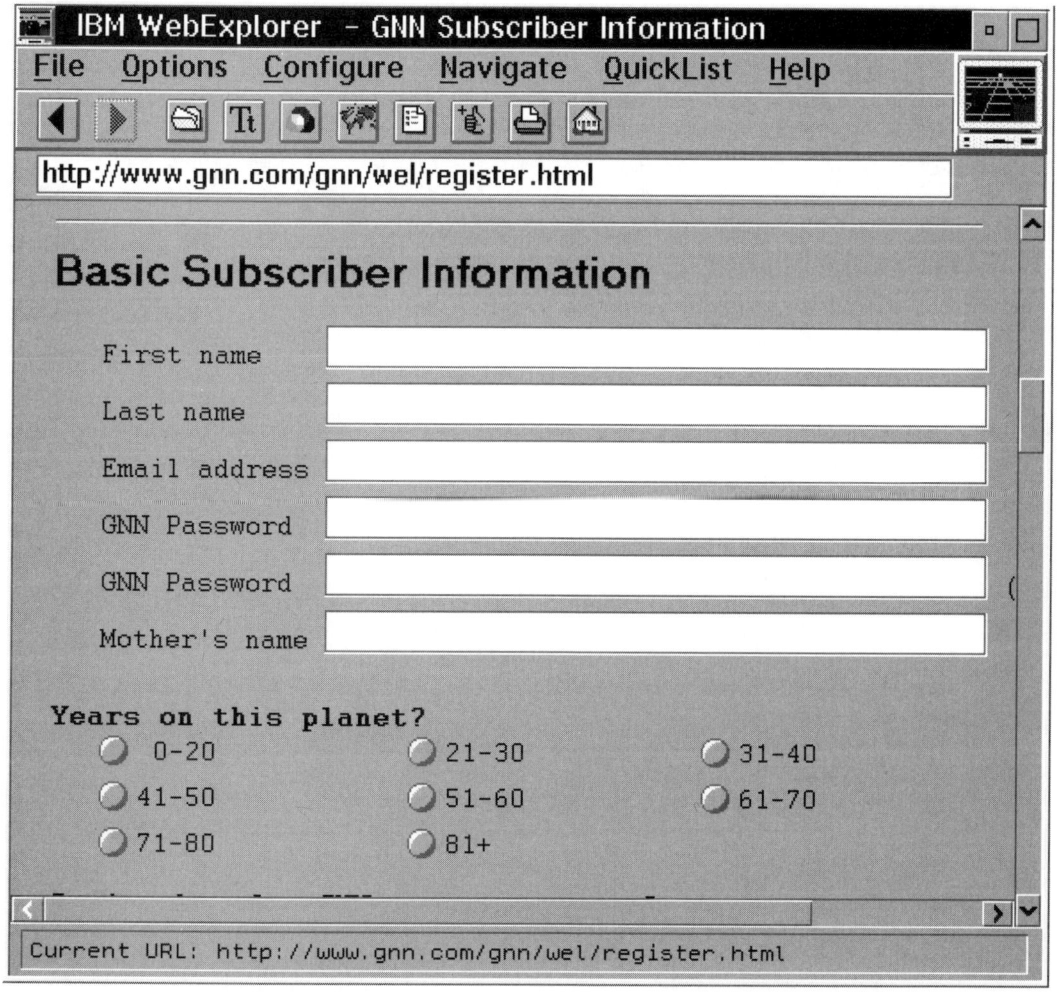

Figure 6-5. GNN subscription form

Configuration forms

Companies that produce Web servers, such as IBM and Netscape, have begun using forms to allow Web administrators to configure the server. These forms provide a more user-friendly interface to configuring the server and, more importantly, allow the server to be configured from remote locations.

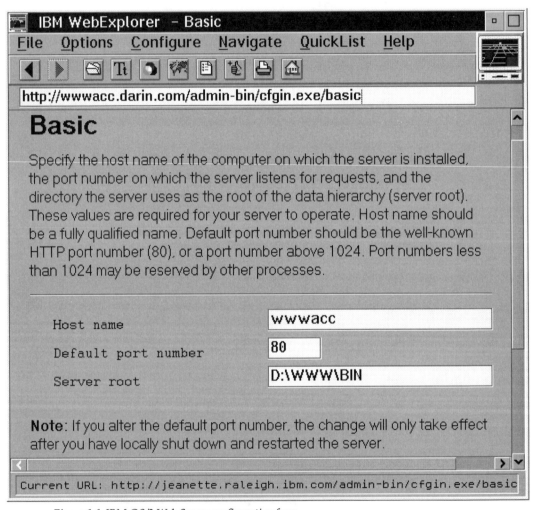

Figure 6-6. IBM OS/2 Web Server configuration form

How forms work

As you have seen, forms can be used for many purposes. The purpose of the form often dictates its complexity. In general, however, all forms work as follows:

1. Someone, typically the Web editor, creates a form using HTML tags and places the form on a Web server. The tags you can use are discussed in the next section.

    At about the same time, the Web administrator creates (or appropriates) a program (or Common Gateway Interface script) suitable for processing the information and places the processing program on the Web server. For example, the program might be designed to take the data supplied by a user and send it as a note to a specified e-mail address. Or, the program might format and forward the data to another program for further processing, such as a configuration program. For more information about CGI scripts, see Chapter 12, "Using the Common Gateway Interface."

2. Using a Web browser, a user fills out the form and clicks on the Submit (or similarly labeled) push button to send the information to the Web server.
3. The Web server receives the information and forwards it to the processing program.
4. The processing program handles the data as instructed.

The steps are fairly simple. The important thing to remember is that forms require processing software at the Web server. This is important because if you do not have access to the appropriate processing software, your form will not work.

Creating a form

A form can be a stand-alone HTML document or it can be included as part of a larger HTML document. You can include more than one form in a document, but you cannot nest forms (include a form within a form).

The tagging for forms consists of form designation tags (a beginning and ending set of tags) and an assortment of form element tags. You can use other HTML tags, such as paragraph and highlighting tags within a form. In fact, you will need to use formatting tags, such as <P> and <br>, to control the look of your form. You cannot, however, use any of the form element tags outside the form designation tags.

Starting a form

To start a form, use the form designation tag, <Form>. This tag marks the beginning of the form and provides the basic information for processing the form.

- Use the ACTION attribute to specify the URL of the processing program. The URL must be HTTP-accessible. You can specify an absolute URL, such as **http://bin.gnn.com/gnnreg/register** or a relative URL, such as **/cgi-bin/pursuit**. If you specify a relative URL, the current server is assumed.

- Use the METHOD attribute to specify the HTTP method that will send the form's data to the processing program. The METHOD can be either GET or POST. GET is the default and is generally used in search forms. POST is, however, the preferred method for forms in which the data is forwarded using electronic mail, such as comment forms.

For example, the form designation tag for the GNN Subscriber Information form is:

```
<Form METHOD=POST ACTION="http://bin.gnn.com/gnnreg/register">
```

And the form designation tag for the Lycos Search form is:

```
<Form ACTION="/cgi-bin/pursuit" METHOD=GET>
```

Including form elements

Remember your first job application? There were probably questions of various types: fill-in-the-blank, multiple-choice, and true-false (or yes-no). Similarly, there are a number of form element tags that you can use to include the same variety of questions in your form.

Fill-in-the-blank questions

To create a fill-in-the-blank question, use the <Input> tag with the TYPE attribute set to "text." This creates a single-line entry field.

- Use the NAME attribute to assign an identifier to the field. This identifier is used by the processing program.

- Use the SIZE attribute to specify the width of the field area, and use the MAXLENGTH attribute to specify the maximum number of characters that can be entered. The MAXLENGTH can be greater than the SIZE. In this case, the field will scroll to the right as the user enters data.

- Use the VALUE attribute to specify a default value for the field.

For example, the IBM OS/2 Web Server Configuration form contains the following fill-in-the-blank field:

```
Host name    <input TYPE="text" NAME="HostName" SIZE=20 MAXLENGTH=256
VALUE="wwwacc">
```

Notice that while the size of the field area is only 20 characters, the user can actually enter up to 256 characters.

There is a unique kind of fill-in-the-blank question for passwords. The information a user types is not displayed. To create a password field, use the <Input> tag with the TYPE attribute set to "password." All other attributes are the same.

For example, the GNN Subscriber Information form contains the following password field:

```
GNN Password   <input SIZE=30 MAXLENGTH=20 NAME="password"
TYPE="password">
```

Single-selection questions

To create a single-selection question, use the <Input> tag with the TYPE attribute set to "radio." This creates an entry preceded by a *radio button*, which is selectable circle.

- Use the NAME attribute to assign an identifier to the field. This identifier is used by the processing program. You can group single-selection entries by assigning the same NAME to each. Users can select only one entry in a single-selection group.

- Use the VALUE attribute to specify the value to be passed if that entry is chosen.

- Use the CHECKED attribute to identify the default selection, if any.

For example, the IBM Networking Home Page Evaluation form contains the following single-selection question:

```
<p>
How did you find the Networking Home Page?
<p>
<input TYPE="radio" NAME="find" VALUE="I">
Through the IBM Corporate Home Page
<br><input TYPE="radio" NAME="find" VALUE="F">
Got URL from friend/associate
<br><input TYPE="radio" NAME="find" VALUE="N">
Ad/newsletter/other hard copy source
<br><input TYPE="radio" NAME="find" VALUE="S">
Search Facility
```

Multiple-selection questions

To create a multiple-selection question, use the <Input> tag with the TYPE attribute set to "checkbox." This creates an entry preceded by a selectable square, a check box.

- Use the NAME attribute to assign an identifier to the field. This identifier is used by the processing program. As with single-selection questions, you can group multiple-selection questions by assigning the same NAME to each. Unlike single-selection questions, however, users can select more than one entry in a multiple-selection group.

- Use the VALUE attribute to specify the value to be passed if that entry is chosen.

- Use the CHECKED attribute to identify the default selection, if any.

For example, the Lycos Search form contains the following multiple-selection question:

```
<b>Terse output:</b><input type="checkbox" name="terse">
```

Multiple-line entry fields

To create a multiple-line entry field, one that allows the user to enter several lines of information, use the <Textarea> and </Textarea> tags. This type of field is useful for allowing users to enter information, such as comments and addresses.

- Use the NAME attribute to assign an identifier to the field. This identifier is used by the processing program.

- Use the ROWS attribute to specify the number of lines of input allowed.

- Use the COLS attribute to specify the number of characters allowed per line.

For example, the Pacifica Blue order form contains the following:

```
<textarea name="e-street" cols=50 rows=2>&lt.&lt. Address &gt.&gt.</
textarea><br>
```

Selection lists

Selection questions prompt you to select one or more items in a list, such as a list of foods you like. To create a selection list box, use the <Select> and </Select> tags.

- Use the NAME attribute to assign an identifier to the field. This identifier is used by the processing program.

- Use the MULTIPLE attribute to allow users to select more than one item in the list.

- Use the SIZE attribute to specify the number of items that should be displayed at any time in the list box. If the number of items listed is greater than the number of items specified by the SIZE attribute, a scroll bar is added to the right of the list box.

To indicate the possible selections, use the <Option> and </Option> tags. <Option> tags must be nested within <Select> and </Select> tags.

- Use the SELECTED attribute to indicate the default selection, if any.

- Use the VALUE attribute to specify the value to be passed if that entry is chosen. If you do not include the VALUE attribute, the text of the option is passed as the value.

For example, the Cheryl's Cheesecakes order form contains the following selection question:

```
Please select the cheesecake you wish to order:
<SELECT NAME="item1" SIZE="3">
<OPTION>Chocolate Brownie</OPTION>
```

```
<OPTION>Peaches-N-Cream</OPTION>
<OPTION>Carrot Cake</OPTION>
<OPTION>Dutch Apple</OPTION>
<OPTION>Mint Chocolate Chip</OPTION>
<OPTION>BlueBerry</OPTION>
<OPTION>Chocolate Turtle</OPTION>
<OPTION>Peanut Butter Truffle</OPTION>
<OPTION>Black Raspberry</OPTION>
<OPTION>Chocolate Chip Banana</OPTION>
<OPTION>German Chocolate</OPTION>
<OPTION>Pumpkin</OPTION>
<OPTION>Sampler</OPTION>
<OPTION>Dual-Duty</OPTION>
</SELECT>
```

Including processing choices

Once a user has filled out a form, he or she can either submit the form for processing or clear the data in the form. These choices are represented by push buttons that you can include in your form.

To provide a push button for submitting the form, use the <Input> tag with the TYPE attribute set to "submit."

To provide a push button for clearing the data in the form, use the <Input> tag with the TYPE attribute set to "reset."

In either case, use the VALUE attribute to indicate the label that should appear on the push button.

For example, the Lycos Search form contains the following push buttons:

```
<input type="submit" value="Start search">
<input type="reset" value="Reset">
```

Ending a form

To end a form, use the </Form> tag.

Chapter 7

Including multimedia in your document

revious chapters discuss how to create HTML documents that include text, images, and forms. But there is more. You can also include *multimedia* in your HTML document. Multimedia includes video and audio clips as well as interactive simulations (virtual reality). The field of multimedia is rapidly growing and changing. New advancements are being made each day. This section is not intended to provide in-depth instructions for creating multimedia, but rather to provide an overview of the types of multimedia, considerations for using multimedia on the Web, and instructions for including multimedia files in an HTML document.

Chapter 7. Including multimedia in your document

Types of multimedia

By formal definition, multimedia is the combined use of two or more communication media. Common usage, however, defines multimedia as any communication medium other than text. Generally speaking, there are four major areas of multimedia on the Web today: video, audio, animation, and virtual reality.

Silicon Graphics maintains a gallery of some of the better samples of multimedia at **http://www.sgi.com/Fun/free/gallery.html**.

Video clips

Video clips are files that contain segments of visual recordings. As the name implies, these tend to be short recordings, a few seconds to a few minutes. Video clips can be used for a variety of purposes, including:

- Entertainment, such as clips from Star Trek movies
  (**http://deathstar.rutgers.edu/people/bochkay/movies.html**)

- Advertising, such as videos from the visitor's booth at the Chicago Mercantile Exchange
  (**http://reagan.eecs.uic.edu/tourism/sightsee/merchant.html**)

- Education, such as videos from the Apollo missions
  (**http://www.univ-rennes1.fr/ASTRO/anim-e.html**)

Video clips come in a variety of formats, depending on how they were created. Some of the more popular formats are:

- QuickTime (.qt), developed by Apple

- Motion Picture Experts Group (.mpg or .mpeg), a lossy file format developed by an ISO subcommittee

- Audio/Visual Interface (.avi), developed by Microsoft

For a sampling of video clips, see
http://www.yahoo.com/Computers/Multimedia/Video/Collections/.

Audio clips

Audio clips are files that contain segments of recorded or created sounds. As with video clips, these tend to be short recordings. Although longer recordings are possible, the lack of effective compression algorithms for sound files limits us to shorter recordings. Audio clips can be:

- Spoken words, such as the discussions on legal subjects provided by Indiana University's LawTalk
  (**http://www.law.indiana.edu/law/lawtalk.html**)

- Music, such as the selection of recordings offered by the Internet Underground Music Archive (**http://www.iuma.com/**)

- Movie soundtracks, such as those stored at SunSITE
  (**http://sunsite.unc.edu/pub/multimedia/sun-sounds/movies/**)

Audio clips are particularly useful for providing information to the visually impaired. They can also be used to convey information that cannot be expressed in text or images, such as bird calls and whale songs. At the moment, however, audio clips are used largely for entertainment purposes, such as providing samplings of the latest recordings of a musical group, segments from a popular radio show, or recordings of interesting sound effects from the latest science-fiction movie.

Audio clips come in many formats. Some of the more popular formats are:

- Audio IFF (.aif), developed by Apple

- Waveform (.wav), developed by Microsoft

- SunAudio (.au), developed by Sun

For a sampling of audio clips, see
http://www.eecs.nwu.edu/~jmyres/other-sounds.html.

Animation

Animation is a series of images joined (or sequenced) in such a way that the objects in the images appear to move. One of the most common forms of animation is the cartoon, such as those contained at Christian Larocque's home page (**http://www.synapse.net/~ob/**). Animation can also be used for other purposes, including:

- Education, such as the simulation of the Shoemaker-Levy comet colliding with Jupiter's surface (**http://newproducts.jpl.nasa.gov/sl9/anim.html**)

- Marketing, such as the demo of IBM's Internet Connection for Windows (**http://www.raleigh.ibm.com/icw/icwdemo.html**)

- Movies and television, such as the opening scene from "Star Trek, the Next Generation" (**http://deathstar.rutgers.edu/people/bochkay/movies.html**)

- Games, such as computer games from Sega (**http://www.segaoa.com/**)

As with other multimedia files, there are several file formats associated with animation. Two of the more popular are:

- Flic (.fli or .flc), which was developed by AutoDesk

- Motion Picture Experts Group (.mpg or .mpeg), a lossy file format developed by an ISO subcommittee

For a sampling of animation files, see
http://pmwww.cs.vu.nl/archive/animations.

Virtual Reality

Virtual reality (VR) is an interactive simulation of a concept or situation. It usually includes animation, video, and audio. Video games and computerized demonstrations have included these three elements for years. But what sets VR apart is the fact that the user is immersed in the simulation and can interact with it. For example, in a VR fencing game, the user can enter a castle, turn left into the great hall, select a foil from the case on the wall, and begin a fencing match with a computer-generated opponent that acts and reacts with life-like movements. For the optimal illusion, a head-mounted display (HMD) and sensor glove are essential.

VR is still in its infancy. HMDs and sensor gloves are not yet common household items. Nevertheless, realizing the potential of VR, Tony Parisi (of Intervista Software) and Gavin Bell (of Silicon Graphics) developed the first specification for the use of VR on the Web. Virtual Reality Modeling Language (VRML) is "a universal description language for multiparticipant simulations."[2] It is designed to be an extensible, platform-independent specification.

VRML got its start in 1994 at the first annual World Wide Web Conference in Geneva, Switzerland. It is based on SGI's Open Inventor, an object-oriented toolkit

---

[2] *Virtual Reality Modeling Language, Version 1.0 Specification*, Tony Parisi and Gavin Bell, May 26, 1995.

for developing interactive, three-dimensional images. Simply put, VRML defines a set of objects (currently numbering 36), called *nodes*, that govern the shape, texture, and relationship of the elements in a simulation. VRML also defines a framework, called a *scene graph*, that provides a hierarchical structure for the nodes.

The significance of VRML is two-fold:

- Unlike "canned" demos, VRML gives the user the ability to control the simulation, allowing the user to select the point of view and zoom level.

- VRML requires less bandwidth to access than full-motion video. With VRML, the 3D image and the accompanying VRML information are transferred to the user and all manipulation of the simulation is handled by the local computer.

The potential uses for VRML are broad-reaching. Possible uses include allowing users to "test drive" new car models, or creating virtual "service desks" where users can "walk" in, choose the door labeled Service, and discuss their concerns with a "virtual service representative." Dave Raggett, of Hewlett Packard Laboratories, has a published proposal for incorporating a VRML system in the Web so users can "walk around (the Web) and push through doors to follow hyperlinks to other parts of the Web."[3] For more information about Dave's proposal, see **http://vrml.wired.com/concepts/raggett.html**.

For more information about VRML in general, see **http://vrml.wired.com/**.

Multimedia requirements

The requirements for multimedia fall into two distinct categories: what is needed to create multimedia and what is needed for *playback.* By playback, we mean listening to, viewing, or interacting with multimedia files.

Multimedia creation

In many cases, you will need additional hardware and software to create multimedia. With the advent of multimedia computers, some companies have begun including basic multimedia development tools with their operating systems. IBM, for example, includes programs for creating audio and video files with their OS/2 Warp BonusPak.

---

[3] *Extending WWW to Support Platform Independent Virtual Reality*, David Raggett.

Even if your operating system supplies programs for creating multimedia, you may want to invest in additional programs to produce professional-quality multimedia. When selecting one, it is a good idea to ensure that it can produce files in one of the popular formats.

There are so many programs and techniques that you can use to create multimedia that we cannot cover them all here. But, for those who are unfamiliar with creating multimedia, we are including descriptions of a sampling of programs. Many of the programs described in this section can be used to produce more than one type of multimedia. But rather than lump them all together, we have categorized them by their *primary* purpose.

Creating video clips

You can create videos using existing image files or using external sources (input from a VCR, camcorder, or laser disk).

To create video clips from existing images, you simply need a video editing program, such as Adobe's Premiere. Premiere, available for Macintosh or Windows, provides an easy-to-use interface for assembling and editing video clips. With Premiere, in addition to basic editing, you can:

- Include animation and special effects created with other programs, such as Adobe's Photoshop

- Superimpose layers of video

- Create transitions between scenes ranging from the simple to the dramatic

For more information about Premiere, see **http://www.adobe.com/Apps/Premiere.html**.

To create video clips from a VCR, camcorder, or laser disk, you need a video capture card and the appropriate software. In general, video capture cards come with the software needed to digitize video images and perform basic editing.

For the Macintosh, VideoVision Studio by Radius provides everything you need to produce 30-frame-per-second video clips in QuickTime format. VideoVision Studio includes a video capture card, connector panels for external video and audio, and a full complement of software to allow you to create and edit video

clips. For more information about VideoVision Studio, see
http://research.radius.com/.

Connectix offers a digital camera, called QuickCam, specifically designed for
creating QuickTime movies. QuickCam plugs directly into a serial port of the
Macintosh.

For Windows, Intel offers Smart Video Recorder Pro. This package also includes
everything you need to produce 30-frame-per-second video clips in a variety of
formats. Smart Video Recorder Pro includes:

- Intel's Indeo video capture card

- Asymetrix's Digital Video Producer, which provides a broad range of editing
  functions

- Tri-Digital's DigiClips, an assortment of video clips and animations

For more information about Smart Video Recorder Pro, see
http://www.intel.com/pc-supp/multimed/indeo/.

QuickTime, by Apple, runs on Macintosh or Windows systems and allows you to
create 30-frame-per-second video clips that can also include sound. QuickTime
also includes features that allow you to perform basic editing of video clips. If you
want to add animation and special effects, try Apple's Quicktime Software
Development Kit. For more information about QuickTime, see
http://quicktime.apple.com/.

For OS/2, IBM offers VideoIN. When used with a video capture card, such as
IBM's Video Capture Adapter/A, you can use VideoIN to create video clips from
external sources. If you do not have a video capture card, you can use VideoIN to
create video clips from bitmaps or animation files. VideoIN is included in the OS/2
Warp BonusPak. For more information about VideoIN, see
http://www.europe.ibm.com/getdoc/psmemea/prodcat/opsys/wn014.html.

For AIX, IBM offers a line of multimedia products called Ultimedia for AIX. One of
the products, Ultimedia Services, allows you to capture, record, edit, manage, and
play video clips. To record video clips from external sources, you will also need a
video capture adapter, such as the Ultimedia Video adapter or the Video Capture
Enhancement adapter. For more information about the Ultimedia for AIX line of
products, see
http://www.austin.ibm.com/software/Apps/ultimedia.html.

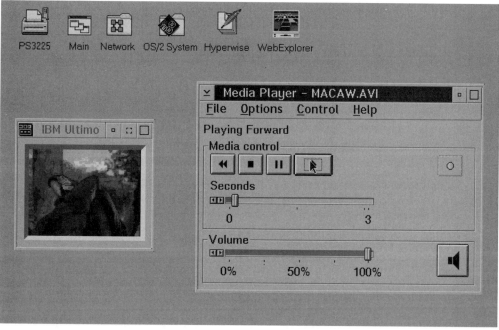

Figure 7-1. VideoIN sample

Creating audio clips

Depending on the content, requirements for creating a video clip vary. Basically, to create audio clips, you must capture the sounds and convert (digitize) them to a format that the computer can understand.

To create an audio clip of spoken words, you can use a microphone and the appropriate software. In most cases, if you have a multimedia computer, you probably already have the software needed to digitize input from a microphone. If not, you can try one of the following:

- For UNIX, the AudioFile client from Digital Equipment Corporation (see **ftp://ftp.dec.com/pub/DEC/AF**)

- For Macintosh, SoundMachine by Rod Kennedy (see **http://wwwhost.ots.utexas.edu/mac/pub-mac-sound.html**)

- For Windows, WHAM by Andrew Bulhak (get the wham133.zip file from **ftp:// ftp.cdrom.com/.22/cica/sounds/** or **ftp://gatekeeper.dec.com/pub/micro/msdos/sounds/**)

- For OS/2 Warp, the sound digitizing program that is included in the BonusPak

- For AIX, Ultimedia Services from IBM (see **http://www.austin.ibm.com/software/Apps/ultimedia.html**)

One of the nice things about these programs is that they can also be used as audio viewers.

In addition, you can use a sound editor, such as Audio Atomizer to create and modify audio clips. Audio Atomizer, from the Walter Shelby Group, runs on Macintosh or Windows systems. It comes with a vast library of recorded words, sentences, and sounds that you can assemble and rearrange using a mouse. For more information about Audio Atomizer, see **http://www.clark.net/pub/listserv/atom1a.html**.

To create an audio clip of music, you can connect a musical instrument (such as an electric keyboard) to a computer that has a *Musical Instrument Digital Interface (MIDI)* port and the appropriate software to create a MIDI file (.mid). MIDI is a protocol that allows musical instruments to communicate with one another and has been adapted to allow computers to record the output from musical instruments. You can then use a conversion program, such as MIDI Renderer, from DiAcoustics, to convert the MIDI files to Waveform files. For more information about MIDI Renderer, see **http://www.iquest.com/~diac/mr-home.html**. For more information about MIDI in general, see **http://www.eeb.ele.tue.nl/midi/**.

As an alternative, you can use your computer to generate the music using a program such as Midiscan. Midiscan for Windows, from Musitek, allows you to create music without playing a note. Midiscan is pattern-recognition software that produces audible music from scanned sheet music. For more information about Midiscan, see **http://www.musitek.com/**.

Creating animation files

When it comes to animation, there is no shortage of good packages available. Many of them are lower-priced versions of animation packages used in the television and film industry.

PowerAnimator, from Alias (which recently merged with Wavefront), runs on Silicon Graphics workstations and provides all the tools necessary to create professional-quality animations, including:

- QuickShade, which allows you to model and animate shaded objects in real-time

- CompuHair, which allows you to give your human figures life-like hair

- ShapeShifter, which allows you to produce full-motion *morphs*. Morphs are images that transform into other images, such as those in the Michael Jackson video, "Black or White"

Alias also offers Animator, a lower-priced (about half that of PowerAnimator) animation package that provides many, but not all, of the features of PowerAnimator. For more information about PowerAnimator and Animator, see **http://www.alias.com/Product/entertainment_products.html**.

Animator Studio, from AutoDesk, is a Windows-based animation authoring program that provides a combination of animation, video, and audio creation and editing tools. It includes a large number of royalty-free animation files, sound clips, and backgrounds. Animator Studio can produce files in a variety of formats, including Flic, AVI, and QuickTime.

For more information about Animator Studio, see **http://www.autodesk.com/prod/mm/animates.htm**.

Creating 3D images

3D images can be used in animation and virtual reality. Therefore, we decided to discuss the programs available for creating 3D images in a separate section. There are several good programs available.

Ez3d-Modeler, from Radiance Software International, is a low-cost software package for 3D modeling and rendering. Currently, it is the only commercial 3D application based directly on SGI's Open Inventor. Ez3d-Modeler runs on Silicon Graphics workstations and allows you to:

- Create complex curved shapes

- Mold an object's surface

- Control the color, material, and texture of an object

- Create beveled 3D text in a wide variety of PostScript fonts

- Produce professional quality ray-traced images with shadows, reflections, texture layering, atmospheric effects, and more

- Control the hierarchy and interaction of objects

Ez3d-Modeler also provides a library of shapes from which you can choose, or you can import your own. For more information about Ez3d-Modeler, see **http://www.radiance.com/~radiance/**.

Home Space Builder, by ParaGraph International, is another low-cost software package for creating 3D images. This easy-to-use 3D authoring program, which runs on Windows systems, allows you to create 3D Web pages that can be viewed with any VRML viewer. In addition to providing 3D creation and editing capabilities, Home Space Builder also allows you to:

- Integrate text, audio, and animation into your 3D image

- Link elements of your 3D image to other resources on the Web

For more information about Home Space Builder, see **http://www.us.paragraph.com/whatsnew/homespce.htm**.

IBM offers a toolkit for *OpenGL* on AIX that allows you to create 3D images. OpenGL is a standard API licensed by Silicon Graphics and controlled by the OpenGL Architecture Review Board, which includes representatives of DEC, Microsoft, and IBM. (For more information about OpenGL, see **http://www.sgi.com/Technology/openGL/opengl.html**.)

IBM's OpenGL requires more programming skills than the other applications listed here. It provides a rendering library, a utility toolkit, a networking protocol, an X11 Window System integration suite, and an OpenGL widget. IBM also recently announced an OS/2 version of OpenGL. For more information about OpenGL offerings from IBM, see **http://www.austin.ibm.com/software/OpenGL/**.

Creating VRML files

Because VRML is relatively new, there are not as many authoring systems available for VRML as there are for HTML. A few are available now, and, as the popularity of VR grows, more are sure to appear.

Radiance Software International was the first to offer a VRML authoring system, Ez3d-VR, which is based on their 3D modeling software, Ez3d-Modeler. In addition to the features offered by Ez3d-Modeler, Ez3d-VR also provides:

- An anchoring tool that allows you to link 3D objects to resources on the Web, including other 3D images, HTML documents, images, video clips, and audio clips

- Support for including local and remote 3D images in-line

- Support for polygons with an unlimited number of vertices

- Support for multiple levels of detail for objects

For more information about Ez3d-VR, see **http://www.radiance.com/~radiance/**.

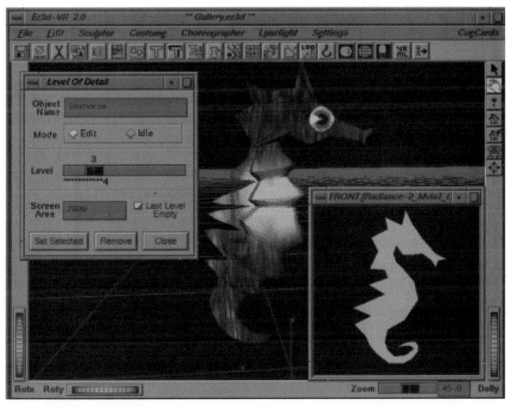

Figure 7-2. Ez3d VR sample

Apple has also announced a VRML authoring system based on their popular QuickTime software. QuickTime VR Authoring Tools Suite is available for Macintosh. Like Ez3d-VR, it allows you to create interactive 3D images and link the images to other resources on the Web. One of the interesting aspects of QuickTime VR is that it also allows you to include real-life images (photographs) in your VR sequence and provides the tools necessary to create 360-degree panoramic sequences based on the photographs.

QuickTime VR is not for the novice, however. It requires experience with image processing and HyperCard scripting. For more information about QuickTime-VR, see **http://quicktime.apple.com/qtvr.html**.

Creating VRML applications

If you need to create your own VRML application, there are several VRML toolkits available that are based on OpenGL. Many hardware manufacturers, including Digital Equipment Corporation, Sony, Silicon Graphics, and IBM, are now providing support for OpenGL for their monitors. Also, a number of companies offer developer's toolkits for developing OpenGL-based applications.

Open Inventor, the basis of VRML, is an OpenGL toolkit. The Open Inventor Development kit is available from Silicon Graphics (for the SGI operating system) and from several vendors (for other platforms) and provides the tools necessary to develop 3D applications based on the OpenGL API. The Open Inventor run-time modules are included with the SGI operating system. The development libraries are available separately from Silicon Graphics. For more information about Open Inventor, see
http://www.sgi.com/Technology/Inventor.html.

Microsoft includes development tools for building OpenGL applications with their Win32 Software Development Kit. This kit also includes instructional documentation and sample source code. For more information about OpenGL offerings from Microsoft, see
http://www.sgi.com/Technology/openGL/vendor/microsoft.html.

Multimedia playback

Multimedia playback requires a multimedia-capable computer, which includes a combination of hardware and software. With the advances in computer hardware, multimedia-capable computers are becoming affordable.

The specific hardware and software requirements depend on the type of com-puter and operating system you are using, but in general, you need a sound card to play audio files and a high-resolution monitor for video and animation. Also, as a rule, the more memory available to your computer, the better the quality of playback. For multimedia over the Web, you need a high-speed connection. Optimally, a LAN connection over a T1 line is best. But if you are accessing the Web via a modem, a speed of 14400 baud or greater is a must.

In addition, you need viewers for the various file formats. Most, if not all, graphi-cal browsers allow you to configure external viewers for various types of files. Some browsers come preconfigured to use multimedia viewers for video, audio, and animation files; for example:

- IBM's WebExplorer is preconfigured to use the viewers provided in the OS/2 Warp BonusPak.

- IBM's WebExplorer Mosaic is preconfigured to use the viewers provided in the IBM Internet Connection for Windows.

- NetScape's Navigator is preconfigured to use viewers that are available from their Helper Applications page (**http://www.netscape.com/assist/helper_apps/**).

If you have a browser that does not come with multimedia viewers, or if you would like to use something other than what has been provided to you, you might want to try one of the viewers mentioned in the following sections.

Viewing video clips and animation files

Most viewers that can play back video clips can also play back animation files. Therefore, we have combined the information on video and animation viewers.

For Windows, viewers for AVI and MPEG files are available from NetScape's Helper Applications page (**http://www.netscape.com/assist/helper_apps/windowhelper.html**).

For Macintosh, you can use Sparkle, by Maynard Handley, to view QuickTime and MPEG files. Sparkle also allows you to convert between the two file formats. For more information about Sparkle, see **http://wwwhost.ots.utexas.edu/mac/pub-mac-graphics.html**.

For UNIX systems running X Windows, try XAnim. XAnim supports playback of several file formats, including FLI/FLC, AVI, QuickTime, and MPEG. It also includes limited, but growing, support for WAV audio files. Although designed for UNIX systems, XAnim has been successfully compiled and used on DOS systems that include support for the X11 library. For more information about XAnim, see **http://www.portal.com/~podlipec/home.html**.

There is also a repository of viewers for Macintosh, MS-DOS, and X11 systems available from the University of Rennes in France (**ftp://ftp.univ-rennes1.fr/pub/Images/ASTRO/anim/soft**).

Viewing audio clips

Yes, it may seem strange to call a program that plays back audio files a *viewer*. But industry convention calls almost any program that provides playback a viewer. The programs previously listed that you can use to digitize audio files can also be used for audio playback; for example:

- For UNIX, the AudioFile client from Digital Equipment Corporation (see **ftp://ftp.dec.com/pub/DEC/AF**)

- For Macintosh, SoundMachine by Rod Kennedy (see **http://wwwhost.ots.utexas.edu/mac/pub-mac-sound.html**)

- For Windows, WHAM by Andrew Bulhak (get the wham133.zip file from **ftp://ftp.cdrom.com/.22/cica/sounds/** or **ftp://gatekeeper.dec.com/pub/micro/msdos/sounds/**)

- For OS/2 Warp, the sound viewer that is included in the BonusPak

- For AIX, Ultimedia Services from IBM (see **http://www.austin.ibm.com/software/Apps/ultimedia.html**)

These viewers will play a variety of audio files, including .wav, .avi, and .aif.

Viewing 3D images and VRML files

There is a limited number of viewers and browsers for VRML.

WebSpace, from Silicon Graphics, is available for SGI workstations. Versions for Windows, Sun Solaris, UNIX, Macintosh, and AIX are, or will shortly be, available from Template Graphics Software. WebSpace is the first commercially available

VRML viewer. It provides an easy-to-use interface to allow users to navigate through 3D images. Although WebSpace runs best on high-end systems, it is designed to adapt to the performance capabilities of systems such as Macintosh.

Figure 7-3. WebSpace sample

For more information about WebSpace, see
http://www.sgi.com/Products/WebFORCE/WebSpace/.

WorldView, from InterVista Software, Inc., is available for Windows, Macintosh, SGI, and Sun OS systems. WorldView is a stand-alone VRML browser that provides powerful 3D rendering capabilities coupled with a high-performance, proprietary, networking function. It can also be used as a viewer in conjunction with Web browsers, such as Netscape.

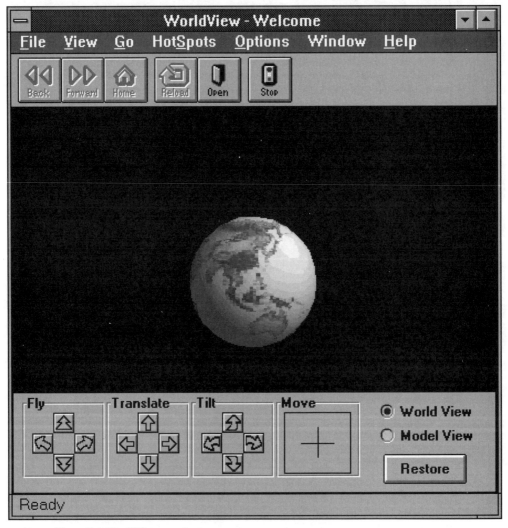

Figure 7-4. WorldView sample

For more information about WorldView, see **http://www.webmaster.com/vrml**.

Apple also provides a viewer as part of their QuickTime VR. Given the proper license, the viewer, or run-time software as they call it, can be distributed with sequences created using QuickTime VR. There are viewers available for Macintosh and Windows. Make note, though, the viewer requires Apple's HyperCard V2.0 or later. For more information about QuickTime VR, see **http://quicktime.apple.com/qtvr.html**.

Linking to multimedia

With the exception of WorldView, which can function as a stand-alone VRML browser, Web browsers do not support in-line multimedia. As the author of an HTML document, you can simply use the anchor tag to give the reader access to a multimedia file.

For example, the following example is an excerpt from a children's story that contains multimedia.

```
<html>
<heading>
<title>Tales from the Toybox</title>
<H1>Tracks of Life</H1>
<p>Gene loved to play with all the toys in his
<a href="/images/VRML/toybox.wrl">toybox</a>.
He was especially fond of his <a href="/images/JPEGs/
stengine.jpg">shiny black steam engine.</a>
It had wheels that moved and a <a href="/images/sounds/
whistle.au">whistle</a>
that sounded like a real train.
<p>Gene spent hours at a time playing with the steam
engine. He would crawl under his bed and imagine he was travel-
ing through a
<a href="/images/movies/tunnel.avi">mountain tunnel.</a>
```

Figure 7-5. Sample HTML document with links to multimedia files

- The first mention of the toybox is linked to a VRML file that allows you to open a child's toybox and look around at the assortment of toys within.

- The description of the train's whistle is linked to an audio clip of a steam engine's whistle.

- The words "mountain tunnel" are linked to a video clip of a train traveling through a tunnel.

In this case, the multimedia files are used to complement the story, not create it. Therefore, the reader can still follow the story even if he or she does not have the capability of viewing one or more of the files.

Chapter 8

Testing and maintaining your document

I f you were to write a book to be published, you would ensure that the content of the book is correct, that any cross-references or index entries are accurate, and that the book looks good (no odd page breaks or misplaced text). Likewise, testing your HTML document is an essential step in publishing an HTML document to the Web. For the benefit of your readers as well as for your reputation (or that of your company or organization), you should ensure that your document is coded properly, that any hypertext links function correctly, and that the document looks as you intended when viewed with a Web browser.

The W3 Consortium provides some helpful tips on testing your document. See **http://www.w3.org/hypertext/WWW/Provider/Style/Testing.html**.

Chapter 8. Testing and maintaining your document

Validating your HTML coding

As discussed in the previous chapters, there are a number of rules of HTML coding that you should follow, for example: You must start an HTML document with <HTML>, an <Input> tag cannot occur outside <Form> tags, an <H1> tag must be ended by an </H1> tag, and so forth. James "Eric" Tilton maintains a list of common HTML coding errors at **http://www.williamette.edu/html-composition/strict-html-ce.html**.

Validation checklist

As a quick review, here is a checklist of some rules of thumb for HTML coding:

- Begin every document with <HTML>, and end every document with </HTML>.

- Include document header information at the top of the document, using <Head> and </Head>.

- Assign a title to every document, using <Title> and </Title>. Place the title in the header of the document.

- If you use relative linking (links using relative URLs), it is a good idea to specify a root URL using <Base>. Specify the root URL in the header of the document.

- After the header, begin the content of the document with <Body>. End the content of the document with </Body>, placed prior to the </HTML> tag.

- Begin the body of the document with a level-one heading, <H1>.

- Do not skip heading levels. For example, the next heading after a level-one heading, <H1>, must be a level-two heading, <H2>.

- Use <P> to separate blocks of text. Do not, however, use <P> in these positions:

  - Prior to or after a heading (<Hx>), address (<Address>), long quote (<Blockquote>), or preformatted text (<Pre>).

  - Between items in a list (<LI>).

  These tags generate their own space; no extra space is needed.

- When using an anchor tag, you must include either the NAME attribute or HREF attribute.

- For attributes that contain user-defined text (such as HREF, NAME, and ALT), surround the attribute value with single or double quotes. Do not, however, surround the value for SRC (the <IMG> attribute) with quotes. With image tags, some browsers interpret the quotes as part of the name of the image and are therefore unable to locate the image.

- Be sure to end all paired tags, such as highlighting tags, with the appropriate end tag.

- If you nest lists, be sure to end the lists in the correct order (ending the most recently started list first).

- Begin a symbol with an ampersand, &, and end it with a semicolon, ;.

- Do not use <Select>, <Textarea>, or <Input> outside the <Form> and </Form> tags.

- Do not use <Option> outside the <Select> and </Select> tags.

Validation programs

Browsing your document with a Web browser is one way to check your HTML coding, but some browsers are more lenient than others and will compensate for errors where others will not. Also, viewing a document with a browser may make you aware that something is wrong, but it will not help you determine the problem. There are several programs available on the Web to assist you with validation and problem determination for HTML documents, such as WebLint and HTMLchek.

WebLint

WebLint, created by Neil Bowers with support from UniPress, is an on-line service to validate HTML coding. You can provide the URL of the document to be validated, or, if you want to check only a part of a document, you can submit just the lines of code you want to validate. If you want to validate an entire document using the on-line version of WebLint, the document must be on a publicly accessible Web server.

If you cannot place your document on a publicly accessible server, you can obtain a copy of WebLint that you can run on your own computer from **ftp://ftp.khoros.unm.edu/pub/perl/www/** or **ftp://ftp.unipress.com/pub/contrib/**.

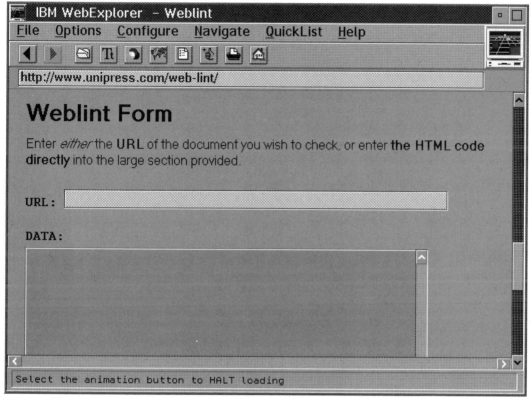

Figure 8-1. WebLint on-line submission form

WebLint performs a fairly thorough check of HTML coding, including checks for:

- Missing required tags, such as the <Title>

- Mismatched tags, such as <OL> paired with </UL>

- Unended tags, such as <Address> without a matching </Address>

- Invalid tags

- Lack of required attributes for certain tags, such as <A> without a NAME or HREF attribute

To access WebLint, see **http://www.unipress.com/web-lint/**.

HTMLchek

HTMLchek, created by H. Churchyard, is a program that you can run on your computer to validate the coding of an HTML document. Versions are available in two programming languages: Awk and Perl.

- Awk is a scripting language designed primarily to search files for a specified string. The original version was written for UNIX, but versions are also available for MS-DOS and OS/2. For more information on Awk, specifically Gnu's version of Awk, see **http://csugrad.cs.vt.edu/manuals/gawk/gawk_toc.html**.

- Perl is also a scripting language designed to scan files and extract information from them. The original version was written for UNIX, but versions are available for other platforms including: MS-DOS, Windows-NT, OS/2, MVS, and Macintosh. For more information about Perl, see **http://www.yahoo.com/Computers_and_Internet/Languages/Perl/**.

HTMLchek validates many of the same aspects of HTML coding as WebLint, such as the order and pairing of tags. It does not, however, validate symbols (such as &) or attribute values.

You can specify whether you want to validate the coding based on HTML 2.0 or HTML 3.0. You can also indicate that the document includes HTML tags proposed by Netscape, which should be ignored in the validation process. HTMLchek also provides options, which you can specify either at the command line or in a configuration file, to instruct the program not to validate certain aspects of the HTML coding.

For more information about HTMLchek, see **http://uts.cc.utexas.edu/~churchh/htmlchek.html**.

Testing the look and feel of your document

In theory, HTML is a vendor- and platform-independent tagging language, which means that the same HTML document can be viewed with any Web browser, regardless of operating system or manufacturer. In reality, however, there are some subtle (and some not-so-subtle) differences in how the various browsers display HTML documents. To ensure that your document has the "look and feel" that you want, you should view it using more than one browser.

For example, while all browsers should support the current level of HTML, Netscape Navigator also supports many proposed future HTML tags. Due to the popularity of Netscape (and in preparation for the future), some document owners are now using these proposed tags, such as tables. If you choose to use any of the proposed tags, be sure to view your document using a browser that supports them, such as Netscape, and one that does not. For those users with browsers that do not yet support the proposed tags, you may want to provide a link to a version of the document (or portion of the document) that uses only approved tags.

Also, different browsers have different ways of displaying certain elements, such as headings, interpreted highlighting, and lists. For example, we wanted to create a list and add some flair by using colored bullets. We use WebExplorer for OS/2 as our primary Web browser. Knowing how WebExplorer for OS/2 displays the various types of lists, we chose to use a <Menu> and include an image at the beginning of each list item. (WebExplorer does not prefix menu list items with anything.) The source for our HTML document looked like this:

```
<html>
<title> Acme Roadrunner WWW Server </title>
<body>
<H1>Acme Roadrunner Project</H1>
<hr>
This server contains information about the Roadrunner project at Acme.
On this server, you will find:
<menu>
<li><img src=ball_pur.gif><a href=rethis.htm>Background on the Roadrun-
ner project</a>
<li><img src=ball_pur.gif><a href=ann.htm>Announcements
regarding recently complete tests</a>
<li><img src=ball_pur.gif><a href='http://wdwfan.raleigh.ibm.com/
sample/icchapt2.htm'>Sample chapter from our latest book</a>
<li><img src=ball_pur.gif><a href=status.htm>Status of WIP (work in
progress) subprojects</a>
<li><img src=ball_pur.gif><a href=ibmp.htm>Information about Acme</a>
<li><img src=ball_pur.gif><a href=meet.htm>Information about the team</
a>
<li><img src=ball_pur.gif><a href=info.htm>Information about how to
join in the fun</a>
<li><img src=ball_pur.gif><a href=proc.htm>Process documents and
guidelines</a>
</menu>
```

Using WebExplorer for OS/2, our document looked like this:

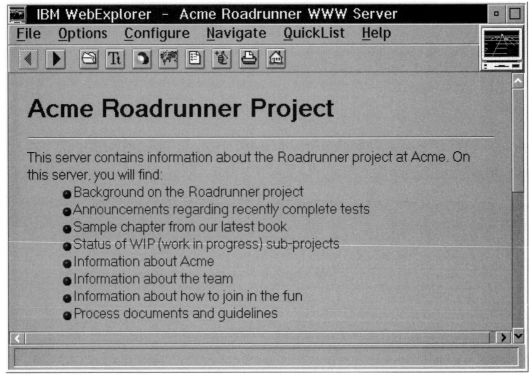

Figure 8-2. Sample document viewed with WebExplorer for OS/2

But when we viewed the document using Netscape Navigator, we discovered that Navigator prefixes each item in a menu with a bullet as shown in Figure 8-3.

Also, note the difference in the size of the text. Because the size of the window and often the size of the text are things that the user can define, it is difficult to judge how much information will fit on a page. But, as a rule of thumb, if it is important, place it near the top of the page.

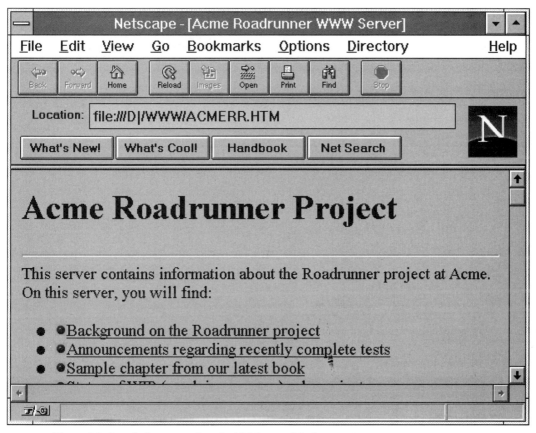

Figure 8-3. Sample document viewed with Netscape Navigator

It is also a good idea to view the document using a text-only browser. This will help ensure that your document is usable and makes sense to those users who have browsers that cannot display images and to users who are visually impaired and must rely on a text-to-speech program to navigate the Web.

Testing your links

When you create an HTML document, in addition to verifying the coding of the document, you should also verify any links contained in your document. This can be a time-consuming process; but it is an essential step. If you doubt the necessity of this step, consider your own frustration if you were to select a hypertext link that you believe will lead you to vitally important information, and you find that the link is invalid.

You can verify the links manually by selecting each hypertext link in each of your documents. Depending on the size and number of documents on your server, this may be a painstaking task, and you might want to enlist the help of your colleagues to complete it.

To speed up the process, you might want to use one of the link-testing tools available on the Web, such as lvrfy or Webxref.

lvrfy

lvrfy, created by Preston Crow, verifies all relative links in a document. It reads the document as input, making note of any links it encounters, then recursively checks all the relative links. During this process, it also verifies the existence of any in-line images. When it is complete, lvrfy creates up to three files. The first file, the OKfile, lists the relative URLs for all the links and images that it could verify. The second file, the BADfile, lists the relative URLs for any links or images that it could not verify. And because lvrfy checks only relative links, the third file, the OFFSITEfile, lists the URLs for any absolute links.

lvrfy runs on UNIX systems only and has several prerequisites. But it is a simple program to use and does a good job of checking relative links. And while it does not check absolute links, it does produce a list of them, which you can then use to check the links manually. For more information about lvrfy, see **http://www.cs.dartmoth.edu/~crow/lvrfy.html**.

Webxref

Webxref, created by Rick Jansen, verifies the links in a document. It also checks links in documents linked to the initial document. It is written in Perl and will run on any system that supports Perl. Upon completion, Webxref returns a list of all documents checked, and, for each document, a list of:

- Images included and whether they could be found

- Internal links and whether they resolved correctly

- Local directories referenced and whether they could be found

- The external URLs referenced, grouped by type (http, mailto, news, ftp, telnet, and gopher), but not whether they could be reached

Plans are in place for Webxref to verify external links in the near future. For more information about Webxref, see **http://www.sara.nl/cgi-bin/rick-acc-webxref**.

Keeping up with shifts in the Web

If you cruise around the Web often, you are likely to encounter one or more invalid hypertext links (links, which when selected, result in an error message stating that the document, directory, or server does not exist). This is because the Web is a dynamic entity. It is constantly growing and changing. Documents and servers are constantly being added, changed, and removed. It is difficult, if not impossible, to predict the stability of a link. Some links are more volatile than others, such as those to information maintained by students, those to news or current events, and those to copied information.

A significant portion of the information on the Web is contributed by college students. Due to the temporary nature of their positions, it is unlikely that the information will be maintained for more than a few months or a few years. Some guidelines warn against linking to information provided by students (which can usually be recognized by a URL pointing to a directory that includes a person's name on a server that ends with .edu, such as **http://cs.ncsu.edu/people/gsmith/**). But, because the information provided by students is often valuable and not found elsewhere, links to these types of documents cannot be avoided.

Many companies place documents about current events, such as product announcements, in a "What's New" directory. For example, IBM places lead stories in a /news/ directory. Because the IBM Web server is updated monthly, a document that you find in the /news/ directory today may not be there next month. A link to a document in a /news/, or similarly named, directory is vulnerable to becoming an invalid link.

Though all authorities on the Web warn against copying documents, some people who maintain a Web site still copy documents to their local server instead of linking to the original. They may or may not keep the copied document in sync with the original. Also, as the person who made the copy develops a better understanding of the Web, he or she may decide to link to the original document and remove the copy from his or her server. Therefore, if possible, it is best to link to an original document. It is not always easy to tell whether a document is a copy or an original. But in some cases, copied documents are identified as such and a reference to the original is given. (Likewise, if you must copy a document to your local server, remember to add a warning at the top of the document, identifying it as a copy and indicating where the original can be found.)

For these reasons and more, it is a good idea to notify the owner if you link to a document and to verify your links on a regular basis. You can verify them manually or you can use the tools discussed in the previous section. If you verify your links manually, you may want to keep a list of vulnerable links to test more frequently.

File   Options   Configure   Navigate   QuickList   Help

http://www.bocaraton.ibm.com/ibmpress/

ADMINISTERING A WEB SITE

IDG BOOKS WORLDWIDE

his part of the book is written to the administrator of the Web server, or Webmaster, and explains how to set up and maintain a Web site. There are five chapters that make up this part of the book.

Chapter 9, "Introduction to Web servers," explains what a Web server is and how it works, and provides an overview of the concepts associated with Web servers.

Chapter 10, "A tour of Web servers," provides brief descriptions of several of the more popular servers.

Chapter 11, "Security on the Web," discusses the need for security and provides an overview of the proposed solutions.

Chapter 12, "Using the Common Gateway Interface," explains what the CGI is and how it works. It also provides brief descriptions of some of the CGI programs currently available, as well as tips on writing your own.

Chapter 13, "Leasing space on someone else's server," provides alternative solutions to maintaining your own Web server.

Chapter 9

Introduction to Web servers

Your Web site can be as simple or as complex as you wish to make it. A simple Web site can consist of a Web server that responds to requests for information that it contains. In addition:

• You can set up your Web server to act as a proxy, making requests to other Web servers, usually on another network, on behalf of a Web browser.

• If your Web server contains sensitive information or performs transactions in which sensitive information is exchanged, such as credit card purchases, you can set up your Web server to use authentication and encryption methods to protect the information.

• You can set up your Web server to interface with other programs, using the Common Gateway Interface. These programs can provide dynamic information, such as the current time or the results of a search. They can exist on the same computer or on other computers that the Web server can access.

Depending on how you want to use your Web site, your Web server may be required to perform one or more of these additional functions.

This chapter provides an overview of the concepts related to a Web site. More detailed information about many of these concepts is provided in the chapters that follow.

Chapter 9. Introduction to Web servers

Web servers

In general, a Web server is a computer that:

- Is connected to a TCP/IP-based network (the Internet or an internal network)

    Note: Although most, if not all, Web servers communicate over a TCP/IP-based network, the HTTP protocol is designed to allow implementation over other types of networks.

- Is running the HTTP daemon (HTTPD)

- Contains information in the form of HTML documents (and associated files, such as images)

- Responds to requests for information from Web browsers

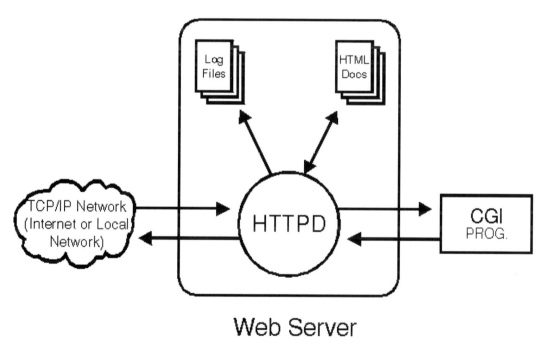

Web Server

Figure 9-1. Overview of a Web site

Because the Web is designed around open protocols, the computer you use can run any operating system for which there is a Web server (HTTPD) program. Currently Web server programs are available for OS/2, Windows, Macintosh, AIX, VMS, and most UNIX systems. Plans are in place to also develop a Web server for MVS.

For an overview of several Web servers, see Chapter 10, "A tour of Web servers."

TCP/IP

Transmission Control Protocol/Internet Protocol (TCP/IP) is the set of protocols used on the Internet to enable communication between clients and servers around the world. The Internet is the basis for the Web and, therefore, the communication on the Web is based on TCP/IP.

TCP/IP was developed by Robert Kahn and Vinton G. Cerf and was originally used by the United States Department of Defense in their effort to connect the computers of companies and universities that were working on military-related projects. There are several categories of TCP/IP protocols, called *layers*. Each layer is designed to address a specific aspect of communication.

- *Network-layer protocols* define how data is transported over a physical network. These protocols define how your computer accesses the network.

- *Internetwork-layer protocols* define the interface between the network layer and the transport layer protocols. These protocols define how control messages are handled and how Internet addresses are mapped to physical adapter addresses.

- *Transport-layer protocols* define how information is exchanged between programs.

- *Application-layer protocols* define how programs should behave. Conformance to these protocols helps ensure that the programs from various vendors can communicate with one another.

Each of the TCP/IP protocols is controlled by a document called a Request for Comments (RFC). A database of RFCs is provided by AT&T through the InterNIC project. For more information, see **http://ds.internic.net/**.

HTTP

The *Hypertext Transfer Protocol (HTTP)* is the protocol that governs communication on the Web. It is a fast, *stateless*, application-layer protocol. Stateless means that the connection between the client (the browser) and the server is maintained only as long as is necessary to process a request.

HTTP is similar to the Multipurpose Internet Mail Exchange (MIME) protocol in the way HTTP allows for transmission of multimedia files. However, there are some significant differences, such as the default character type for text files (MIME uses US-ASCII, and HTTP uses ISO88591), that prevent HTTP from being MIME-compliant.

The HTTP specification defines how:

*   The Web browser requests information from the Web server

*   The Web server responds to the browser's request

It also defines the confirmation and error messages that can be used. For a copy of the HTTP specification, see
http://www.w3.org/hypertext/WWW/Protocols/Overview.html.

Requests to a server

The request from the browser must be sent in a standard format as defined by the HTTP specification. There are two formats for requests: a Simple-Request and a Full-Request. At a minimum, the request must specify the method and the identifier of the requested information.

With a Simple-Request, the only possible method is GET. With a Full-Request, the method can be GET, HEAD, or POST.

With either of the formats, the identifier of the requested information is similar to the URL; however, the identifier generally includes only the path and file name. The protocol is assumed to be the protocol used to make the request, and the server is assumed to be the server receiving the request.

A Full-Request may also include additional information, such as the date and any authorization information.

Responses from a server

The response from the server must also be sent in a standard format as defined by the HTTP specification. There are two formats for responses: a Simple-Response and a Full-Response.

A Simple-Response can be sent only in response to a Simple-Request and can include only the body of the response.

A Full-Response can also include additional information, such as the content type and content length of the response.

Messages from a server

The HTTP specification defines the following standard messages that a server program should use to confirm a request, indicate a redirection of the request, or return an error. Depending on how the browser handles these messages, a user may or may not see some of them.

Confirmation messages

Message	Meaning
200 OK.	The request has been accepted and processed.
201 Created.	The request has been accepted and a new resource has been created. Only used with POST requests.
202 Accepted.	The request has been accepted but not yet processed.
204 No Content.	The request has been accepted and processed, but there is no information to include in the response.

Redirection messages

Message	Meaning
300 Multiple Choices.	The requested information is not available using the current URL but is available from several other URLs, which should be listed in the message.
301 Moved Permanently.	The requested information has been permanently moved to a new URL, which should be listed in the message.

Message	Meaning
302 Moved Temporarily.	The requested information has been temporarily moved to a new URL, which should be listed in the message.
304 Not Modified.	A conditional GET request has been made, but the requested information has not changed.

Client error messages

Message	Meaning
400 Bad Request.	The syntax of the request was incorrect, and the request could not be processed.
401 Unauthorized.	The user is not authorized to access the requested information.
404 Not Found.	The URL indicated in the request could not be found.

Server error messages

Message	Meaning
500 Internal Server Error.	The server encountered an unexpected error and could not process the request.
501 Not Implemented.	The function requested has not been implemented on the server.
502 Bad Gateway.	The server received an invalid response from the gateway.
503 Service Unavailable.	The server is temporarily unable to process the request.

HTTPD

The *Hypertext Transfer Protocol daemon (HTTPD)* is the program that runs on the Web server and communicates with the Web browser. It controls the connection and processes the browser's requests.

There are two primary implementations of HTTPD on which many Web servers are based: CERN HTTPD (the CERN Web server) and NCSA HTTPD (the NCSA Web server). Both of these are discussed in Chapter 10, "A tour of Web servers." For more information about CERN's implementation, see **http://www.w3.org/hypertext/WWW/Daemon/User/Guide.html**. For more information about NCSA's implementation, see **http://hoohoo.ncsa.uiuc.edu/docs/Overview.html**.

HTML documents

An HTML document is a file containing information that is coded with the Hypertext Markup Language. *Hypertext Markup Language (HTML)* is a set of markup tags that you include in a file to govern the formatting of the information and the behavior of selectable elements. Specifically:

- Formatting tags govern the font, size, and placement of information. For example, heading tags placed around a string of text cause the text to be displayed on a separate line in a larger, bold font.

- Behavior tags govern the interaction between the reader and the Web. For example, anchor tags placed around a string of text cause the Web browser to link to the specified information when the reader selects the text.

HTML is based on Standard Generalized Markup Language (SGML), a developing standard for word-processing programs. HTML documents are stored on Web servers in an unformatted state. Upon request, the Web server sends a copy of the HTML source file to the browser, which interprets the HTML coding in the file and formats the information.

For more information on how to create HTML documents, see Part One, "Writing for the Web."

Proxy servers

Depending on how your network is set up, you may want (or need) your Web server to act as a *proxy server*. A proxy server forwards requests from Web browsers to other Web servers, and then forwards the responses back to the browsers. Many Web server products provide options that allow you to configure them as a proxy server.

The most common use of a proxy server is on a *firewall*. A firewall is a computer that connects a private network to another network, such as the Internet, and controls communication between the two. Using a proxy server on a firewall, you can allow users inside a private network to access information on the Web without jeopardizing the security of your private network.

To aid in performance and response time, many Web servers that can be configured as proxy servers can also be set up to store, or cache, the documents that they forward. When documents are held in cache, the proxy server can respond to subsequent requests for the same document more quickly.

Many of the Web servers described in Chapter 10, "A tour of Web servers," can be configured as a proxy server or a caching proxy server.

Web security

The Web is built on a set of "open" protocols. This fact has allowed numerous individuals and companies to develop information and programs for the Web, which accounts for its rapid growth over the past few years. However, this openness has also made the Web vulnerable to a number of security problems.

There are basic mechanisms for protecting data on a server, such as storing all your programs in the cgi-bin subdirectory. These mechanisms, however, are often not sophisticated enough to block attempts by knowledgeable users who wish to bypass them. This creates a hole through which users can access (what should be) protected information. Also, the lack of data checking could allow corrupted data to be stored using accepted access methods, such as the PUT method used in some forms. To solve this problem, there must be a way to confirm the identity of the user and to restrict access to the data: user authentication and access control.

In addition, the Web's popularity and accessibility have also made it a new avenue for commerce. Many companies are beginning to use the Web to advertise their products and services and allow customers to purchase them over the Web. The customer wants to be confident that the order (which may include a credit card number) is being sent to the correct Web server without chance of interception. And the company receiving the order needs to be sure that the information they receive has not been tampered with or otherwise corrupted. To solve this problem, there must be a way to confirm the identity of the server and to ensure the integrity of the data: server authentication and data encryption.

There are several security schemes that attempt to provide one or more of these types of protection. Many manufacturers of Web servers and browsers have begun offering secure products that use one of these security schemes.

For more information about Web security, see Chapter 11, "Security on the Web."

Common Gateway Interface

Web servers are designed to respond to requests for information. Typically, this information is stored on the server in a file, such as an HTML document. In this case, the server simply sends a copy of the file to the requesting browser. There are instances, however, when users may want to request other types of information, such as a list of all the documents on a specific topic. This type of information is not generally stored in a file; it is created by a separate search program. The *Common Gateway Interface (CGI)* allows the Web server to pass parameters to a separate, external program, such as a search program, and return the results to the requesting browser.

CGI programs are not limited to returning search results. CGI simply defines how information will be passed from the server and how it must be returned to the server. The nature of the program is up to you. For example, you could write a program that processes input from forms, performs conversions (such as converting an RGB value to its hexadecimal equivalent), or extracts information from a relational database (such as DB2 or Ingres).

For more information about CGI, see Chapter 12, "Using the Common Gateway Interface."

Presence providers

There are several companies that allow you to place your HTML documents on their server for a fee. These companies, called *presence providers*, may also offer other services, such as:

- Assistance with designing your documents to help you get the most out of your leased space

- Server monitoring and security to protect your information and any data sent or received

- Analysis of the server log information to let you know if your home page is reaching its intended audience

For more information about presence providers, see Chapter 13, "Leasing space on someone else's server."

A tour of Web servers

entral to setting up a Web site is selecting a Web server. Today, there are several Web servers available, and the number is growing. All require a TCP/IP-based network connection, and all can serve HTML documents using HTTP. The difference between them is the options and features they provide.

Which server is right for you will depend on how you intend to use the server. For example, if you plan to allow users to order products from you using HTML forms, you will need a server that provides transaction security to protect the users' information (such as their credit card numbers). If you plan to use the server to allow users of your protected internal network to obtain documents from servers on the Internet, you will need a server that can act as a proxy.

You also, of course, need to take into consideration the volume of traffic you expect (some servers provide better performance than others) and the operating system you want to use.

This chapter gives an overview of some of the currently available Web servers, their features, their availability, and where you can go to get more information. Yahoo also maintains a list of available server software with links to more information. See **http://www.yahoo.com/Computers/World_Wide_Web/HTTP/Servers/**.

Chapter 10. A tour of Web servers

CERN Web server

CERN initiated the Web and was naturally the first to create a Web server. The CERN Web server is part of the *public domain*, which means it is placed on public servers on the Internet and is freely available to anyone who wishes to use it. In addition, it is the basis for many of the commercially available servers, such as IBM's Internet Connection servers.

Features

For many people, the biggest selling feature of the CERN Web server is that it is free. More than that, however, it is a reliable, well-designed Web server. It doesn't have all the "bells and whistles" of its commercial descendants, but it does provide most of the functions that many people need, including support for CGI and options for configuring many aspects of the server, including:

- Running the server as a caching proxy server

- Restricting access to data on the server

- Mapping virtual resource names to actual resources

- Logging requests

- Controlling how directories are displayed at the browser

Using other programs with the server

You can use the CERN Web server to do much more than just store and serve static HTML documents. Because the CERN server supports CGI, you can write programs, or scripts, that enable your server to build and return customized information. These programs can perform searches, process forms, process image maps, and interact with databases.

CERN provides several CGI programs, such as htimage (for processing image maps) and cgiparse (a generic parser for CGI input), that you can get from **http://www.w3.org/hypertext/Dist/httpd/**.

Running the server as a caching proxy

The CERN Web server can be configured to run as a proxy server, forwarding requests and responses between a browser and a server (usually on different networks). In addition, the proxy server can be configured to cache the documents that it forwards, allowing the server to respond more quickly to other requests for the same document.

Within an internal network, you can set up the server as a caching proxy to reduce the amount of traffic on the network. In large networks, you can connect a hierarchy of caching proxies. Requests are forwarded through the hierarchy of servers until the document is retrieved from a server's cache or from the actual server where the document resides.

You can also set up your server to be a proxy on a firewall. A firewall is connected to both your internal network and the external Internet. Users of the internal network are inside the firewall, but the server allows them to have access to the Internet. The firewall can also be set up to prevent external machines from accessing your internal network.

Restricting access

Most likely, you will not want everyone to be able to access all the information on your Web server. For example, you probably would not want everyone to be able to access your CGI programs.

The CERN Web server allows you to restrict access based on user name or IP address. Access authorization is controlled using one or more files, including:

- A Password file, which allows you to define individual user access

- A Group file, which allows you to define access for a group of users

- An Access Control List (ACL), which allows you to define access for individual files or groups of files

For more information about restricting access on the CERN Web server, see **http://www.w3.org/hypertext/WWW/Daemon/User/Config/AccessAuth.html**.

Mapping resources

The CERN Web server supports *resource mapping*, which allows you to assign aliases to real path names. With resource mapping, each URL request that comes to the server is checked against a list of aliases to determine the actual location of the requested resource. This allows you to create a virtual hierarchy of Web resources that is independent of the physical structure.

Logging requests

When you establish a presence on the Web, you will probably have some idea of how often the server will be accessed and by whom. To assist you in determining whether projections were correct, the CERN Web server provides an option that you can use to record the requests that are made to your server.

Controlling how directories are displayed

If you allow readers to access a directory instead of an HTML document, such as a directory where freeware programs are stored, you have some control over how the directory information is displayed. For example, you can control the information that describes each file as well as the placement of general directory information.

Depending on the purpose of the directory, the types of files included, the anticipated needs of your users, and your own personal preferences, you may want to specify what information is displayed about each file. The CERN Web server provides several configuration options that allow you to select what information is displayed, including:

- The file date

- The file size

- The permission attributes assigned to the file

Also, you may want to provide the reader with information about that directory. For example, you may want to list the files contained in the directory and identify the contents of each. You may also want to provide instructions for decompressing or unzipping the files. Typically, such information is included in a file called a *README*. The CERN server provides a configuration option that allows you to specify whether the text of the README is included at the top or bottom of the directory listing, or not included at all.

Configuration

All configuration information must be maintained in a configuration file. The CERN Web server does not provide a graphical interface to assist in configuration. (Remember, this is a free server.) There are, however, some sample configuration files that you can use:

- **httpd.conf** is the default.

- **prot.conf** allows you to configure a protected server, one with access control.

- **proxy.conf** allows you to configure a proxy server, without caching.

- **caching.conf** allows you to configure a proxy server with caching.

If you obtain one of the compiled versions, you can find the sample configuration files in cern_httpd/config. If you obtain the source code, you can find the sample configuration files in WWW/server_root.

Availability

Compiled versions of the CERN Web server are available for most UNIX systems, including Digital, Hewlett-Packard, Next, Sun, and SGI.

For those of you who are not using one of these systems, the source for the CERN server is also available. Compiled versions and the source code of the CERN server can be found at **http://www.w3.org/hypertext/Dist/httpd/**. If you obtain the source code, you will need to compile it using a BUILD script, which is provided with the W3C Reference Library. If you do not have a copy of this library, you can obtain one from **http://www.w3.org/hypertext/Dist/libwww/**.

Additional information, including instructions for compiling the source code and instructions for installing the server, can be found at **http://www.w3.org/hypertext/WWW/Daemon/**.

NCSA Web server

NCSA, the creators of Mosaic, also offers a Web server that is available free of charge.

Features

Like the CERN Web server, the NCSA server is a free, reliable, well-designed Web server. It is a full-function server that provides support for CGI and options for configuring many aspects of the server, including:

- Restricting access to data on the server

- Mapping virtual resource names to actual resources

- Logging requests and errors

Using other programs with the server

Like most Web servers, the NCSA server supports the Common Gateway Interface. This means you can write programs that can interact with the NCSA Web server. NCSA provides several sample CGI programs that you can use, including:

- archie, a program that provides an interface (using ISINDEX) to *Archie*, a standard Internet search tool that searches anonymous FTP servers for files that match the specified criteria.

- date, a program that displays the current date.

- query, a generic form response program.

- imagemap, a program for processing information from mapped images. Source for this CGI program is also available from NCSA at **http://hoohoo.ncsa.uiuc.edu/docs/tutorials/imagemap.txt**.

In addition, NCSA allows you to generate dynamic documents using server side includes. *Server side includes* are execs that are launched from within an HTML document. They can be used if you want to include dynamic information, such as the current date, in your document. For more information about server side includes, see **http://hoohoo.ncsa.uiuc.edu/docs/tutorials/includes.html**.

Restricting access

As with the CERN server, you can restrict access to the information on your NCSA Web server.

The NCSA Web server allows you to restrict access based on host name (host filtering) or user name (user authentication).

With *host filtering*, you can limit access to certain files to only those users on certain machines. For example, you might limit access to some documents to only users in your company (users of machines that are within your company's domain).

With *user authentication*, you can limit access to certain files to a specific user (user file) or group of users (group file), as specified in the access.conf file. Each defined user must be assigned a password. The NCSA Web server package includes a command, htpasswd, that you can use to maintain user password files.

For more information about restricting access on the NCSA Web server, see **http://www.w3.org/hypertext/WWW/Daemon/User/Config/AccessAuth.html**.

Mapping resources

Like the CERN server, the NCSA server supports resource mapping. With the NCSA Web server, each URL request that comes to the server is checked against the aliases specified in the srm.conf file to determine the actual location of the requested resource.

Logging requests and errors

To assist you in determining who is accessing your server and how your server is operating, the NCSA Web server provides configuration options that you can use to record the requests that are made to your server and any errors that result.

Configuration

All configuration information must be maintained in a configuration file. The NCSA server does not provide a graphical interface to assist in configuration. (Remember, this is a free server.) There are, however, some sample configuration files that you can use:

- **httpd.conf** is the server operation configuration file. It allows you to configure basic operating parameters, such as the host name of the server. A template for this file, called httpd.conf-dist, is included with the NCSA server in the conf directory.

- **srm.conf** is the resource configuration file. It allows you to configure parameters pertaining to the documents on your server, such as the literal path assigned to an alias. A template for this file, called srm.conf-dist, is included with the NCSA server in the conf directory.

- **access.conf** is the access configuration file. It allows you to configure access authorization, such as which users can access certain files.

Availability

Compiled versions of the NCSA Web server are available for most UNIX systems, including Digital, Hewlett-Packard, Sun, and SGI, as well as one for IBM's AIX system. For access to the compiled versions, see **http://hoohoo.ncsa.uiuc.edu/docs/setup/PreCompiled.html**.

For those of you who are not using one of these systems, the source for the NCSA server is also available. The source code can be found at **ftp://ftp.ncsa.uiuc.edu/Web/httpd/Unix/ncsa_httpd/current/**.

Additional information, including instructions for compiling the source code and instructions for installing the server, can be found at **http://hoohoo.ncsa.uiuc.edu/docs/Overview.html**.

IBM Internet Connection servers

IBM currently offers Web servers for AIX and for OS/2 and has announced plans for developing servers for other systems. The IBM Internet Connection servers provide the foundation for building a presence on the Internet. Each of these servers can be used as a Web server for the Internet or as an internal server for your company or organization.

Features

The IBM Internet Connection Servers are based on the CERN Web server. They include functions similar to those of the CERN server along with many additional features. The servers are also backed by IBM's world-wide service and support teams.

The IBM Internet Connection Server supports CGI and provides configuration and administration utilities that make it easy to:

- Use the server as a caching proxy server on a firewall

- Restrict access to the server and its information

- Map requests sent to the server to other resources

- Log requests and error messages

Using other programs with the server

Like the CERN server, the Internet Connection Server supports CGI, which allows you to create programs that interface with your server and perform tasks such as searching and forwarding e-mail messages.

To assist you in writing programs that use CGI, the Internet Connection Server includes utilities for extracting forms data, writing document headers, and processing image maps.

For more information about CGI, see Chapter 12, "Using the Common Gateway Interface."

Running the server as a caching proxy

As with the CERN server, the Internet Connection Server can be configured as a caching proxy server. This will improve performance as well as allow users of your internal network to access documents on the Internet.

The Internet Connection Server allows you to specify:

- Which files you want (and do not want) to store in cache

- The maximum and minimum sizes for files stored in cache

- The maximum amount of space allotted to cache storage

It also allows you to configure automatic reclamation of cache storage space as well as reroute requests to other proxy servers.

Restricting access

Like the CERN server, the Internet Connection Server allows you to restrict access to specific files or directories to only authenticated users. You can restrict access based on IP address or user name.

Also, IBM has announced plans to produce secure versions of their AIX and OS/2 Web servers. The products, called IBM Internet Connection Secure Server for AIX and IBM Internet Connection Secure Server for OS/2, will support two of the most popular emerging security protocols: SSL and S-HTTP.

For more information about SSL and S-HTTP, see Chapter 11 "Security on the Web."

Mapping resources

The Internet Connection Server also allows you to use resource mapping to create a virtual hierarchy of Web resources.

As part of the Internet Connection Server configuration, you can specify *resource mapping rules*, which associate the actual path to a document or resource with an alias. Each URL request that comes to the server is checked against these rules to determine if the request should be accepted and where the requested resource is actually located.

Logging requests and errors

To help you determine whether or not your Internet message is reaching the intended audience, the Internet Connection Server maintains logs showing who is accessing your server and when. It can also maintain logs of requests for cached files (if the server is a caching proxy), and logs of internal server errors.

Because the logs are written in a format that is common to most Web servers, you can use any of several standard statistical programs to analyze the log contents.

Controlling how directories are displayed

Like the CERN server, the Internet Connection Server provides several configuration options that allow you to specify how the file information is displayed and where README text is displayed.

Installation and Configuration

The Internet Connection Servers for AIX and OS/2 are delivered on both 3.5-inch diskettes and CD-ROM. You can easily install the servers from either of these media. The servers follow standard installation procedures for their respective operating systems:

- The Internet Connection Server for AIX uses the Installp feature of SMIT.

- The Internet Connection Server for OS/2 uses the OS/2 installation tool, Software Installer.

After installing the IBM Internet Connection Server for AIX or OS/2, you can start it using the configuration values you specified during installation. Default values are supplied for all the other configuration values. Using a Web browser, you can then connect to the server.

By default, your server uses the Internet Connection Server Front Page as its home page. The front page provides a valuable assortment of tools and information.

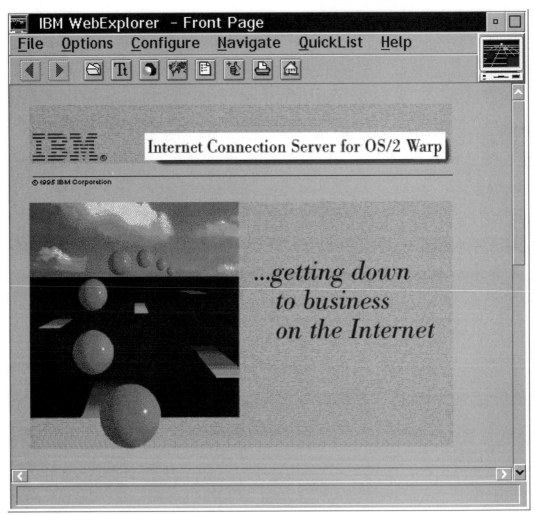

Figure 10-1. IBM Internet Connection Server Front Page

One of the most useful features of the IBM Internet Connection Servers is the on-line Configuration and Administration tool. This tool allows you, or other authorized personnel, to configure your server remotely by entering information in a series of HTML forms. When you click on the link to the Configuration and Administration Forms from the Front Page, you see a list of links to each of the tool's input forms.

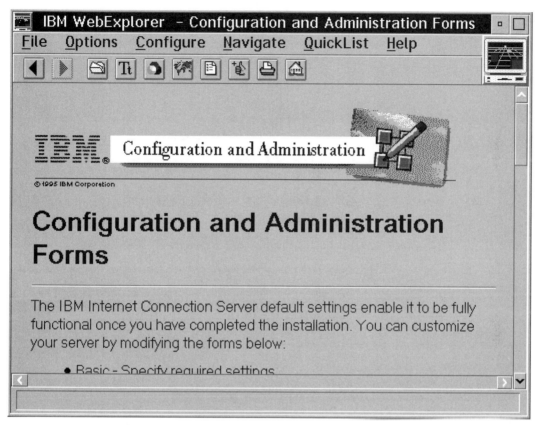

Figure 10-2. IBM Internet Connection Server Configuration and Administration Forms

When you link to a form, it is shown with the current values in the input fields. You can then change the values on the form to configure a part of your server. The forms provide instructions and links to on-line help to assist you in deciding what changes to make. For example, you would use the following form to control how the server displays information when returning a directory list to a browser.

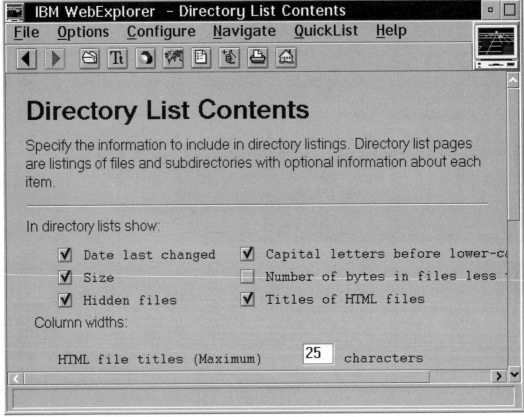

Figure 10-3. IBM Internet Connection Servers Directory List Contents form

After making changes to a form, click on the Apply push button. Once your input is accepted, you are given the option of restarting the server to have your changes take effect immediately.

Availability

The IBM Internet Connection Server for AIX and the IBM Internet Connection Server for OS/2 are available now. The AIX operating system runs on IBM's RISC System/6000 workstations and the IBM Power Series Family. The OS/2 operating system runs on desktop and laptop computers. Plans are in place for the Internet Connection Server for AIX to support Scaleable POWERparallel Systems (SP2).

IBM has also announced plans to make the Internet Connection Server available on its MVS and OS/400 operating systems. MVS runs on IBM S/390 mainframe computers. OS/400 runs on IBM AS/400 business computers. The IBM Internet Connection Server for MVS will enable companies to use a portion of their S/390 mainframe Web server. The IBM Internet Connection Server for OS/400 will take advantage of OS/400 features including an integrated database and integrated security authorization.

The following is an overview of the system requirements for the currently available IBM Internet Connection Servers. For the exact requirements, refer to the product documentation.

The IBM Internet Connection Server for AIX has the following hardware and software requirements:

- A RISC System/6000 or IBM Power Series Family

- Approximately 6 MB of free disk space

- A 3.5-inch 1.44 MB diskette drive or a CD-ROM drive for installation

- A mouse or compatible pointing device (although all functions can be performed with the keyboard, a pointing device is recommended)

- Any communication hardware adapter supported by the TCP/IP protocol stack to make network connections

- AIX 4.1.3 or later

The IBM Internet Connection Server for OS/2 has the following hardware and software requirements:

- Any personal computer or PS/2 computer that can support OS/2 Warp V3.0

- A mouse or compatible pointing device

- A Local Area Network (LAN) adapter that is supported by OS/2 Warp V3.0

- Approximately 2 MB of free disk space

- A 3.5-inch 1.44 MB diskette drive or a CD-ROM drive for installation

- OS/2 Warp Version 3.0 or later

- One of the following:

  - TCP/IP Version 3.0, which is a part of Warp Connect

  - Internet Connection for OS/2, which is included in all versions of Warp including Warp Connect. (See the product documentation for service level requirements.)

- TCP/IP Version 2.0. (See the product documentation for service level requirements.)

- A partition formatted using the High Performance File System (HPFS). Only the server needs to be on the HPFS partition, not the entire operating system.

For more information, see **http://www.ibm.com/Internet/**.

Netscape servers

Netscape offers several servers designed to suit different needs, including the Communications Server, the Proxy Server, and the Commerce Server.

Netscape Communications Server

The Communications Server is Netscape's basic Web server. It can be used as a Web server for the Internet or as an internal server for your company or organization.

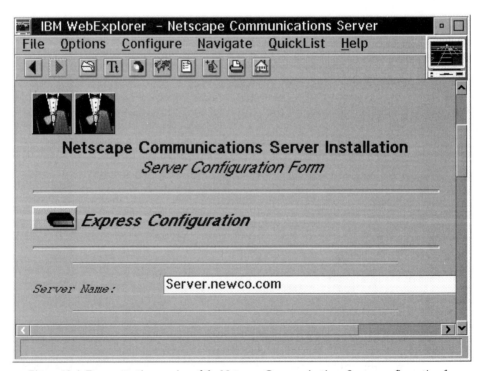

Figure 10-4. Demonstration version of the Netscape Communications Server configuration form

Features

Like the IBM Internet Connection Servers, the Netscape Communications Server provides an easy-to-use, forms-based interface for remote configuration and administration of the server. This interface allows you to restrict access, specify logging options, and adjust performance parameters.

One of the performance parameters that you can adjust is the maximum number of processes to be maintained. Unlike many other servers that create a new process to fulfill each request, the Netscape Communications Server can hold a certain number (as configured) of processes in memory. This allows the server to run more efficiently and respond more quickly to requests.

In addition to the Common Gateway Interface, the Netscape Communications Server supports the Netscape Server Application Programming Interface (NSAPI). Like CGI, this API enables communication between the Web server and external programs. However, the design of the NSAPI provides better performance and efficiency than CGI.

Availability

The Communications Server is available for UNIX and Windows NT systems. Memory requirements vary, but in general, the Communications Server for UNIX requires 32 MB, and the Communications Server for Windows NT requires 16 MB.

For more information, see
http://www.netscape.com/comprod netscape_commun.html.

Netscape Proxy Server

The Proxy Server is Netscape's caching proxy server.

Features

In addition to the features offered by the Communications Server, the Proxy Server provides enhanced security and improved network performance.

The Netscape Proxy Server provides controlled access between two networks. In addition, the Netscape Proxy Server supports SSL and can also be used for secure communication between a secure browser on one network and a secure server on another. If the browser making the request does not support SSL, the Proxy Server will establish a secure connection for the browser. In addition to HTTP requests, the Proxy Server can forward other protocol requests, including FTP and Gopher.

The Proxy Server can also be configured to cache, or store, requested documents. Additional requests for those documents can then be answered more quickly.

Availability

The Proxy Server is available for UNIX systems. Memory requirements vary, but in general, the Communications Server for UNIX requires 32 MB.

For more information, see **http://www.netscape.com/comprod/proxy_server.html**.

Netscape Commerce Server

The Commerce Server is Netscape's secure Web server designed for those who wish to conduct business on the Web.

Features

In addition to the features offered by the Communications Server, the Commerce Server provides enhanced security for the protection of sensitive data.

Through the use of SSL, the Commerce Server uses security certificates and encryption algorithms to ensure server authentication and data privacy and integrity. For more information about SSL, see Chapter 11 "Security on the Web."

Availability

The Commerce Server is available for UNIX and Windows NT systems. Memory requirements vary, but in general, the Communications Server for UNIX requires 32 MB, and the Communications Server for Windows NT requires 16 MB.

For more information, see
http://www.netscape.com/comprod/netscape_commerce.html.

SPRY Internet Office Web servers

SPRY, a subsidiary of Compuserve, offers two versions of its Internet Office Web server: secure and nonsecure. Either can be used on the Internet or as an internal server for your company or organization.

Features

Similar to the IBM Internet Connection servers and the Netscape servers, the Internet Office Web Server provides an easy-to-use graphical interface for configuring and administering the server. In addition, there is a command line configuration tool, which is useful for small changes.

The secure Internet Office Web Server supports both SSL and S-HTTP. It supports both server and client (browser) authentication as well as data encryption. For flexibility, it provides three types of security databases: a Certificate database, a Shared Secret database, and an Access Control List database. For more information about SSL and S-HTTP, see Chapter 11 "Security on the Web."

To provide improved performance, the Internet Office Web Server allows you to start multiple occurrences of the HTTP daemon at server startup. This allows the server to respond more quickly to requests.

In addition to supporting CGI, the Internet Office Web Server provides built-in support for Structured Query Language (SQL) queries, which allows the server to communicate with your existing SQL databases.

Availability

The Internet Office Web Servers are available for UNIX and Windows NT systems.

For more information, see
http://www.compuserve.com/prod_services/corp_solutions/ioff_server.html.

Chapter 11

Security on the Web

etwork security is not a new issue. With the advent of the Internet and the Web, however, it became much more difficult to achieve.

At one time, each corporate and organization network was a world in itself—disconnected from the rest of the world, like islands in a sea. Security, while an important consideration, was a containable issue. Access to a private network from the outside was difficult, if not impossible. However, once these discrete, private networks established connections to the Internet, it was like building bridges between the islands. While well intended, these "bridges" not only let local people venture outside their "island network," they also made the "island network" vulnerable to uninvited and malicious intruders. Security became one of the foremost concerns in every network administrator's mind.

The advantages of being connected to the Web far outweigh the security problems that must be tackled. In this chapter, we focus on two aspects of Web security: protecting your network and protecting your Web site.

Security on the Web

Protecting your network

Regardless of whether your company or organization has a Web site or is connected to the Internet for other reasons, one of the best mechanisms for protecting your private network is a *firewall*. A firewall provides access control between a private network, such as a corporate network, and a public network, such as the Internet. A firewall typically consists of a computer, which is connected to both networks, and a program or programs that:

- Permit users of the private network to access the public network

- Restrict access from the public network to the private one

With respect to the Web, you can allow users of your private network to access information on the Web by installing a proxy Web server on your firewall. A proxy server receives a request from a Web browser and forwards it to the appropriate Web server. It then receives the response and forwards it to the requesting browser. As mentioned in Chapter 10, "A tour of Web servers," many Web server programs can be configured as a proxy server on a firewall.

For more information on firewalls, see the following:

- Information Warehouse, Inc., provides a copy of Marcus Ranum's FAQ on firewalls at **http://www.iwi.com/pubs/faq.htm**. They also offer an instructor-led tutorial on network security. See **http://www.iwi.com/iw-clas.html**.

- Great Circle Associates also offers an instructor-led tutorial on Internet firewalls. See **http://www.greatcircle.com/gca/tutorial/main.html**.

- Livermore Software Laboratories offers an on-line tutorial on firewalls and network security. The tutorial was written in support of the PORTUS firewall, developed by Freemont Avenue Software, but it also contains general discussions on firewalls and network security. See **http://www.lsli.com/**.

We describe some of the firewall products in this chapter. Cathy Fulmer maintains an extensive list of firewall products at **http://www.access.digex.net/~bdboyle/firewall.vendor.html**.

IBM Internet Connection Secured Network Gateway

IBM offers a firewall called the Internet Connection Secured Network Gateway for AIX (formerly the Network Security Program, NetSP), which is part of IBM's family of Internet products.

The Internet Connection firewall allows users in your private network to access servers outside the network using standard TCP/IP applications, such as FTP or Telnet. It also allows you to permit authorized users on the outside to access specific resources in your private network, while protecting the rest of the network from unauthorized access. You can specify who is allowed access into and out of your network based on IP address, user name, or the application being used.

In addition, the Internet Connection firewall provides secure communication between firewalls by encrypting data that must travel across unsecured networks. The Internet Connection firewall encrypts the IP packets, which carry the data, creating a private IP "tunnel."

The Internet Connection firewall also provides:

- An easy-to-use graphical interface and a command line interface for configuration and administration.

- A facility to monitor security events at the firewall and notify the network administrator of any problems.

- Advanced filtering capability, which can be used to limit access based on criteria, such as a range of acceptable addresses for the source or destination of a request.

- Support for the Software Common Knowledge IR System (SOCKS) API. The SOCKS API is used by some applications as a means of controlling access to the Internet, while, at the same time, hiding the IP addresses of the internal network from the outside world.

- A mail service, which forwards authorized e-mail messages to an e-mail server in your private network.

- Strong user authentication, based on passwords or on more sophisticated methods, like Digital Pathways' SecureNet card or Security Dynamics' SecurID card.

The Internet Connection firewall requires a RISC System/6000 running AIX/6000 Version 3.2.5 or 4.1.3 with 1 GB disk space and at least 32 MB of memory. Additional disk space is required for log files.

TIS GAUNTLET Internet Firewall

Trusted Information Systems (TIS) offers the GAUNTLET Internet Firewall. Like the Internet Connection firewall, the GAUNTLET firewall provides:

- Access control

- Encryption of communication between firewalls

- Security monitoring and notification

- Strong user authentication

The design of the GAUNTLET firewall is based on a minimalist approach to security: "That which is not expressly permitted is prohibited." Assuming that you want to block communication from more users than you permit, this approach reduces the amount of configuration required and helps ensure that there are no holes in your access control.

The GAUNTLET firewall is an integrated product, including both the hardware and the software. TIS does, however, offer the software separately. For more information about the GAUNTLET firewall, see **http://www.tis.com/**.

PORTUS

Livermore Software Laboratories offers PORTUS, whose name is derived from that of the Roman god, Portunus, protector of gates, doorways, and harbors. Developed by Freemont Avenue Software, PORTUS was designed to provide security without complexity.

PORTUS provides many of the same security features as the Internet Connection firewall and the GAUNTLET firewall, including:

- Access control

- Strong user authentication, including support for single-use passwords

- Secure forwarding of e-mail messages

- Built-in FTP and Telnet proxy support

In addition, PORTUS provides proxy servers for news, Web, Gopher, and search requests.

To simplify configuration, PORTUS:

- Was designed so any access not explicitly permitted is denied (similar to the GAUNTLET firewall)

- Does not permit packet filtering (due to the complexity of the configuration and the potential for error)

- Uses familiar tools for configuration: Systems Management Information Tool (SMIT) for AIX systems and System Administration Manager (SAM) for HP-UNIX systems

For more information on PORTUS, see **http://www.lsli.com/**.

Protecting your Web site

Protecting your Web site includes protecting the Web server, its data, and any transactions that may take place between the server and a client (or browser). Therefore, you need programs that will provide: access control, authentication, and encryption.

- *Access control* allows you to limit access to the files and directories on your Web server.

- *Authentication* provides a way for the browser to verify the identity of the server. This is useful when you need to make sure that your browser is communicating with the correct server. Authentication can allow the server to verify the identity of the browser.

- *Encryption* provides a way to protect sensitive data, such as a credit card number. With encryption, data is scrambled using an algorithm known only to the corresponding browser and server.

As we discussed in Chapter 10, "A tour of Web servers," many of the servers provide mechanisms for controlling access to the data stored on a server. Access control can be based on *who* is requesting access or *what* they are requesting access to.

To address the aspects of transaction protection (authentication and encryption), there are several methods, or schemes, being proposed or already in use. Two of the more popular security schemes are: Secure Sockets Layer (SSL) and Secure Hypertext Transfer Protocol (S-HTTP).

Secure Sockets Layer (SSL)

The SSL protocol was developed by Netscape. It is designed to provide secure communications by ensuring the following:

- The authenticity of the server (and optionally the browser)

- The privacy of the communication

- The reliability of the data

For identity authentication, SSL uses certificates and keys:

- From the server perspective, if you want to set up a secure Web server, you must obtain a *certificate* from a Certifying Authority (CA), such as VeriSign. A certificate is a digital document that binds a public key to the certificate owner. When a secure server responds to a request, it sends an encrypted response that can only be read by those who have a copy of the appropriate key.

- From the browser perspective, if you want to communicate with a secure Web server, your Web browser must have access to the appropriate key (usually a preconfigured public key). The *key* is used to decrypt the server's response and verify the identity of the server. In some cases, the browser might also be required to have a certificate for the purpose of client authentication.

To ensure privacy, all communication is encrypted using a secret session key, which is agreed upon by the browser and the server after authentication.

To ensure reliability, the server performs an integrity check on all data received. An integrity check ensures that the message received is the same message that was sent— no data has been changed, added, or deleted.

When connecting to (or coding a hypertext link to) a Web server that supports SSL, the URL must begin with https (rather than http). For more information about SSL, see **http://www.netscape.com/info/SSL.html**. For more information about certificates and keys, see the FAQ maintained by RSA Data Security at **http://www.rsa.com/rsalabs/faq/faq_km.html**.

Secure Hypertext Transfer Protocol (S-HTTP)

Secure Hypertext Transfer Protocol (S-HTTP) was developed by Enterprise Integration Technologies (EIT). It is based on HTTP and adds message-based security.

Like SSL, S-HTTP uses certificates and keys to ensure the following:

- The authenticity of the server and the browser

- The privacy of the communication

- The reliability of the data

There are some differences, however, in how S-HTTP makes these assurances:

- S-HTTP requires both the server and the browser to have certificates. This means that the browser user must request and receive a certificate from a Certifying Authority (CA), such as VeriSign.

- For encryption, S-HTTP requires the server and the browser to agree upon an encryption method. If the browser does not support any of the methods used by the server, no further communication can take place.

- S-HTTP also requires the browser to have a private and public key pair.

When connecting to (or coding a hypertext link to) a Web server that supports S-HTTP, the URL must begin with shttp (rather than http). Also, with S-HTTP, the cryptographic options are specified in the URL. For more information about S-HTTP, see **http://www.eit.com/creations/s-http/**. For more information about certificates and keys, see the FAQ maintained by RSA Data Security at **http://www.rsa.com/rsalabs/faq/faq_km.html**.

Using the Common Gateway Interface

f the Web were simply made up of thousands of machines that contained numerous documents all linked together, that in itself would be an accomplishment. But the Web is much more. It is an interactive medium that allows users to give feedback to a company about its products, use search utilities to locate information on a certain topic, use conversion programs to convert one value to another, and more. The Web server software does not perform these tasks. They are performed by external programs using information passed to them by the Web server. The Common Gateway Interface (CGI) allows the server and the external program to communicate.

This chapter discusses what the Common Gateway Interface is, why you might want to use it, and how it works. Also, there is a tutorial on CGI at **http://hoohoo.ncsa.uiuc.edu/**.

Chapter 12. Using the Common Gateway Interface

What CGI is (and is not)

The *Common Gateway Interface (CGI)* is not a piece of hardware or software. It is not even a protocol. It is a specification or standard, supported by almost all Web servers, that defines how information is exchanged between a Web server and an external program (CGI program).

CGI programs can be written in any language supported by the operating system on which it is run. The language can be a programming language, like C++, or it can be a scripting language, like Perl. Programs written in programming languages need to be compiled, and typically run faster than uncompiled programs. On the other hand, programs written in scripting languages tend to be easier to write, maintain, and debug.

The functions and tasks that the CGI programs can perform range from the simple to the very advanced. In general, those that perform the simple tasks are called *CGI scripts* (because they tend to be written in a scripting language). Those that perform more complex tasks are called *gateway programs* (because they tend to be written in a programming language). In this chapter, we refer to both types as *CGI programs*.

Given the wide choice of languages and the variety of functions, the possibilities for CGI programs seem almost endless. How you use them is up to you. Once you understand the CGI specification, you will know how the server will pass the input to your program and how the server will expect the output.

Uses for CGI

There are many uses for CGI programs. Basically, they are designed to handle dynamic information. Now, in some sense, most of the information on the Web can be considered dynamic. Very few documents go unchanged for an extended period of time. But in this context, dynamic means temporary information that is created for a one-time use and not stored anywhere on the Web. This information may be a document, an e-mail message, or the results of a conversion program.

CGI and dynamic documents

There are many types of files that exist on the Web. Primarily they fall into one of the following categories: images, multimedia, and documents. In Part One of this book, we discussed the various types of images and multimedia that can be used.

We also discussed documents, which are always HTML documents. However, from the server perspective, there are two types of HTML documents: static and dynamic. *Static documents* are ones that exist in source form on the Web server. *Dynamic documents* are ones that are created as temporary documents to satisfy a specific, individual request.

Consider the process of "serving" these two types of documents. Responding to requests for static documents is fairly simple. For example, Sam User accesses the Acme Web server to get information on their Model X Rocket. He clicks on Products, then on Rockets, and finally on Model X. Each time Sam clicks on a link, the Web browser uses the URL to request a specific document from the Web server, and the server responds by sending a copy of the document to the browser.

What if Sam then decides he wants to search through the information on the Acme Web server for all documents that contain information on Acme rockets, such as news articles, press releases, price listings, and service agreements. This is a more difficult request to process. This is not a request for an existing document. Instead, it is a request for a dynamically generated list of documents that meet certain criteria. This is where CGI comes in.

You can use a CGI program to parse the request, search through the documents on your Web server, and create a list with hypertext links to each of the documents that contain the specified word or string.

CGI and e-mail

HTML allows you to access resources on the Internet using other protocols by specifying the protocol in the URL. One such protocol is mailto. If you code a link with mailto followed by an e-mail address, the link will result in a generic mail form.

What if you wanted your customers to provide specific information, such as how often they use the Web and how they heard about your company? Rather than using the generic mailto form, you can create a form that asks these questions and more. You can then use a CGI program to interpret the information, include it in an e-mail message, and send it to the appropriate person.

Other uses for CGI

CGI programs are not limited to processing search requests and e-mail. They can be used for a wide variety of purposes. Basically, anytime you want to take input from the reader and generate a response, you can use a CGI program. The input may even be transparent to the reader. For example, many people are interested in how many other people have visited their home page. As a fun way to keep count of this, you can create a CGI program that keeps track of the number of requests for your home page and displays the new total each time someone links to your home page.

Similarly, you could write a program that takes English text (received through an HTML form) and converts it to Spanish.

How the process works

The process involves three players: the Web browser, the Web server, and the CGI program. Let's take an on-line survey as an example. We will assume that the Web browser has already requested the form and the Web server has provided it.

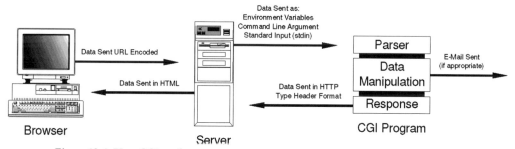

Figure 12-1. How CGI works

The user enters some information and clicks on the submission push button. The Web browser then sends the data to the Web server in an encoded format. (Do not confuse encoded with encrypted. The information is always encoded and may or may not be encrypted. Encoding by itself provides no security.) In our example, the data consists of responses to questions on an HTML form.

Upon receiving the data, the Web server converts the data to a format compliant with the CGI specification for input and sends it to the CGI program.

The CGI program then decodes the data, processes it per its own instructions, and formulates a response. In our example, the data processing step produces an e-mail message containing the information from the survey that is sent to the customer service department.

This response is sent back to the Web server in a form that is compliant with the CGI specification for output. In our example, the response is a generic message confirming that the e-mail message has been sent and thanking the user for the input.

The Web server interprets the response and forwards it to the Web browser.

How information is sent to the server

When you fill out a form or enter a phrase in a search field and click on the submission push button, the Web browser sends the request to the server in a format described as *URL-encoded*. In URL-encoded information:

- The URL starts with the URL of the processing program.

- Attached data, such as name=value information from a form, is appended to the URL and preceded by a question mark.

- Fields are separated by an ampersand (&).

- Spaces are represented by a plus sign (+).

- Special characters, such as a period or slash, are represented by a percent sign (%) followed by the ASCII hexadecimal equivalent of the symbol. For more information about ASCII hexadecimal equivalents for special characters, see Appendix B, "Understanding URL formats."

- Multiple values for a field, such as check boxes, are sent as a string separated by a null character (\0).

Let's use the following form as shown in Figure 12-2.

Here is the HTML source of this form:

```
<HTML>
<Head>
<Title>Acme Mailing List Application</Title>
</Head>
<Body>
<H1>Acme Mailing List Application</H1>
<FORM METHOD=POST ACTION="http://www.acme.com/cgi-bin/mlist">
Please provide the following information so we may add you to our
mailing list.<P>
```

```
Your name: <INPUT TYPE="text" NAME="name" SIZE=45 MAXLENGTH=50
VALUE="Enter your name here"><P>
Your e-mail address: <INPUT TYPE="TEXT" NAME='ADDR' SIZE=45
MAXLENGTH=50 VALUE="Enter your e-mail address here">
Your interests include:<P>
<INPUT TYPE="checkbox" NAME="Interest" VALUE="R"> Rockets
<INPUT TYPE="checkbox" NAME="Interest" VALUE="C"> Catapults
<INPUT TYPE="checkbox" NAME="Intetest" VALUE="T"> Fake tunnels
<INPUT TYPE="checkbox" NAME="Interest" VALUE="O"> Other<P>
<p><INPUT TYPE="submit" Value="SEND"> <INPUT TYPE="reset"><P>
</FORM>
</Body>
</HTML>
```

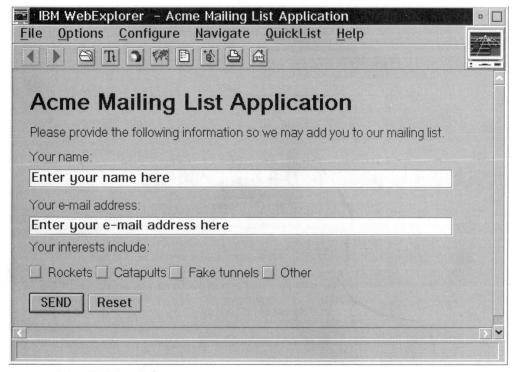

Figure 12-2. Sample form

In the source, note that:

- The ACTION attribute of the form is set to http://www.acme.com/cgi-bin/mlist. (FORM METHOD=POST ACTION="http://www.acme.com/cgi-bin/mlist")

- The field "Your name" is assigned a name of NAME.

- The field "Your e-mail address" is assigned a name of ADDR.

- Each of the check boxes in the field "Your interests include" is assigned a name of INTEREST, and a value as follows:

    - "Rockets" has a value of R.

    - "Catapults" has a value of C.

    - "Fake tunnels" has a value of T.

    - "Other" has a value of O.

After it is filled out and the user clicks on the submission push button, the URL-encoded information is sent as follows:

```
http://www.acme.com/cgi-bin/
mlist?NAME=Eugene+T%2E+Fox&ADDR=etfox%7Cibm.net&INTEREST=R\0C\0O
```

How input is passed to a CGI program

Before writing your CGI program, you need to understand the format in which the server will pass the data. The server receives the URL-encoded information and, depending on the type of request, passes the information to the program using environment variables, command line arguments, or standard input.

For all requests, regardless of type, certain information is passed using the following environment variables:

- SERVER_SOFTWARE

    Specifies the name and version of the server, such as IBM/1.0.

- SERVER_NAME

    Specifies the host name or IP address of the server, such as www.acme.com.

- GATEWAY_INTERFACE

  Specifies the version of CGI that the server is using, such as CGI/1.1.

- SERVER_PROTOCOL

  Specifies the name and version of the protocol used to make the request, such as HTTP/1.0.

- SERVER_PORT

  Specifies the port number to which the request was sent, such as 80.

- REQUEST_METHOD

  Specifies the method (as specified with the METHOD attribute) used to send the request, such as GET or POST.

- PATH_INFO

  Specifies the additional path information as sent by the Web browser.

- PATH_TRANSLATED

  Specifies the decoded or translated version of the path information contained in PATH_INFO.

- SCRIPT_NAME

  Specifies the name of the processing script. This information is useful if you want to create a dynamic document that will contain a link to the CGI program, such as a document that contains search results and allows the user to initiate another search.

- REMOTE_HOST

  Specifies the host name of the Web browser, if available.

- REMOTE_ADDR

  Specifies the IP address of the Web browser.

- AUTH_TYPE

  If the server supports client authentication and the script is protected, this environment variable specifies the method used to authenticate the client.

- REMOTE_USER

  If the server supports client authentication and the script is protected, this environment variable specifies the username passed for authentication.

- REMOTE_IDENT

  If the server supports the Authentication Protocol, RFC 931, this environment variable specifies the name of the remote user.

The format of any attached data, such as forms data, varies depending on the type of request.

For requests from standard search (ISINDEX) documents

ISINDEX is an HTML tag that identifies the document as a standard search document and causes the browser to automatically generate an entry field. When information is sent from an ISINDEX document, the server takes the appended data (the information following the ?), breaks it at the pluses (+), and sends the data to the CGI program as command line arguments (argv).

For requests with a method of POST

When information is sent using a method of POST, the server takes the appended data and sends it to the CGI program as stdin (standard input). It also includes useful information using the following environment variables:

- CONTENT_TYPE

  Specifies the type of data included, such as application/x-www-form-urlencoded.

- CONTENT_LENGTH

  Specifies the number of characters of data. Servers typically do not send an end-of-file flag when they forward the information using stdin. If needed, you can use the CONTENT_LENGTH value to determine the end of the input string.

For requests with a method of GET

When information is sent using a method of GET, the server takes the appended data and sends it to the CGI program using the following environment variable:

- QUERY_STRING

  Specifies the information in a query that follows the ?. This information should not be decoded by the server, but must be decoded by the CGI program.

How a CGI program works

In general, when you write a CGI program, you should include the following three stages: parsing, data manipulation, and response generation.

Parsing

Parsing is the first stage of a CGI program. In this stage, the program takes the data in one or more of the possible formats (environment variables, command-line arguments, or stdin), breaks it into components, and decodes the information in the components.

For example, if the following were received using the environment variable QUERY_STRING:

```
NAME=Eugene+T%2E+Fox&ADDR=etfox%7Cibm.net&INTEREST=R\0C\0O
```

The program would break the fields at the ampersands and decode the ASCII hexadecimal characters. The result would be:

```
NAME=Eugene T. Fox
ADDR=etfox@ibm.net
INTEREST=RCO
```

Many servers include a generic parsing program called cgiparse. This program is also available from CERN at **http://www.w3.org/hypertext/Dist/httpd/**.

Data manipulation

Data manipulation is the second stage of a CGI program. In this stage, the program takes the parsed data and performs the appropriate action. For example, a CGI program designed to process a mailing list application form might:

1. Take the input from the parsing stage
2. Convert abbreviations into more meaningful information, such as changing RCO to "Rockets, Catapults, Other"
3. Plug the information into an e-mail template
4. Call the sendmail program
5. Send the filled-in template to a specified e-mail address

Response generation

Response generation is the final stage of a CGI program. In this stage, the program formulates its response back to the Web server, which forwards it to the Web browser. The type of response varies depending on the type of request. With a search, the response might be the URLs of all the documents that met the search criteria. With a request that results in e-mail, the response might be a message confirming that the e-mail was sent.

How output is returned from a CGI program

When the CGI program is done, it passes the resulting response to the Web server using standard output (stdout). The Web server interprets the response and sends it to the Web browser.

Note: If you do not want the Web server to interpret the response, but just to forward it to the Web browser, the name of your CGI program should begin with nph- (no parse header).

The first line of the response must be in MIME-type header format. The content of the response will vary depending on the type of request.

If the response is a static document, the program returns the URL of the document using the HTTP Location header. For example:

```
Location: http://www.acme.com/products.html
```

Upon receiving this information from the CGI program, the Web server will retrieve the specified document and send a copy of it to the Web browser.

If the response is a dynamic document, such as a list of hypertext links to documents that meet specified criteria, the program should indicate that the response is an HTML document, using the Content-type header followed by a blank line, and then include links to the documents in HTML format. For example:

```
Content-type: text/html

<HEAD>
<TITLE>Documents Found</TITLE>
</HEAD>
<BODY>
<H1>Documents Found</H1>
The following documents meet the specified criteria:<P>
<a HREF="http://www.acme.com/Products/rockmodx.html">
Rocket Model X </a><P>
<a HREF="http://www.acme.com/Products/rockmodz.html">
Rocket Model Z </a><P>
<a HREF="http://www.acme.com/news/modxrevu.html">
Times review of Acme Rocket Model X </a><P>
<a HREF="http://www.acme.com/pressrel/annmodz.html">Announcing
Acme Rocket Model Z</a><P>
<a HREF="http://www.acme.com/service/modxwarr.html">
Rocket Model X: Warranty</a><P>
<a HREF="http://www.acme.com/service/modzwarr.html">
Rocket Model Z: Warranty</a><P>
<a HREF="http://www.acme.com/Prices/rockmodz.html">
Price listing: Rocket Model Z</a><P>
<a HREF="http://www.acme.com/Prices/rockmodx.html">
Price listing: Rocket Model X</a><P>
</Body>
```

If the response is a text file, such as a confirmation message, the program should indicate that the response is a text file, using the Content-type header followed by a blank line, and then include the text. For example:

```
Content-type: text/plain

Your message has been forwarded to our customer service depart-
ment. Thank you for participating in our survey.
```

Obtaining a CGI program

Depending on the intended use, you may be able to use an existing CGI program or you may have to write your own.

Using an existing program

Many Web servers provide some basic CGI programs. For example, the CERN Web server includes htimage (a program for processing image maps) and cgiparse (a generic parser for CGI input). These programs are also available from **http://www.w3.org/hypertext/Dist/httpd/**. The NCSA server includes archie (a program that provides an interface to Archie), date (a program that displays the current date), query (a generic form-response program), and imagemap (a program for processing image maps). Imagemap is also available from **http://hoohoo.ncsa.uiuc.edu/docs/tutorials/imagemap.txt**.

There are also several CGI programs available for free or for purchase. Yahoo maintains a list of links to freeware and shareware CGI programs. There is an assortment of programs written in various languages, for various platforms, and for various purposes. You can find the Yahoo list at **http://www.yahoo.com/Computers_and_Internet/World_Wide_Web/CGI_Common_Gateway_Interface/**.

Commercial gateway programs are also starting to hit the market. IBM recently announced two new gateway programs: CICS Internet Gateway and DB2 World Wide Web Connection.

- CICS applications receive and send information using a host-specific format called the 3270 data stream. As you know, the format of information on the Web is HTML. The CICS Internet Gateway, positioned between the Web server and the CICS application, transforms the 3270 data stream into HTML. Thus, with the CICS Internet Gateway, companies and organizations that run CICS applications can make those applications available to the world over the Web.

For more information about the CICS Internet Gateway, see **http://www.hursley.ibm.com/cics/saints/index.html**.

- DB2 is a popular database used by thousands of companies to store important data. Information in a DB2 database can be accessed using the Structured Query Language (SQL). Using the DB2 WWW Connection and standard SQL and HTML coding, you can write applications that allow users to access information in your DB2 database through a Web browser.

  For more information about the DB2 WWW Connection, see **http://www.torolab.ibm.com/data/db2/db2wannc.html**.

IBM also recently announced a revolutionary Web search solution that uses the Common Gateway Interface. Query By Image Content (QBIC) uses a combination of a gateway program and an image server to allow users to search for images that meet specified criteria (in terms of color content, color placement, texture, or pattern). This technology has many uses. For example, if you wanted to place a short story set in New England on the Web and you needed some scenes of the countryside, you could use QBIC to search a database of images for an image with a blue sky and green fields. Or, for example, QBIC could be set up to search through images in a clothes catalogue for a tie with a certain texture, pattern, and color to match the new suit you bought.

For more information about QBIC, see **http://wwwqbic.almaden.ibm.com/**.

Tips on writing your own CGI program

How you write your CGI program will depend on the language you use and on the purpose of the program. As previously mentioned, CGI programs can be written in any language that is supported by the operating system on which they are intended to run. And the purposes are even more varied than the languages. Therefore, we cannot provide explicit instructions for writing a CGI program. Basically, your program needs to be able to handle the input as formatted by the server, and generate output that can be interpreted by the server (as described in previous sections). There are, however, some tips, or guidelines, that we would like to pass along.

Protect your programs

All CGI programs should be placed in a subdirectory called cgi-bin. Storing your programs in this subdirectory provides some level of protection as typical users do not have access to the cgi-bin subdirectory. In most cases, this is sufficient.

However, there are some smart, but devious users out there who can figure out how to use your CGI program to "break into" your server. To guard against this, you must understand and make adjustments for the limitations and vulnerable areas of your code. For example, if a Perl program encounters an escape character as input, it will abort and dump the user out to the machine's root directory. Therefore, if you do not take measures to compensate for this, it is possible for a user to send escape character in the URL-encoded data as input to a Perl program in order to gain root access to your server.

Be generic

CGI programs are not necessarily difficult to write, but there is no sense in writing three or four if one will do. For example, let's assume you wanted to place three different survey forms on your Web server and you wanted the data from each to be sent to a different e-mail address, one to someone in service, one to someone in sales, and one to someone in research and development. You could write three CGI programs, each with the e-mail address of the recipient hard-coded in the program. But this takes up valuable space on your server and requires you to modify the CGI program if one of the e-mail addresses should change.

A better solution would be to use a hidden field, <INPUT TYPE=HIDDEN>, in the form to specify the e-mail address. This means you will have three different survey forms (which you probably have anyway) rather than 3 CGI programs. It also allows others to change the e-mail address, if needed. This will save you space and time.

Another means of saving time is to write parsing code that, regardless of the type of data sent, simply breaks data at the pluses and translates the ASCII hexadecimal characters. This code can then be reused in other CGI programs (written in the same language).

Watch the time

When you write a CGI program, remember that while your program is running, a user is waiting, staring at their Web browser. If your program takes too long, the user may give up and go elsewhere. If possible, it is a good idea to test your CGI program using a modem connection. 9600 baud should be sufficient. Because modem connections tend to be the slowest of all the connection types, using one to test your program will give you a good sense of "worst case" response time.

Chapter 13

Leasing space on someone else's server

or individuals and small businesses, the cost of the hardware, software, and connection to the Internet may make owning your own Web server difficult. Even large businesses may find it difficult to afford a Web site if they must hire someone with the skills to set up and maintain a Web server. But you can have a presence on the Web without having your own Web server. You can lease space on someone else's server.

Companies that lease space on their server are called *presence providers*. There are several presence providers located worldwide. In this chapter, we describe a few of them, but there are many more. And the list grows daily. For additional information, see Yahoo's Presence Provider list, which is available at **http://www.yahoo.com/Business/Corporations/Internet_Presence_Providers/**.

Chapter 13. Leasing space on someone else's server

BBS One OnLine Service

BBS One OnLine Service is a full-service presence provider and is located at **http://www.prgone.com/**.

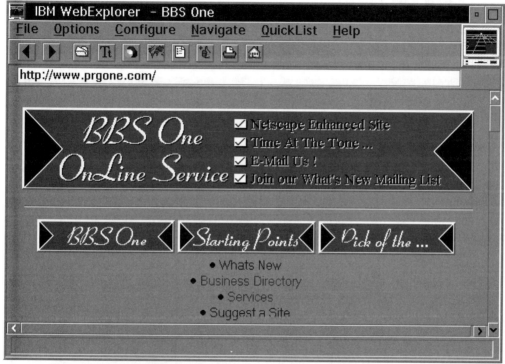

Figure 13-1. BBS One OnLine Service

BBS One OnLine Service, run by Jim Diefendorff and Jeremy Cowgar, offers a wide range of services in various packages.

The top-of-the-line, the Professional Site, includes everything you need in a Web site. For an initial setup fee and a monthly leasing fee, BBS One will design and code your HTML documents, provide a Web site with up to 25 MB of space, provide an FTP site with up to 10 MB of space, provide a mailing list, send an automated reply to users who send requests, and provide a monthly activity report.

At the other end of the spectrum, if you would prefer to do some of the work yourself (or if your funds are limited), you can opt for the Create Your Own Site. With this package, you provide the coded HTML documents and pay only the initial setup fee and a smaller monthly leasing fee (for a Web site of up to 5 MB of space). Other options, such as a monthly activity report can be added for an additional fee.

The Web Factory

The Web Factory is also a full-service presence provider and is located at **http://usa.net/factory/**.

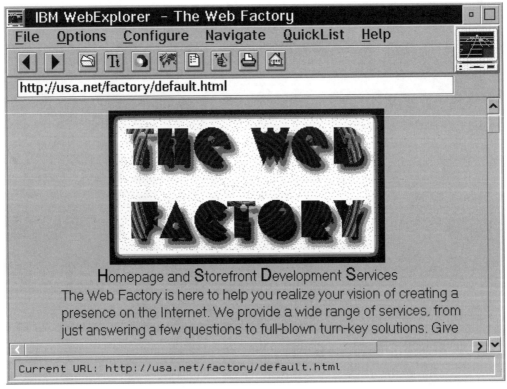

Figure 13-2. The Web Factory

Like BBS One OnLine Services, the Web Factory offers a wide range of services through a number of packages, or plans. They have packages to accommodate the needs of individuals, small businesses, midsize businesses, and large corporations. They also offer a Virtual Catalog plan for those who want to offer a variety of products or services via the Web.

Limitless Technical Dimensions, Ltd.

Limitless Technical Dimensions is a presence provider in the UK and is located at **http://www.limitless.co.uk/**.

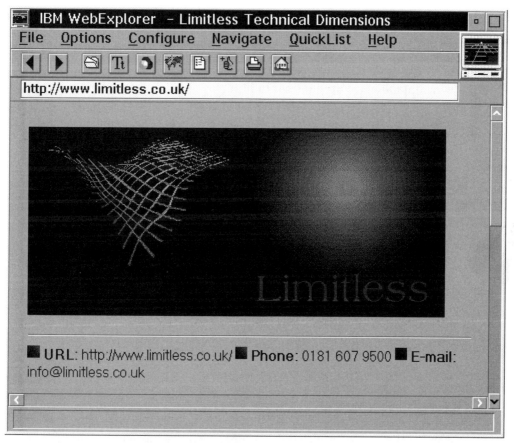

Figure 13-3. Limitless Technical Dimensions

In addition to providing design and creation of HTML documents and leasing space on their Web server, Limitless Technical Dimensions will also forward any e-mail to you via e-mail, fax, or pager. They also provide consulting services for those who want to set up and maintain their own Web server.

Dataplace

Dataplace is another full-service presence provider and is located at **http://www.dataplace.nl/**.

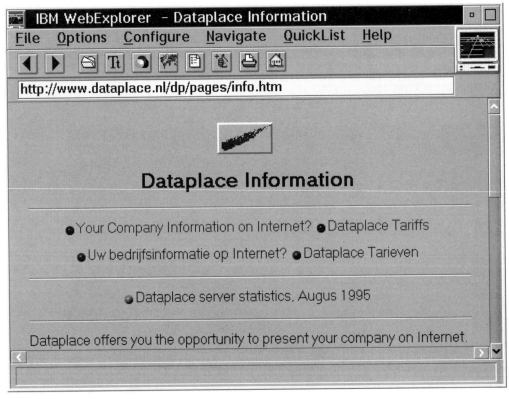

Figure 13-4. Dataplace

Dataplace, located in the Netherlands, offers design, setup, and maintenance of your Web site on their Web server. While other presence providers base their fees on space usage, Dataplace charges on a per page basis, a page being equal to the amount of information that will fit on a single printed A4-size page. (A4 is a standard paper size in Europe.)

Designed more for businesses than individuals, Dataplace generally asks you to supply one of your printed brochures. From that, they provide design solutions for making the most of your Web presence, implement the approved design, and ensure that your new Web site is listed with all the popular search utilities.

WebTowers

WebTowers is a low-cost presence provider and is located at
http://emporium.turnpike.net/W/webtower/.

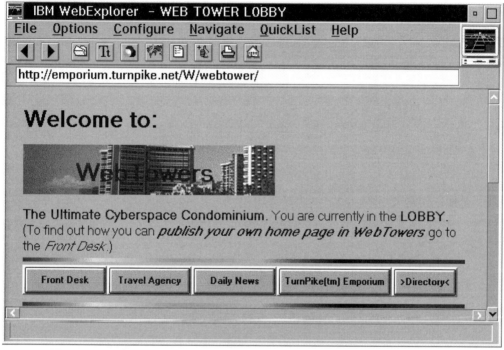

Figure 13-5. WebTowers

The services and space provided by WebTowers (and the fees charged) are geared toward individuals and small businesses. Currently, they lease space in quantities of 30 KB, 60 KB, and 100 KB. Design assistance is available for an additional fee. They offer monitoring and monthly reports, and will assist in advertising your new site on the Web.

PART THREE

REFERENCE

n this part of the book, we provide useful reference information. There are four appendices that make up this part of the book.

Appendix A, "HTML tagging reference," describes each of the HTML 2.0 tags and their attributes. It also lists symbols that can be used with HTML 2.0.

Appendix B, "Understanding URL formats," describes the formats used to identify the resources on the Web, including Web servers, FTP servers, Gopher servers, and more.

Appendix C, "Resource listing," lists several useful resources on the Web. Links to these resources are contained in an HTML document on the CD in the back of this book. The document is WWWRES.HTM.

Appendix D, "Samples," illustrates several sample HTML documents and sample CGI scripts that you can use. Each of these samples is contained on the CD in the back of the book.

Appendix A

HTML tagging reference

This section describes each of the currently available HTML 2.0 tags and symbols.

For more information about creating an HTML document, read Chapter 4 "Creating an HTML document."

Appendix A. HTML tagging reference

Tags to define document structure

Document structure tags affect the entire HTML document by helping to organize the information within the document. Although they are not all required, it is good practice to include them in your document. We recommend that you use the following template, or create one of your own. Using a template will reduce the amount of tagging that you have to do and help maintain consistency in your documents.

Sample HTML tagging:

```
<HTML>
<!- Comments regarding this document ->
<Head>
<Base href="base_URL">
<Title>Enter the title of the document here.</Title>
</Head>
<Body>
<H1>First heading</H1>
Include the text and images of the document here.
</Body>
</HTML>
```

HTML

Purpose: The HTML tag identifies the file as an HTML document.

Starting and ending tags: <HTML>...</HTML>

Attributes: None.

Usage notes: Only one pair of HTML tags is allowed per document. Make them the first and last tags in the document.

Head

Purpose: The head tag identifies the section of the document that contains general document information, such as the title and root URL of the document.

Starting and ending tags: <Head>...</Head>

Attributes: None

Usage notes: Only one pair of head tags is allowed per HTML document.

Base

Purpose: The base tag identifies the root URL of the document, which is used with relative linking. This information is necessary in cases where the document has been copied to another URL.

Tag: <Base>

Attributes: The base tag takes the following attribute:

- HREF. Required. Identifies the original URL of the document. In cases where the document has been moved from its original URL, this string is appended to any relative links.

Usage notes: The base tag is a single tag; it does not consist of a pair of starting and ending tags. It is optional. However, if included, it must occur within the HEAD tags.

Title

Purpose: The title identifies the document.

Starting and ending tags: <Title>...</Title>

Attributes: None

Usage notes: The title must occur within the HEAD tags. It cannot contain any links, highlighting, or paragraph tags. And, there can only be one title per document.

Titles should be as specific as possible. However, due to the limited amount of space that most browsers allow for a title, we recommend that you not use titles longer than 50 characters.

Expected output: In most browsers, the title is displayed in the window title bar. Also, many browsers display the title in their history list or hot list.

Body

Purpose: The body tags identify the section of the document that contains the text and images.

Starting and ending tags: <Body>...</Body>

Attributes: None.

Usage notes: Only one pair of body tags is allowed per HTML document.

Tags to enable searching

Purpose: The searchable index tag indicates to the Web server that this page provides an interface for keyword searches.

Tag: <ISINDEX>

Attributes: None.

Usage notes: The searchable index tag is a single tag; it does not have a paired starting and ending tag. The tag, if used, should occur in the BODY of the HTML document.

Expected output: The searchable index tag automatically generates an entry field and instructions for using it.

Sample HTML tagging for Figure A-1:

```
<HTML>
<Head>
<Title>Example of Searchable Index</Title>
</Head>
<Body>
<H1>Example of a Searchable Index</H1>
<ISINDEX>
</Body>
</HTML>
```

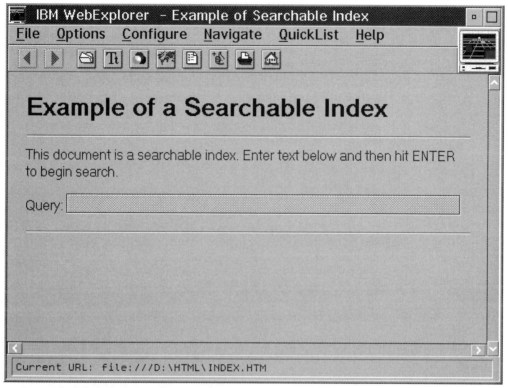

Figure A-1. Example of Searchable Index

Tags to create headings

Purpose: Heading tags distinguish the headings in a document from the text by generating a change in font and line spacing.

Starting and ending tags: <H1>...</H1>, <H2>...</H2>, <H3>...</H3>, <H4>...</H4>, <H5>...</H5>, <H6>...</H6>

Attributes: None.

Usage notes: You should begin each document with a primary heading, <H1>. You should not skip head levels within a document. For example, if the first heading is an H1, subordinate information should begin with an H2, not an H3.

Expected output: The treatment of headings varies between browsers, but the HTML specification describes the following as the expected output:

H1   Centered text in very large, bold letters followed by two blank lines.

H2   Flush left text in large, bold letters preceded by two blank lines and followed by two blank lines.

H3   Indented text in large, italic letters preceded by two blank lines and followed by two blank lines.

H4   Indented (more than the H3) text in bold letters preceded by one blank line and followed by one blank line.

H5   Indented (equal to H4) text in italic letters preceded by one blank line.

H6   Indented (more than H5) text in bold letters preceded by one blank line.

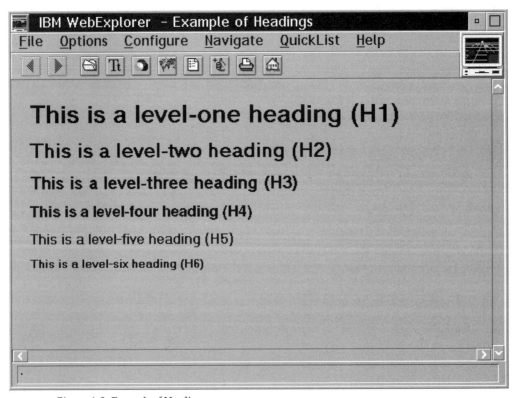

Figure A-2. Example of Headings

Sample HTML tagging for Figure A-2:

```
<HTML>
<Head>
<Title>Example of Headings</Title>
</Head>
<Body>
<H1>This is a level-one heading (H1)</H1>
<H2>This is a level-two heading (H2)</H2>
<H3>This is a level-three heading (H3)</H3>
<H4>This is a level-four heading (H4)</H4>
<H5>This is a level-five heading (H5)</H5>
<H6>This is a level-six heading (H6)</H6>
</Body>
</HTML>
```

Tags to create paragraphs

Purpose: Paragraph tags vertically separate two bodies of text, as you would separate two paragraphs on a printed page.

Starting and ending tags: <P>...</P>

Attributes: None

Usage notes: You can also use the paragraph tag as a single tag, <P>. If you use the single tag, place the paragraph tag at the end of a paragraph or the beginning of one, but not both. Do not use a paragraph tag in conjunction with tags that also generate a blank line. For example, the following is correct HTML coding:

```
<H1>Mary's Lamb</H1>
Mary had a little lamb, his fleece was black as soot. And, every-
where that Mary went, his sooty foot he put.<P>
He followed her to school one day, which was against the rules. It
made the children laugh and play to see a lamb in school.
```

The following is incorrect:

```
<H1>Mary's Lamb</H1>
<P>
Mary had a little lamb, his fleece was black as soot. And, every-
where that Mary went, his sooty foot he put.<P>
He followed her to school one day, which was against the rules. It
made the children laugh and play to see a lamb in school.
```

Because level-one headings (<H1>) generate space after the heading text, you do not need to use a paragraph tag at the beginning of the paragraph that follows the heading. Likewise, you need not use paragraph tags before lists, block quotes, or address style elements.

Expected output: In general, a paragraph tag generates a blank line or blank half line of space before the next body of text. With some browsers, a paragraph tag will also cause the first line of the paragraph to be slightly indented.

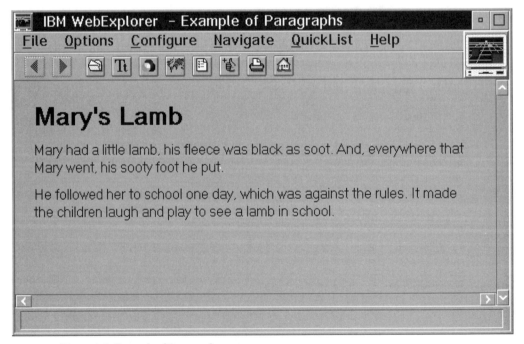

Figure A-3. Example of Paragraphs

Sample HTML tagging for Figure A-3:

```
<HTML>
<Head>
<Title>Example of Paragraphs</Title>
</Head>
<Body>
<H1>Mary's Lamb</H1>
Mary had a little lamb, his fleece was black as soot. And, every-
where that Mary went, his sooty foot he put.<P>
He followed her to school one day, which was against the rules. It
made the children laugh and play to see a lamb in school.
</Body>
</HTML>
```

Tags to link information

Purpose: Linking (or anchor) tags establish a connection between two pieces of information. Depending on the attributes used, the text that the tags surround can be either a launch point or a destination.

Starting and ending tags: <A>...</A>

Attributes: Linking (or anchor) tags can take the following attributes:

- NAME. Optional. Used to assign an ID to text you want to link to (a destination). For example:

```
<H3><A NAME="ingred">Ingredients</A></H3>
```

- HREF. Optional. Used to identify the URL or ID of the information you are linking to.

  If the destination is outside the current page, the identifier is the URL of the destination surrounded by quotation marks. This URL can be absolute or relative. Explicit URLs specify the protocol, the name of the server, and location (path and filename) of the linked file. Relative URLs specify only the location (path and filename) of the linked file and must begin with a slash /. For example:

```
I.M. Pei may best be known for his controversial addition
to the
<A HREF="http://mistral.enst.fr/~pioch/louvre/">Louvre
museum</A>.
```

If the destination is inside the current page, the identifier is the ID assigned to the destination text (the value of the NAME attribute) preceded by a pound sign (#) and surrounded by quotation marks. For example:

```
Before you begin, make sure you have all the necessary
<A HREF="#ingred">ingredients.
```

- TITLE. Optional. When used with the HREF attribute, indicates the title of the destination. If the destination document or page has a title, this attribute is informational only. If the destination document or page does not have a title, as with some Gopher servers, many browsers will display the value of this attribute as the title.

Usage notes: While all attributes are optional, you must include either HREF or NAME for the linking tags to be functional. Link tags can be used around a text string or around an image.

Expected output: When used with the NAME attribute, linking tags have no visual effect. When used with the HREF attribute, linking tags have the following effect:

- If the link is a text string, the surrounded text is highlighted per the browser's convention, such as colored and underscored.

- If the link is an image, the image appears to be surrounded by a three-dimensional frame.

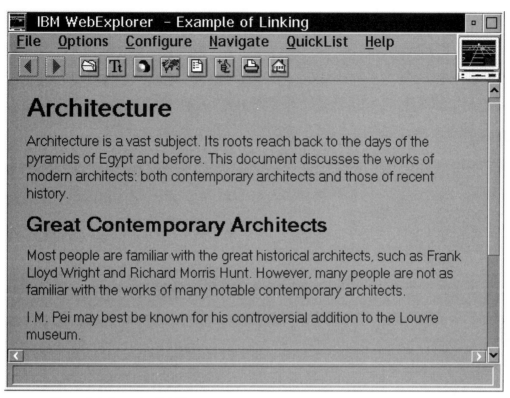

Figure A-4. Example of Linking

Sample HTML tagging for Figure A-4:

```
<HTML>
<Head>
<Title>Example of Linking</Title>
</Head>
<Body>
<H1>Architecture</H1>
Architecture is a vast subject.  Its roots reach back
to the days of the pyramids of Egypt and before.  This document
discusses the works of modern architects: both
<A HREF="#contemp">contemporary architects</A> and those
of <A HREF="#hist">recent history</A>.
<H2><A Name="contemp">Great Contemporary Architects</A></H2>
Most people are familiar with the great historical architects, such
as Frank Lloyd Wright and Richard Morris Hunt.  However, many
```

```
people are not as familiar with the works of many notable contempo-
rary architects.
<P>I.M. Pei may best be known for his controversial addition to the
<A HREF="http://mistral.enst.fr/~pioch/louvre/">Louvre museum</
A>.<P>
  .
  .
  .


<H2><A Name="hist">Great Architects of Recent History</A></H2>
  .
  .
  .


</Body>
</HTML>
```

This example shows the tagging necessary to link to information inside the current document and outside the current document. If this were a real HTML document, the link to the heading "Great Contemporary Architects" might be unnecessary because it is so close to the top of the page.

Tags to highlight text

Purpose: Tags for highlighting text distinguish certain text from the rest of the document by displaying the text in a different manner. There are two types of highlighting: explicit and interpreted. *Explicit highlighting* instructs the browser to display the text in a specific manner. *Interpreted highlighting* instructs the browser to display the text in whatever manner it determines is appropriate for the given emphasis. For example, <EM>...</EM> instructs the browser to give emphasis to the surrounded text. Many browsers interpret this as requiring an italic font, but the interpretation is up to the browser. If a browser does not know how to interpret a highlighting tag, it will not highlight the surrounded text.

Usage notes: Highlighting tags do not cause a paragraph break.

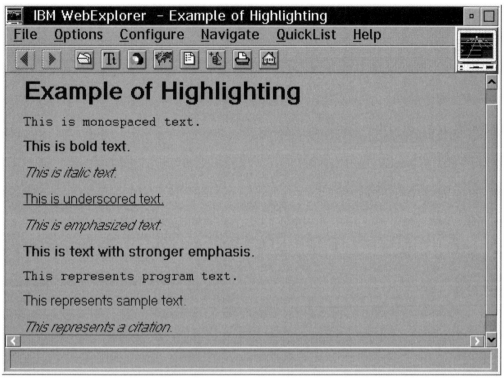

Figure A-5. Example of Highlighting

Sample HTML tagging for Figure A-5:

```
<HTML>
<Head>
<Title>Example of Highlighting</Title>
</Head>
<Body>
<H1>Examples of Highlighting</H1>
<TT>This is monospaced text.</TT><P>
<B>This is bold text.</B><P>
<I>This is italic text.</I><P>
<U>This is underscored text.</U><P>
<EM>This is emphasized text.</EM><P>
<STRONG>This is text with stronger emphasis.</STRONG><P>
<CODE>This represents program text.</CODE><P>
<SAMP>This represents sample text.</SAMP><P>
```

```
<CITE>This represents a citation.</CITE><P>
</Body>
</HTML>
```

This browser did not recognize the <SAMP> tag and therefore did not highlight the text.

Monospaced

Starting and ending tags: <TT>...</TT>

Attributes: None.

Expected output: Monospaced (or teletype) is an explicit highlighting that causes the surrounded text to be displayed in a font resembling that of a typewriter where every character (whether it is an "I" or a "w") occupies the same amount of horizontal space.

Bold

Starting and ending tags: <B>...</B>

Attributes: None.

Expected output: Bold is an explicit highlighting that causes the surrounded text to be displayed in a bold version of the default font.

Italic

Starting and ending tags: <I>...</I>

Attributes: None.

Expected output: Italic is an explicit highlighting that causes the surrounded text to be displayed in an italic (slanted) version of the default font.

Underscored

Starting and ending tags: <U>...</U>

Attributes: None.

Expected output: Underscored is an explicit highlighting that causes the surrounded text to be displayed in the default font with a line drawn beneath.

Emphasis

Starting and ending tags: <EM>...</EM>

Attributes: None.

Expected output: Emphasis is an interpreted highlighting that causes the surrounded text to be displayed with emphasis. In general, most browsers will display the text in italic.

Strong emphasis

Starting and ending tags: <STRONG>...</STRONG>

Attributes: None.

Expected output: Strong is an interpreted highlighting that causes the surrounded text to be displayed with stronger emphasis than <EM>. In general, most browsers will display the text in bold.

Code simulation

Starting and ending tags: <Code>...</Code>

Attributes: None.

Expected output: Code is an interpreted highlighting that causes the surrounded text to be displayed as simulated code. In general, most browsers will display the text in a monospaced font.

Sample simulation

Starting and ending tags: <SAMP>...</SAMP>

Attributes: None.

Expected output: Sample is an interpreted highlighting that causes the surrounded text to be displayed as a simulated sample. In general, most browsers will display the text in a monospaced font.

Keyboard simulation

Starting and ending tags: <KBD>...</KBD>

Attributes: None.

Expected output: Keyboard is an interpreted highlighting that causes the surrounded text to be displayed as simulated keyboard entry text. In general, most browsers will display the text in a monospaced font.

Variables

Starting and ending tags: <VAR>...</VAR>

Attributes: None.

Expected output: Variable is an interpreted highlighting that causes the surrounded text to be displayed with emphasis indicating it is a variable (information that can be changed, such as the value of a parameter). In general, most browsers will display the text in italic.

Definitions

Starting and ending tags: <DFN>...</DFN>

Attributes: None.

Expected output: Definition is an interpreted highlighting that causes the surrounded text to be displayed with emphasis indicating it is a term or phrase defined in text. In general, most browsers will display the text in bold or bold italic.

Citations

Starting and ending tags: <CITE>...</CITE>

Attributes: None.

Expected output: Citation is an interpreted highlighting that causes the surrounded text to be displayed with emphasis indicating that it cites a reference, such as a book title. In general, most browsers will display the text in italic.

Tags to create lists

HTML provides tags that allow you to create several types of lists, such as numbered and bulleted lists.

Numbered (ordered) lists

Purpose: Ordered list tags generate a sequential list of individual items. Use an ordered list when the items must be addressed in a specific sequence, such as the steps of a procedure.

Starting and ending tags: <OL>...</OL>

Attributes: None.

Usage notes: Place the beginning and ending tags on separate lines. The first line after the starting tag (<OL>) must be a list item and begin with <LI>. Each item in the list must be preceded by <LI>.

Expected output: Each item begins on a separate line and is preceded by a number and a period.

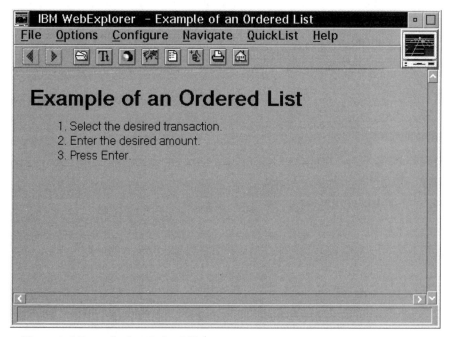

Figure A-6. Example of an Ordered List

Sample HTML tagging for Figure A-6:

```
<HTML>
<Head>
<Title>Example of an Ordered List</Title>
</Head>
<Body>
<H1>Example of an Ordered List</H1>
<OL>
<LI>Select the desired transaction.
<LI>Enter the desired amount.
<LI>Press Enter.
</OL>
</Body>
</HTML>
```

Bulleted (unordered) lists

Purpose: Unordered list tags generate a bulleted list of individual items. Use an unordered list when the sequence of the items is unimportant, such as a list of benefits.

Starting and ending tags: <UL>...</UL>

Attributes: None.

Usage notes: Place the beginning and ending tags on separate lines. The first line after the starting tag (<UL>) must be a list item and begin with <LI>. Each item in the list must be preceded by <LI>.

Expected output: Each item begins on a separate line and is preceded by a solid bullet (•) and a space.

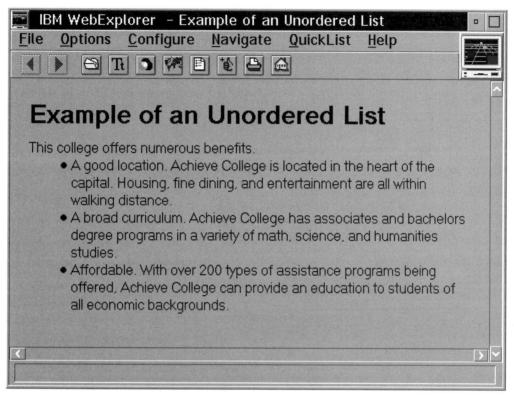

Figure A-7. Example of an Unordered List

Sample HTML tagging for Figure A-7:

```
<HTML>
<Head>
<Title>Example of an Unordered List</Title>
</Head>
<Body>
<H1>Example of an Unordered List</H1>
This college offers numerous benefits.
<UL>
<LI>A good location. Achieve College is located in the heart of the
capital.  Housing, fine dining, and entertainment are all within
walking distance.
<LI>A broad curriculum.  Achieve College has associates and bach-
elors degreeprograms in a variety of math, science, and humanities
studies.
```

```
<LI>Affordable.  With over 200 types of assistance programs being
offered, Achieve Collegean provide an education to students of
all economic backgrounds.
</UL>
</Body>
</HTML>
```

Menus

Purpose: Menu tags generate a list of individual items without numbers or bullets. Use a menu list when the items are brief (usually no more than one line) and sequence of the items is unimportant, such as a shopping list.

Starting and ending tags: <MENU>...</MENU>

Attributes: None.

Usage notes: Place the beginning and ending tags on separate lines. The first line after the starting tag (<MENU>) must be a list item and begin with <LI>. Each item in the list must be preceded by <LI>.

Expected output: Each item begins on a separate line. In many browsers, there is not as much vertical space between menu items as there is with unordered list items.

Sample HTML tagging for Figure A-8:

```
<HTML>
<Head>
<Title>Example of a Menu</Title>
</Head>
<Body>
<H1>Example of a Menu</H1>
<Menu>
<LI>Apples
<LI>Oranges
<LI>Pineapples
</Menu>
</Body>
</HTML>
```

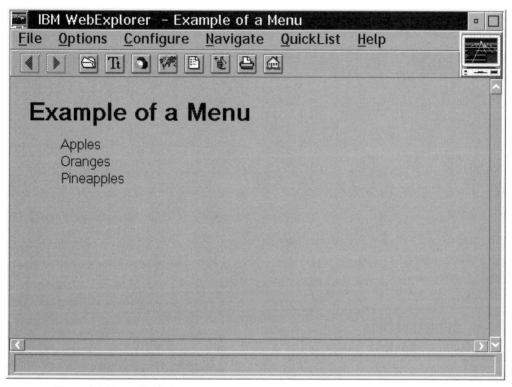

Figure A-8. Example of a Menu

Directories

Purpose: Directory tags generate a tabular list of individual items. Use a directory list when items need to be displayed in columns, such as a price list.

Starting and ending tags: <DIR>...</DIR>

Attributes: None.

Usage notes: Place the beginning and ending tags on separate lines. The first line after the starting tag (<DIR>) must contain the items of the first row. Each item in the list must be preceded by <LI>. Few browsers support this type of list.

Expected output: Each row of items begins on a separate line. In most cases, a column is limited to about 25 characters.

Sample HTML tagging:

```
<HTML>
<Head>
<Title>Example of a Directory</Title>
</Head>
<Body>
<H1>Example of a Directory</H1>
<DIR>
<LI>Item<LI>Price
<LI>Shirt<LI>24.99
<LI>Shoes<LI>49.50
<LI>Hat<LI>34.50
</DIR>
</Body>
</HTML>
```

Definition lists

Purpose: Definition list tags generate a list of paired items. Use a definition list when you want to list and describe items, such as a list of glossary terms and definitions.

Starting and ending tags: <DL>...</DL>

Attributes: Definition list tags can take the following attribute:

- COMPACT. Optional. Removes the vertical spacing between the term and its description.

Usage notes: Place the beginning and ending tags on separate lines. Each term must be preceded by <DT>. Each description must be preceded by <DD>. For each <DT> you must have a corresponding <DD>.

Expected output: Each term begins on a separate line. Each description begins on a separate line indented below the corresponding term.

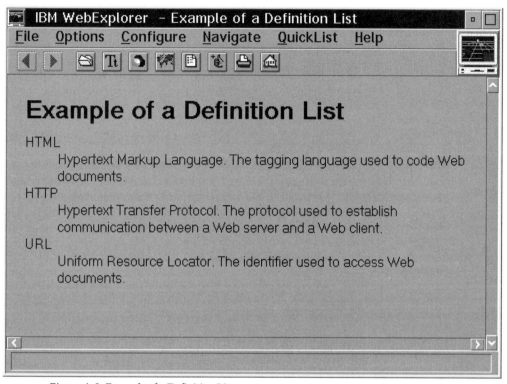

Figure A-9. Example of a Definition List

Sample HTML tagging for Figure A-9:

```
<HTML>
<Head>
<Title>Example of a Definition List</Title>
</Head>
<Body>
<H1>Example of a Definition List</H1>
<DL>
<DT>HTML
<DD>Hypertext Markup Language.  The tagging language used to code
Web documents.
<DT>HTTP
<DD>Hypertext Transfer Protocol.  The protocol used to establish
communication between a Web server and a Web client.
```

```
<DT>URL
<DD>Uniform Resource Locator.  The identifier used to access Web
documents.
</DL>
</Body>
</HTML>
```

Tags to cause line breaks

Purpose: Line break tags cause the text to break and resume on the next line with no vertical space between. Use line break tags to control the formatting (line length) of information such as an address.

Tag:

Attributes: None.

Usage notes: The line break tag is a single tag; it does not have paired starting and ending tags.

Expected output: Text following the <BR> is placed on the next line. No additional vertical space is generated.

Sample HTML tagging for Figure A-10:

```
<HTML>
<Head>
<Title>Example of Line Breaks</Title>
</Head>
<Body>
<H1>Example of Line Breaks</H1>
<Address>
Meghan Morrison<br>
Chess Champions, Inc.<br>
1985 Auburn Blvd<br>
Cary, NC 27511
</Address>
</Body>
</HTML>
```

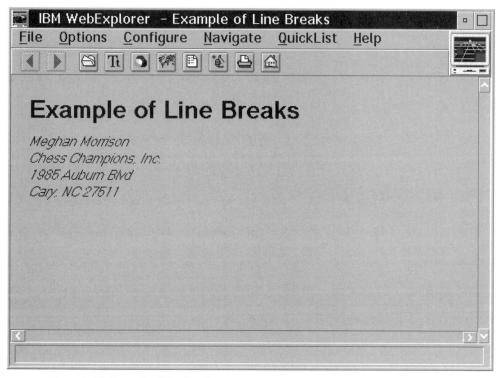

Figure A-10. Example of Line Breaks

Tags to create horizontal rules

Purpose: Horizontal rule tags generate a line across the page. Use horizontal rule tags to create a visual break in the page.

Tag: <HR>

Attributes: None.

Usage notes: The horizontal rule tag is a single tag; it does not have paired starting and ending tags.

Expected output: A horizontal line of medium weight extends the width of the page.

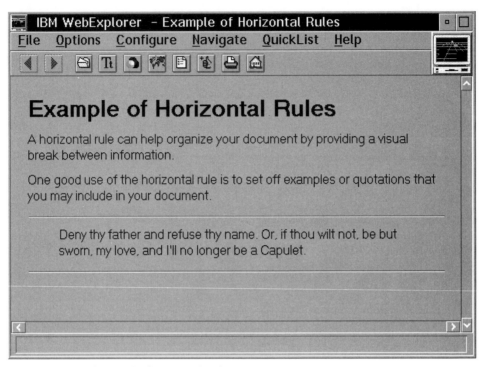

Figure A-11. Example of Horizontal Rules

Sample HTML tagging for Figure A-11:

```
<HTML>
<Head>
<Title>Example of Horizontal Rules</Title>
</Head>
<Body>
<H1>Example of Horizontal Rules</H1>
A horizontal rule can help organize your document by
providing a visual break between information.<P>
One good use of the horizontal rule is to set off examples
or quotations that you may include in your document.<P>
<HR>
<BLOCKQUOTE>
Deny thy father and refuse thy name, if thou wilt not, be but
sworn, my love, and I'll no longer be a Capulet.
</BLOCKQUOTE>
<HR>
```

```
</Body>
</HTML>
```

Tags for special formatting

Within the body of your document, most information can be formatted as a paragraph or list. Some information, such as an address, requires special formatting. Special formatting tags allow you to specify that certain information should be interpreted and formatted in a different manner from the rest.

Address

Purpose: Address tags combine interpreted highlighting and paragraph formatting. Use address tags to set off document identification information and addresses.

Starting and ending tags: <Address>...</Address>

Attributes: None.

Usage notes: Paragraph tags used within address tags act as line break tags. They do not generate additional vertical space. To generate a stacked address format, similar to the format of an address on an envelope, use line break tags inside the address tags.

Expected output: As with interpreted highlighting tags, such as <CITE>, the browser controls the emphasis that is placed on the surrounded text. In general, most browsers will display the text in italic. Also, the ending address tag acts as a paragraph tag, causing a line break and generating additional vertical space prior to any following information.

Sample HTML tagging for Figure A-12:

```
<HTML>
<Head>
<Title>Example of an Address</Title>
</Head>
<Body>
<H1>Example of an Address</H1>
<Address>
Chloe Morrison<br>
```

```
Acme Services<br>
1983 Hepburn Way<br>
Cary, NC 27511
</Address>
</Body>
</HTML>
```

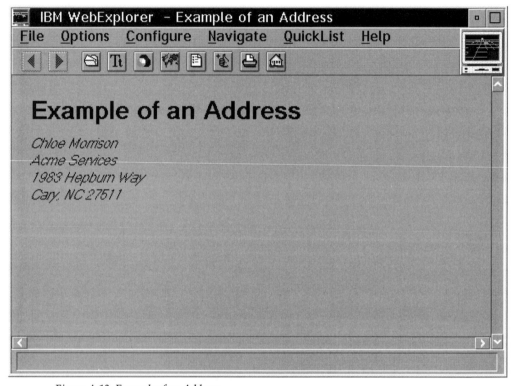

Figure A-12. Example of an Address

Long quotes

Purpose: Long (or block) quote tags combine interpreted highlighting and paragraph formatting. Use block quote tags to set off information quoted from other sources.

Starting and ending tags: <Blockquote>...</Blockquote>

Attributes: None.

Expected output: As with interpreted highlighting tags, such as <CITE>, the browser controls the emphasis that is placed on the surrounded text. In general, most browsers will display the text in italic. Some also indent the margins for the surrounded text. Also, the ending block quote tag acts as a paragraph tag, causing a line break and generating additional vertical space prior to any following information.

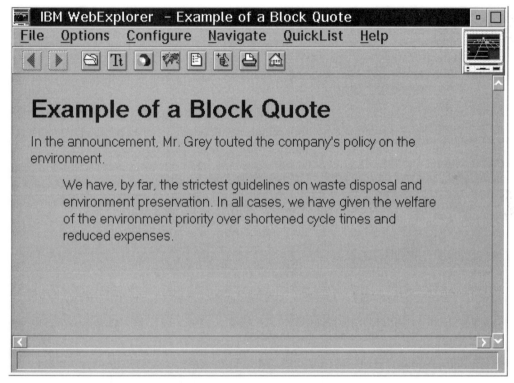

Figure A-13. Example of a Block Quote

Sample HTML tagging for Figure A-13:

```
<HTML>
<Head>
<Title>Example of a Block Quote</Title>
</Head>
<Body>
<H1>Example of a Block Quote</H1>
```

```
In the announcement, Mr. Grey touted the company's
policy on the environment.<p>
<BLOCKQUOTE>
We have, by far, the strictest guidelines on waste disposal
and environment preservation.  In all cases, we have given the
welfare of the environment priority over shortened cycle times and
reduced expenses.
</BLOCKQUOTE>
</Body>
</HTML>
```

Preformatted text

Purpose: Preformatted text tags combine interpreted highlighting and line breaks. Use preformatted text tags to set off information that needs to be displayed as it is in the HTML file, for example, lines from a program or sample file.

Starting and ending tags: <Pre>...</Pre>

Attributes: Preformatted text tags can take the following attribute:

- WIDTH. Optional. Specifies the maximum allowable number of characters that can appear on a line. Browsers should use this specification to determine the optimal font to be used. The format of this attribute is:

```
<PRE WIDTH="x">
```

Where x is the number of characters.

Usage notes: HTML tags included within preformatted text tags are interpreted as tags. If you want to include an example that shows HTML tagging, you must use the HTML symbols to create the tag delimiters (<>). Highlighting and linking can be used within preformatted text. However, headings and formatting tags, such as paragraph and address tags, should not be used within preformatted text.

Expected output: As with interpreted highlighting tags, such as <CITE>, the browser controls the emphasis that is placed on the surrounded text. In general, most browsers will display the text in a monospaced font. Line breaks are preserved in the output as they are in the source HTML file. The ending preformatted text tag acts as a paragraph tag, causing a line break and generating additional vertical space prior to any following information.

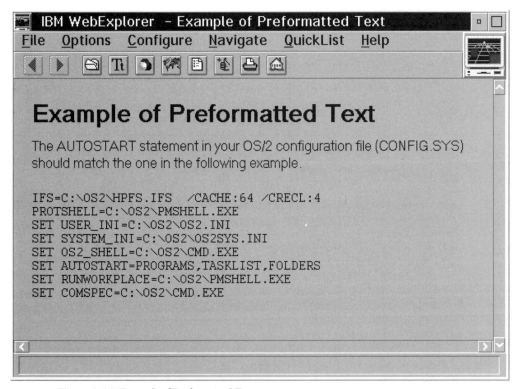

Figure A-14. Example of Preformatted Text

Sample HTML tagging for Figure A-14:

```
<HTML>
<Head>
<Title>Example of Preformatted Text</Title>
</Head>
<Body>
<H1>Example of Preformatted Text</H1>
The AUTOSTART statement in your OS/2 configuration file
(CONFIG.SYS)should match the one in the following example.<P>
<PRE WIDTH="80">
IFS=C:\OS2\HPFS.IFS  /CACHE:64 /CRECL:4
PROTSHELL=C:\OS2\PMSHELL.EXE
SET USER_INI=C:\OS2\OS2.INI
SET SYSTEM_INI=C:\OS2\OS2SYS.INI
```

```
SET OS2_SHELL=C:\OS2\CMD.EXE
SET AUTOSTART=PROGRAMS,TASKLIST,FOLDERS
SET RUNWORKPLACE=C:\OS2\PMSHELL.EXE
SET COMSPEC=C:\OS2\CMD.EXE
</PRE>
</Body>
</HTML>
```

Tags to include images

Purpose: Image tags allow you to include pictures in your document.

Tag: <IMG>

Attributes: Image tags can take the following attributes:

- SRC. Required. Specifies the source file of the in-line image. The SRC attribute is followed by a character string (identifier) that identifies the image file and its location.

- ALIGN. Optional. Specifies how the image should be aligned vertically. Possible values are TOP, MIDDLE, and BOTTOM.

- ALT. Optional. Specifies the label for the image that is to be displayed if the browser does not support in-line images.

- ISMAP. Optional. Specifies that the image contains defined areas that, when selected, link to other URLs. For more information about creating mappable images, read Chapter 5, "Including images in your document."

Usage notes: The image tag is a single tag. It is not a paired set of starting and ending tags. Some browsers cannot display in-line images, but can display linked images. If an image is crucial to a document, you may want to link to it rather than include it in-line.

Expected output: For browsers that can display images in-line, the image is left-justified. If a series of images is specified, the images are displayed on the same line, if possible. For browsers that cannot display images in-line, the label, if any, is displayed.

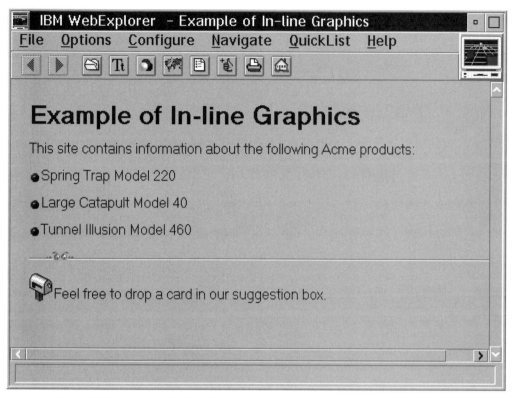

Figure A-15. Example of In-Line Graphics

Sample HTML tagging for Figure A-15:

```
<HTML>
<Title>Example of In-line Graphics</Title>
<Body>
<H1>Example of In-line Graphics</H1>
This site contains information about the following Acme products:
<p>
<img src=ball_pur.gif><a href='st200.html'>Spring Trap Model 220</
a><p>
<img src=ball_pur.gif><a href='cat40.html'>Large Catapult Model
40</a><p>
<img src=ball_pur.gif><a href='tun460.html'>Tunnel Illusion Model
460</a><P>
<img src=lineeyes.gif><p>
```

```
<img src=mailbox.gif>Feel free to drop a card in our
<A href='mal2acme.html'>suggestion box</A>.
</Body>
</HTML>
```

Tags to create forms

Form tags allow you to create input forms. Data from these forms can be submitted to a Web server for processing and analysis.

For more information about creating forms, read Chapter 6, "Including forms in your document."

Sample HTML tagging for Figures A-16 and A-17:

```
<HTML>
<Head>
<Title>Example of a Form</Title>
</Head>
<Body>
<H1>Example of a Form</H1>
<FORM METHOD=POST ACTION="/Forms/cgi-bin/">
Please complete this survey so that we may better improve our
service.<P>
Name: <INPUT TYPE="text" NAME="name" SIZE=45 MAXLENGTH=50
VALUE="Enter your name here"><P>
Address: <TEXTAREA NAME='address' COLS=40 ROWS=3>
Enter your address here.
</TEXTAREA><P>
Account ID: <INPUT TYPE="text" NAME="acctID" SIZE=30><P>
Password: <INPUT TYPE="password" NAME="password" SIZE=10><P>
Which applications do you use?<P>
<INPUT TYPE="checkbox" NAME="apps" VALUE="Gopher"> Gopher
<INPUT TYPE="checkbox" NAME="apps" VALUE="Newsreader"> NewsReader
<INPUT TYPE="checkbox" NAME="apps" VALUE="Ultimail"> UltiMail
<INPUT TYPE="checkbox" NAME="apps" VALUE="WExplorer"> WebExplorer
<INPUT TYPE="checkbox" NAME="apps" VALUE="Archie"> Archie
```

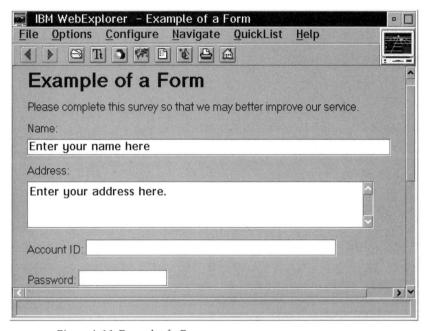

Figure A-16. Example of a Form

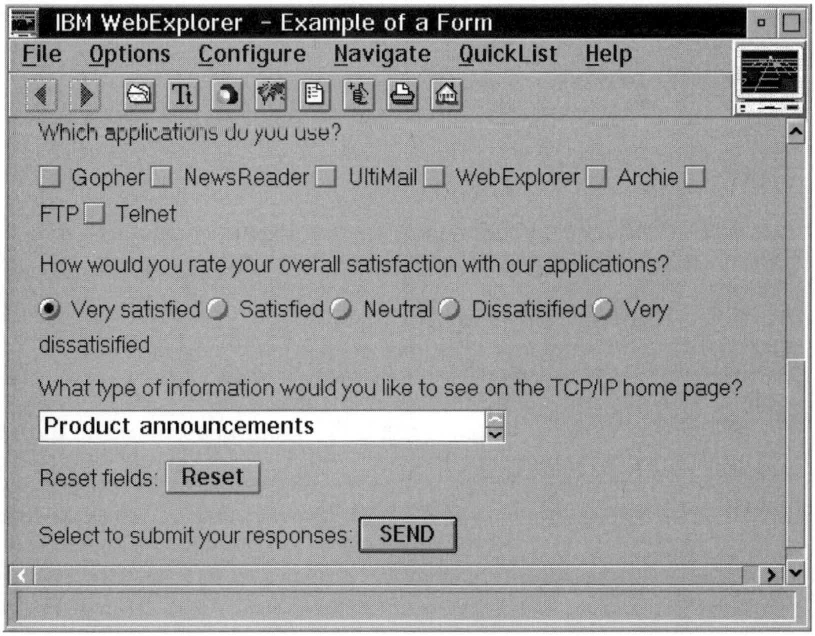

Figure A-17. Example of a Form

```
<INPUT TYPE="checkbox" NAME="apps" VALUE="FTP"> FTP
<INPUT TYPE="checkbox" NAME="apps" VALUE="Telnet"> Telnet<P>
How would you rate your overall satisfaction with our
applications?<P>
<INPUT TYPE="radio" NAME="rating" VALUE="1"> Very satisfied
<INPUT TYPE="radio" NAME="rating" VALUE="2"> Satisfied
<INPUT TYPE="radio" NAME="rating" VALUE="3"> Neutral
<INPUT TYPE="radio" NAME="rating" VALUE="4"> Dissatisfied
<INPUT TYPE="radio" NAME="rating" VALUE="5"> Very dissatisfied<P>
What type of information would you like to see on the TCP/IP home
page?
<Select MULTIPLE NAME="info" SIZE=1>
<Option>Product announcements</Option>
<Option>CSD information</Option>
<Option>Frequently asked questions</Option>
<Option>Tips and techniques</Option>
<Option>Related information</Option>
</select><p>
Reset fields: <INPUT TYPE="reset"><P>
Select to submit your responses: <INPUT TYPE="submit" Value="SEND">
</FORM>
</Body>
</HTML>
```

Form

Purpose: Form tags indicate that the surrounded information is part of a data entry form.

Starting and ending tags: <Form>...</Form>

Attributes: Form tags can take the following attributes:

- METHOD. Required. Indicates the HTTP method used to send the data to the server. Possible values are GET and POST. We recommend you use POST.

- ACTION. Optional. Specifies the URL of the processing script. The URL must be enclosed in quotation marks. If the ACTION attribute is not specified, the default is the URL of the document.

- ENCTYPE. Optional. Specifies how the input data is encrypted. At this time, the only possible value is application/x-www-form-urlencoded. This is also the default.

Usage notes: You can include more than one set of form tags in a document. You cannot, however, nest them.

Input

Purpose: Input tags create elements in an HTML document that accept user input. These elements may be in the form of selections or entry fields.

Starting and ending tags: <Input>...</Input>

Attributes: The attributes that an input tag can take depend upon the input TYPE.

- TYPE. Required. Specifies the type of field to be displayed. Possible values are:

  - CHECKBOX. Displays a "box" that can be selected. Use check boxes for Boolean selections (on or off, yes or no). Multiple check boxes can be grouped together. And, one or more check boxes in a group may be selected.

    Required attributes: NAME and VALUE

    Optional attribute: CHECKED

  - HIDDEN. Does not accept nor display any information to the user. Hidden form fields are used to send state information to the server.

    Required attribute: NAME

    Optional attribute: VALUE

  - IMAGE. Displays an image, which, when selected, submits the data to the specified URL. Because IMAGE may, in the future, be obsolete, we recommend you use the SUBMIT form type.

Required attributes: NAME and SRC

Optional attribute: ALIGN

–   PASSWORD. Displays a single-line entry field. Password fields are similar to Text fields except information entered in this field is not displayed.

Required attribute: NAME

Optional attributes: MAXLENGTH, SIZE, and VALUE

–   RADIO. Displays a radio button (a circle that can be selected). Use radio for multiple choice selections where only one in a series can be selected. All radio buttons in a group should be assigned the same NAME.

Required attributes: NAME and VALUE

Optional attribute: CHECKED

–   RESET. Displays a push button, which, when selected, returns all the form's fields to their original values. Use the VALUE attribute to define the label for the push button. The default label is RESET.

Optional attributes: VALUE

–   SUBMIT. Displays a push button, which, when selected, submits the data. Use the VALUE attribute to define the label for the push button. The default label is SUBMIT. You can also use the SRC attribute to include an image on the push button.

Optional attributes: NAME, SRC, and VALUE

–   TEXT. Displays a single-line entry field. If you require a multiple-line entry field, use the Textarea tag.

Required attribute: NAME

Optional attributes: MAXLENGTH, SIZE, and VALUE

•   SRC. Required with TYPE="image." Specifies the URL of the image to be displayed.

•   ALIGN. Optional. Specifies how the image should be aligned vertically. Possible values are TOP, MIDDLE, and BOTTOM.

•   CHECKED. Optional. Indicates the default selection.

- MAXLENGTH. Optional. Indicates the maximum number of characters that can be entered into a field. If MAXLENGTH is greater than SIZE, the entry field will allow the field to scroll as information is entered.

- NAME. Required. The identifier assigned to a field. When a form is submitted, the name of a field is paired with its value.

- SIZE. Optional. Specifies the width in characters of a field area.

- VALUE. Required with TYPE="checkbox" and TYPE="radio." For entry fields, VALUE is used to specify the initial setting. For check boxes and radio buttons, VALUE is used to specify the value assigned to a selection. For SUBMIT and RESET, VALUE is the label to appear on the push button.

Usage notes: The input tag is a single tag. It is not a paired set of starting and ending tags. Input tags cannot occur outside form tags.

Textarea

Purpose: Textarea tags create multiple-line entry fields.

Starting and ending tags: <Textarea>...</Textarea>

Attributes: Textarea tags can take the following attributes:

- ROWS. Required. Indicates the number of rows of input allowed.

- COLS. Required. Indicates the number of characters allowed for each row.

- NAME. Required. The identifier assigned to a field. When a form is submitted, the name of a field is paired with its value.

Usage notes: The textarea tag is not an attribute of the input tag; it is a separate tag. Textarea tags cannot occur outside the form tags.

Select

Purpose: Select tags are used with option tags to create a list box of choices, similar to the radio or check box input types.

Starting and ending tags: <Select>...</Select>

Attributes: Select tags can take the following attributes:

- MULTIPLE. Optional. Indicates that multiple selections are allowed.

- SIZE. Optional. Indicates the number of items displayed in the selection list at a time. If SIZE is less than the number of items listed, a scroll bar is displayed to the right of the field, allowing users to scroll through the other items in the list.

- NAME. Required. The identifier assigned to a field. When a form is submitted, the name of a field is paired with its value.

Usage notes: The select tag is not an attribute of the input tag; it is a separate tag. Select tags cannot occur outside the form tags.

Option

Purpose: Option tags are used with select tags to create a list of choices, similar to the radio or check box input types.

Starting and ending tags: <Option>...</Option>

Attributes: Option tags can take the following attributes:

- SELECTED. Optional. Indicates that this option is the default.

- VALUE. Optional. The value to be paired with the name if this option is chosen. If no VALUE is specified, the text associated with the option is sent as the value.

Usage notes: The option tag is not an attribute of the select tag; it is a separate tag. Option tags cannot occur outside select tags.

HTML symbols

In addition to the tags, HTML includes a number of symbols (or entities) that represent certain characters. These are characters that you might not otherwise be able to include in your document either because they have a special meaning in HTML or because your keyboard does not include them.

All symbols are preceded by an ampersand (&) and followed by a semicolon (;). Unlike the HTML tags, the symbols are case-sensitive. For example, Á will produce a different symbol than á.

Reserved characters

In HTML, certain characters are reserved for use in tags, such as the greater than and less than signs that are used as tag delimiters. If you want to use one of the characters in the text of your document, use the corresponding symbol (as indicated in the following table).

Character	Symbol	Description
<	<	Less than sign
>	>	Greater than sign
&	&	Ampersand
"	"	Double quotation marks

Special characters

There are a number of characters that may not be available on your keyboard, for example, an upper-case A with an acute accent (Á). If you want to include one of these characters in your document, use the corresponding symbol (as indicated in the following tables).

Added Latin 1

This table includes the Added Latin 1 entity set as derived from the ISO Standard 8879:1986.

Character	Symbol	Description
Á	Á	Upper-case A, acute accent
À	À	Upper-case A, grave accent
Â	Â	Upper-case A, circumflex accent
Ã	Ã	Upper-case A, tilde
Å	Å	Upper-case A, ring
Ä	Ä	Upper-case A, dieresis or umlaut mark
Æ	Æ	Upper-case AE diphthong (ligature)
Ç	Ç	Upper-case C, cedilla

Character	Symbol	Description
É	É	Upper-case E, acute accent
È	È	Upper-case E, grave accent
Ê	Ê	Upper-case E, circumflex accent
Ë	Ë	Upper-case E, dieresis or umlaut mark
Í	Í	Upper-case I, acute accent
Ì	Ì	Upper-case I, grave accent
Î	Î	Upper-case I, circumflex accent
Ï	Ï	Upper-case I, dieresis or umlaut mark
Ð	Ð	Upper-case Eth, Icelandic
Ñ	Ñ	Upper-case N, tilde
Ó	Ó	Upper-case O, acute accent
Ò	Ò	Upper-case O, grave accent
Ô	Ô	Upper-case O, circumflex accent
Õ	Õ	Upper-case O, tilde
Ö	Ö	Upper-case O, dieresis or umlaut mark
Ø	Ø	Upper-case O, slash
Ú	Ú	Upper-case U, acute accent
Ù	Ù	Upper-case U, grave accent
Û	Û	Upper-case U, circumflex accent
Ü	Ü	Upper-case U, dieresis or umlaut mark
Ý	Ý	Upper-case Y, acute accent
Þ	Þ	Upper-case THORN, Icelandic
ß	ß	Lower-case sharp s, German (sz ligature)
á	á	Lower-case a, acute accent

Character	Symbol	Description
à	à	Lower-case a, grave accent
â	â	Lower-case a, circumflex accent
ã	ã	Lower-case a, tilde
å	å	Lower-case a, ring
ä	ä	Lower-case a, dieresis or umlaut mark
æ	æ	Lower-case ae diphthong (ligature)
ç	ç	Lower-case c, cedilla
é	é	Lower-case e, acute accent
è	è	Lower-case e, grave accent
ê	ê	Lower-case e, circumflex accent
ë	ë	Lower-case e, dieresis or umlaut mark
í	í	Lower-case i, acute accent
ì	ì	Lower-case i, grave accent
î	î	Lower-case i, circumflex accent
ï	ï	Lower-case i, dieresis or umlaut mark
∂	ð	Lower-case eth, Icelandic
ñ	ñ	Lower-case n, tilde
ó	ó	Lower-case o, acute accent
ò	ò	Lower-case o, grave accent
ô	ô	Lower-case o, circumflex accent
õ	õ	Lower-case o, tilde
ö	ö	Lower-case o, dieresis or umlaut mark
ø	ø	Lower-case o, slash
ú	ú	Lower-case u, acute accent

Character	Symbol	Description
ù	ù	Lower-case u, grave accent
û	û	Lower-case u, circumflex accent
ü	ü	Lower-case u, dieresis or umlaut mark
ý	ý	Lower-case y, acute accent
þ	þ	Lower-case thorn, Icelandic
ÿ	ÿ	Lower-case y, dieresis or umlaut mark

Numeric character references

This table includes the Numeric Character Reference set as derived from the ISO Standard 8859-1, the 8-bit single-byte coded graphic character set.

Character	Symbol	Description
None			Horizontal tab

None	
	Line feed

	 	Space
!	!	Exclamation mark
"	"	Quotation mark
#	#	Number sign
$	$	Dollar sign
%	%	Percent sign
&	&	Ampersand
'	'	Apostrophe
(	(	Left paren
)	)	Right paren
*	*	Asterisk
+	+	Plus sign

Character	Symbol	Description
,	,	Comma
-	-	Hyphen
.	.	Period (fullstop)
/	/	Solidus (slash)
0 - 9	0 - 9	Digits 0 through 9
:	:	Colon
;	;	Semicolon
<	<	Less than
=	=	Equal sign
>	>	Greater than
?	?	Question mark
@	@	Commercial at sign
A - Z	A - Z	Upper-case letters A through Z
[	[	Left square bracket
\	\	Reverse solidus (backslash)
]	]	Right square bracket
^	^	Caret
—	_	Horizontal bar
`	`	Grave accent
a - z	a - z	Lower-case letters a through z
{	{	Left brace
|	|	Vertical bar
}	}	Right brace
~	~	Tilde

Character	Symbol	Description
¡	¡	Inverted exclamation
¢	¢	Cent sign
£	£	Pound sterling
¤	¤	General currency sign
¥	¥	Yen sign
¦	¦	Broken vertical bar
§	§	Section sign
¨	¨	Umlaut (dieresis)
©	©	Copyright
ª	ª	Feminine ordinal
«	«	Left angle quote, guillemotleft
¬	¬	Not sign
-	­	Soft hyphen
®	®	Registered trademark
¯	¯	Macron accent
°	°	Degree sign
±	±	Plus or minus
²	²	Superscript two
³	³	Superscript three
´	´	Acute accent
µ	µ	Micro sign
¶	¶	Paragraph sign
·	·	Middle dot
¸	¸	Cedilla

Character	Symbol	Description
¹	¹	Superscript one
º	º	Masculine ordinal
»	»	Right angle quote, guillemotright
¼	¼	Fraction one-fourth
½	½	Fraction one-half
¾	¾	Fraction three-fourths
¿	¿	Inverted question mark
Á	À	Upper-case A, acute accent
À	Á	Upper-case A, grave accent
Â	Â	Upper-case A, circumflex accent
Ã	Ã	Upper-case A, tilde
Å	Ä	Upper-case A, ring
Ä	Å	Upper-case A, dieresis or umlaut mark
Æ	Æ	Upper-case AE diphthong (ligature)
Ç	Ç	Upper-case C, cedilla
É	È	Upper-case E, acute accent
È	É	Upper-case E, grave accent
Ê	Ê	Upper-case E, circumflex accent
Ë	Ë	Upper-case E, dieresis or umlaut mark
Í	Ì	Upper-case I, acute accent
Ì	Í	Upper-case I, grave accent
Î	Î	Upper-case I, circumflex accent
Ï	Ï	Upper-case I, dieresis or umlaut mark
Ð	Ð	Upper-case Eth, Icelandic

Character	Symbol	Description
Ñ	&#209;	Upper-case N, tilde
Ó	&#210;	Upper-case O, acute accent
Ò	&#211;	Upper-case O, grave accent
Ô	&#212;	Upper-case O, circumflex accent
Õ	&#213;	Upper-case O, tilde
Ö	&#214;	Upper-case O, dieresis or umlaut mark
×	&#215;	Multiply sign
Ø	&#216;	Upper-case O, slash
Ú	&#217;	Upper-case U, acute accent
Ù	&#218;	Upper-case U, grave accent
Û	&#219;	Upper-case U, circumflex accent
Ü	&#220;	Upper-case U, dieresis or umlaut mark
Ý	&#221;	Upper-case Y, acute accent
Þ	&#222;	Upper-case THORN, Icelandic
ß	&#223;	Lower-case sharp s, German (sz ligature)
á	&#224;	Lower-case a, acute accent
à	&#225;	Lower-case a, grave accent
â	&#226;	Lower-case a, circumflex accent
ã	&#227;	Lower-case a, tilde
ä	&#228;	Lower-case a, dieresis or umlaut mark
å	&#229;	Lower-case a, ring
æ	&#230;	Lower-case ae diphthong (ligature)
ç	&#231;	Lower-case c, cedilla
é	&#232;	Lower-case e, acute accent

Character	Symbol	Description
è	`&#233;`	Lower-case e, grave accent
ê	`&#234;`	Lower-case e, circumflex accent
ë	`&#235;`	Lower-case e, dieresis or umlaut mark
í	`&#236;`	Lower-case i, acute accent
ì	`&#237;`	Lower-case i, grave accent
î	`&#238;`	Lower-case i, circumflex accent
ï	`&#239;`	Lower-case i, dieresis or umlaut mark
ð	`&#240;`	Lower-case eth, Icelandic
ñ	`&#241;`	Lower-case n, tilde
ó	`&#242;`	Lower-case o, acute accent
ò	`&#243;`	Lower-case o, grave accent
ô	`&#244;`	Lower-case o, circumflex accent
õ	`&#245;`	Lower-case o, tilde
ö	`&#246;`	Lower-case o, dieresis or umlaut mark
÷	`&#247;`	Division sign
ø	`&#248;`	Lower-case o, slash
ú	`&#249;`	Lower-case u, acute accent
ù	`&#250;`	Lower-case u, grave accent
û	`&#251;`	Lower-case u, circumflex accent
ü	`&#252;`	Lower-case u, dieresis or umlaut mark
ý	`&#253;`	Lower-case y, acute accent
þ	`&#254;`	Lower-case thorn, Icelandic
ÿ	`&#255;`	Lower-case y, dieresis or umlaut mark

Understanding URL formats

he Uniform Resource Locator (URL) indicates the location of a resource on the Web (or other part of the Internet). A resource can be a file, a server, a newsgroup, an e-mail address, or an HTML document. In an HTML document, a URL is used as part of an anchor tag to identify a linked document or resource. A URL can also be specified in a Web browser window to access the resource directly (without using a hypertext link).

The URL includes two parts. The first part specifies the protocol used by the type of server you want to access. The second part is a string that uniquely identifies the resource. The format of the second part depends on the protocol specified in the first part. This appendix explains the most commonly used formats for URLs used to access different types of resources. For more information about URL formats, see
http://www.w3.org/hypertext/WWW/Addressing/URL/.

Note: Although capitalization of HTML tags is not important, the capitalization of a URL might be. The file systems of some operating systems are case-sensitive. For example, the UNIX file system distinguishes between a file called Overview.html and one called overview.html. Therefore, to be on the safe side, when you find a resource that you want to access or link to, take care to make note of the exact URL, including capitalization. In the examples in this chapter, the terms in italics are placeholders; you replace them with actual names or numbers.

Appendix B. Understanding URL formats

Web servers

The URL format for accessing information (a document or file) on a Web server is as follows:

```
http://server_name:port_number/directory/file_name
```

- http

  Required. Specifies the protocol used by Web servers. Always include the :// after http.

- *server_name*

  Required. Specifies the host name of the Web server, for example, www.ibm.net.

- *port_number*

  Optional. Specifies the protocol port to which the request should be sent. If you specify a port number, include a colon to separate it from the server name. If no port number is specified, the well-known port is used. In most cases, you will not need this information.

- *directory*

  Optional. Specifies the directory on the Web server. If no directory is specified, the server's default directory is assumed.

- *file_name*

  Optional. Specifies the document or file on the Web server. If no file is specified, the default file (usually named index.html) in the directory specified, if any, is displayed.

If you do not specify a file, end the URL with a slash, /.

Examples

http://www.ibm.net/user.html

Requests the file named user.html that is located in the default directory of the Web server known as www.ibm.net.

http://www.w3.org/

Requests the default file in the default directory of the Web server known as www.w3.org.

FTP servers

The URL format for accessing files on an FTP server is as follows:

`ftp://login@server_name:port_number/directory/file_name`

- ftp

  Required. Specifies the protocol used by FTP servers. Always include the :// after ftp.

- *login*

  Optional. Specifies the user ID and password to be used to access the server. The format is *userid:password@*. If you are linking to an FTP server from an HTML document and you include the login information, remember that users can easily access the source of your HTML document and see the password. If no login information is specified, anonymous is assumed as the user ID and the user's e-mail address is assumed as the password.

- *server_name*

  Required. Specifies the host name of the FTP server, for example, ftp.cdrom.com.

- *port_number*

  Optional. Specifies the protocol port to which the request should be sent. If you specify a port number, include a colon to separate it from the server name. If no port number is specified, the well-known port is used. In most cases, you will not need this information.

- *directory*

  Optional. Specifies the directory on the FTP server. If no directory is specified, the server's default directory is assumed.

- *file_name*

  Optional. Specifies the file on the FTP server. If no file is specified, a list of the contents of the specified directory is displayed.

  If you do not specify a file, end the URL with a slash, /.

Examples

ftp://software.watson.ibm.com/pub/tcpip/tcpnewv4.txt

Sends anonymous as the user ID and the user's e-mail address as the password, and requests the file named tcpnewv4.txt located in the /pub/tcpip/ directory of the FTP server known as software.watson.ibm.com. (This file happens to be the June 1995 issue of IBM's TCP/IP newsletter.)

ftp://ftp.cdrom.com/

Sends anonymous as the user ID and the user's e-mail address as the password, and requests a list of the files and subdirectories in the default directory of the FTP server known as ftp.cdrom.com.

ftp://tonym:piano@ftp.acme.com/rrunner/

Sends tonym as the user ID and piano as the password, and requests a list of the files in the /rrunner/ directory of the FTP server known as ftp.acme.com.

Gopher servers

The URL format for accessing information (document or file) on a Gopher server is as follows:

```
gopher://server_name:port_number/gopher_type_gopher_selector
```

- gopher

  Required. Specifies the protocol used by Gopher servers. Always include the :/ / after gopher.

- *server_name*

  Required. Specifies the host name of the Gopher server, for example, gopher.cup.cam.ac.uk.

- *port_number*

  Optional. Specifies the protocol port to which the request should be sent. If you specify a port number, include a colon to separate it from the server name. If no port number is specified, the well-known port is used. In most cases, you will not need this information.

- *gopher_type_gopher_selector*

  Optional. Specifies the information to be requested from the Gopher server. If no gopher type or selector is specified, a list of the items in the server's default directory is displayed.

  The *gopher_type* specifies the single character or number assigned to the type of information you are requesting. Because the gopher type tells the Web browser how the returned information should be formatted, you should always specify a gopher type if you specify a gopher selector. The most commonly used gopher types are: 0 (for a text file), 1 (for an item list, or *menu*), and 7 (for a search program).

  The *gopher_selector* specifies the name of an item on the Gopher server. The item name may be a directory or a directory and file name. With Gopher, directories and files can be represented by literal names, such as /assist/help.staff, or *symbolic names*. Symbolic names may include spaces. If symbolic name includes a space, the space is represented as %20 (the ASCII hexadecimal equivalent of a space) in the URL. For example, a symbolic name of Satellite Discussion would be Satellite%20Discussion when specified in a URL. When setting up a Gopher server, some people include the gopher type as part of the selector. In these cases, the selector number is repeated in the URL.

If you do not specify a file, end the URL with a slash, /.

Examples

gopher://gopher.almaden.ibm.com/

Requests the default item list, or menu, of the Gopher server known as gopher.almaden.ibm.com.

gopher://wx.atmos.uiuc.edu/11/States/Alabama/

Requests the list of the items (indicated by the 1 following the server name) in the /States/Alabama/ directory of the Gopher server known as wx.atmos.uiuc.edu. In this case, the gopher selector included a 1; therefore, the gopher type appears to be repeated.

gopher://wiretap.spies.com/00/Library/Article/Sports/soccer.rul

Requests the text file (indicated by the 0 following the server name) named soccer.rul located in the /Library/Article/Sports/ directory of the Gopher server known as wiretap.spies.com.

gopher://wx.atmos.uiuc.edu/00/Latin%20America/Temp%20and%20Weather

Requests the text file (indicated by the 0 following the server name) with a symbolic name of "Temp and Weather" in the directory with a symbolic name of "Latin America" of the Gopher server known as wx.atmos.uiuc.edu.

News servers

Most, if not all, Web browsers provide a configuration option that allows you to specify the name of the news server that you want to use for all news requests. Also, in theory, all Usenet news servers have access to the same information. Therefore, the format of a request for information from a news server does not include the server name. The URL format for accessing a news group is as follows:

```
news:newsgroup_name
```

- news

  Required. Specifies that this is a request to a news server. Always include the : after news.

- *newsgroup_name*

  Required. Specifies the name of the newsgroup, for example, rec.arts.disney. To request a list of all newsgroups, use an asterisk (*).

Examples

news:misc.writing.screenplays

Requests a list of the articles in the newsgroup named misc.writing.screenplays.

news:*

Requests a list of all newsgroups.

Local files

Using URLs for local files is useful for testing files and documents on your computer, but you should not use them in HTML documents published on the Web. The URL format for accessing a local file (a file on your computer) is as follows:

```
file:///drive:/directory/file_name
```

- file

  Required. Specifies that this is a request for a local file. Always include the :/// after file. Note that in the URL for a local file there are three slashes after the colon.

- *drive*

  Required. Specifies the drive on your computer.

- *directory*

  Optional. Specifies the directory on your computer. If no directory is specified, the root directory of the specified drive is assumed.

- *file_name*

  Required. Specifies the file on your computer.

Examples

file:///d:/wwwtest/sample.html

Requests the file named sample.html that is located in the /wwwtest/ directory in the d drive of your computer.

E-mail

Many Web browsers allow you to send e-mail messages. The format of a request to send an e-mail message does not include the server name. The URL format for sending an e-mail message is as follows:

```
mailto:e-mail_address
```

- mailto

  Required. Specifies that this is a request to send an e-mail message. Always include the : after mailto.

- *e-mail_address*

  Required. Specifies the e-mail address, such as tcpipnews@vnet.ibm.com, of the intended recipient.

Examples

mailto:webmaster@w3.org

Indicates that you want to send an e-mail message to the address of webmaster@w3.org.

URL-encoded information

Information sent to a Web server, such as user input from a form, is sent as a single string of data using a special format. This special format is described as **URL-encoded**. In URL-encoded information:

- The URL starts with the URL of the processing program.

- Attached data, such as name=value information from a form, is appended to the URL and preceded by a question mark.

- Fields are separated by an ampersand (&).

- Spaces are represented by a plus sign (+), such as "A+long+value."

- Multiple values for a field, such as check boxes, are sent as a string separated by a null character (\0), such as "B\0C\0D."

- Special characters, such as a period or slash, are represented by a percent sign (%) followed by the ASCII hexadecimal equivalent of the symbol, such as "John+Q%2E+Doe." See "ASCII hexadecimal equivalents."

Example

http://www.xxx.com/cgi-bin/
cgiprog?name1=X&name2=A+long+value&name3=B\0C\0D&name4=John+Q%2E+Doe

ASCII hexadecimal equivalents

The following lists many of the commonly used special characters and their ASCII hexadecimal equivalents.

Character	ASCII hex		Character	ASCII hex
!	21		;	3B
"	22		<	3C
#	23		=	3D
$	24		>	3E
%	25		?	3F
&	26		@	40
'	27		[	5B
(	28		\	5C
)	29		]	5D
*	2A		¬ or ^	5E
+	2B		_	5F
,	2C		'	60
-	2D		{	7B
.	2E		¦	7C
/	2F		}	7D
:	3A		~	7E

Resource listing

his appendix provides a list of resources on the Web that may be helpful to you. This list is also provided as an HTML document (named **wwwres.htm**) on the CD in the back of this book.

Appendix C. Resource listing

Web concepts

This section lists resources that contain general information about the Web.

Overview of the World Wide Web

The following Web documents contain useful information about the Web in general.

Title: The World Wide Web Initiative: The Project

URL: http://www.w3.org/

Description: This document, written by Tim Berners-Lee, provides an introduction to the World Wide Web. It contains links to additional information, such as the history of the Web, an overview of the W3 Consortium, lists of Web client and server software, and on-line versions of specifications for HTTP and HTML.

Title: World Wide Web FAQ

URL: http://sunsite.unc.edu/boutell/faq/www_faq.html

Description: This document, maintained by Thomas Boutell, provides answers to frequently asked questions about the Web. The answers cover topics of interest to users of all levels of expertise, such as explanations of Web concepts, instructions for obtaining a Web browser, information about how to set up a Web server, and instructions for using the more advanced features of the Web.

Title: CERN's World Wide Web FAQ

URL: http://www.w3.org/hypertext/WWW/FAQ/List.html

Description: This document, written by Tim Berners-Lee, provides answers to frequently asked questions about the Web. Fewer questions are addressed here than in the FAQ described above.

Web etiquette

Title: Etiquette for Information Providers

URL: http://www.w3.org/hypertext/WWW/Provider/Etiquette.html

Description: This document, written by Tim Berners-Lee, provides some tips for creating and maintaining a user-friendly Web document.

Title: The Webiquette

URL: http://www.cosy.sbg.ac.at/www-doku/standards/webiquette.html

Description: This document, written by Brigitte Jellinek, provides a short but useful list of recommendations for Web documentation.

Understanding URL formats

Title: An Overview of URLs

URL: http://www.w3.org/hypertext/WWW/Addressing/URL/URI_Overview.html

Description: This document provides the specifications for identifying resources on the Internet.

Title: A Beginner's Guide to URLs

URL: http://www.ncsa.uiuc.edu/demoweb/url-primer.html

Description: This document describes the various types of URLs in terms that a novice can understand.

Title: UR* and The Names and Addresses of WWW objects

URL: http://www.w3.org/hypertext/WWW/Addressing/Addressing.html

Description: This document, maintained by the W3 Consortium, discusses how resources on the Web can be named using URIs, URLs, and URNs.

General guides for Information Providers

Title: How to Put Information on the Web

URL: http://www.w3.org/hypertext/WWW/Provider/Overview.html

Description: This document, maintained by the W3 Consortium, provides tips and recommendations for those who wish to make information available on the Web. The document is divided into three sections, addressing three levels of information providers: the author, the WebMaster, and the system administrator.

Title: The Web Developer's Virtual Library

URL: http://www.stars.com/

Description: This document, maintained by Alan Richmond, provides links to close to 1000 documents related to all phases and facets of providing information on the Web, including tutorials and images.

Title: Running a WWW Service

URL: http://info.mcc.ac.uk/CGU/SIMA/handbook/handbook.html

Description: This document, written by Brian Kelly, provides instructions for establishing a presence on the World Wide Web. It includes links to several browsers and utilities as well as discussions on the future of the Web and current legal concerns.

Title: Style Guide for On-line Hypertext

URL: http://www.w3.org/hypertext/WWW/Provider/Style/Overview.html

Description: This document, written by Tim Berners-Lee, provides guidelines for creating on-line information, including recommendations on document structure and document testing.

Title: The EIT Webmaster's Starter Kit

URL: http://wsk.eit.com/wsk/doc

Description: This document, provided by Enterprise Integration Technologies Corporation, provides instructions for setting up a Web site, including links to many of the programs that you will need.

Document creation

This section lists resources that contain information about document creation.

HTML style and reference documents

Title: HyperText Markup Language (HTML): Working and Background Materials

URL: http://www.w3.org/hypertext/WWW/MarkUp/MarkUp.html

Description: This document, maintained by Daniel Connolly, provides links to documents that discuss all levels of HTML: past (HTML 1.0), present (HTML 2.0), and future (HTML 3.0).

Title: HTML 2.0 Specification (Internet Draft)

URL: http://www.w3org/hypertext/WWW/Markup/html-spec/html-spec_toc.html

Description: This document is a hypertext version of the Internet Draft that describes the specifications of HTML version 2.0.

Title: HyperText Markup Language Specification Version 3.0

URL: http://www.hpl.hp.co.uk/people/dsr/html/CoverPage.html

Description: This document is a hypertext version of the Internet Draft that describes the specifications of HTML version 3.0.

Title: Learning HTML

URL: http://union.ncsa.uiuc.edu/HyperNews/get/www/html/learning.html

Description: This document, maintained by Daniel LaLiberte, provides links to more than a dozen documents describing HTML, including an HTML tutorial.

Title: A Beginner's Guide to HTML

URL: http://www.ncsa.uiuc.edu/General/Internet/WWW/HTMLPrimer.html

Description: This document, maintained by NCSA, is a primer for HTML. It covers the basic elements of HTML documents and provides links to information about the more advanced elements.

Title: Common Errors

URL: http://www.willamette.edu/html-composition/strict-html-ce.html#break

Description: This document, written by James "Eric" Tilton, provides helpful troubleshooting tips. It describes the symptoms and solutions for errors that occur most often in HTML coding.

Title: HTML, the Complete Guide

URL: http://www.chem.emory.edu/html.html

Description: This document provides a high-level overview of HTML and how it is used to provide information on the Web.

Title: Elements of HTML Style

URL: http://bookweb.cwis.uci.edu:8042/Staff/StyleGuide.html

Description: This document, written by J.K. Cohen, provides formatting tips for on-line documents. This document is designed to supplement Tim Berners-Lee's *Style Guide for Online Hypertext*.

Title: Composing Good HTML

URL: http://www.willamette.edu/html-composition/strict-html.html

Description: This document, written by James "Eric" Tilton, discusses what constitutes a "good" HTML document. Included in the document is a list of common errors and recommendations for "things to avoid."

Title: Creating a Home Page

URL: http://nearnet.gnn.com/gnn/news/feature/netizens/create.html

Description: This document provides some suggestions for creating a home (or welcome) page.

Title: Home Page Template

URL: http://nearnet.gnn.com/gnn/news/feature/netizens/template.html

Description: This document is an HTML template that you can download.

HTML tools

Title: Yahoo's List of HTML Converters

URL: http://www.yahoo.com/Computers/World_Wide_Web/HTML_Converters/

Description: This document provides links to more than 30 programs that convert information in various formats (including many desktop publishing formats) to HTML.

Title: Yahoo's List of HTML Editors

URL: http://www.yahoo.com/Computers/World_Wide_Web/HTML_Editors/

Description: This document provides links to more than 30 programs available for numerous operating systems that aid in the creation and editing of HTML documents.

Using images in your document

Title: Graphics formats for WWW

URL: http://www.w3.org/hypertext/WWW/Graphics/Overview.html

Description: This document, maintained by the W3 Consortium, discusses many of the image file formats that can be used on the Web.

Title: NCSA Imagemap Tutorial

URL: http://hoohoo.ncsa.uluc.edu/docs/setup/admin/Imagemap.html

Description: This document provides step-by-step instructions for creating mapped images.

Title: CERN Server Clickable Image Support

URL: http://www.w3.org/hypertext/WWW/Daemon/User/CGI/HTImageDoc.html

Description: This document, maintained by Ari Luotonen, provides step-by-step instructions for using the htimage program.

Using forms in your document

Title: Web Communications HTML Tutorial: WWW Fill-out Forms

URL: http://www.webcom.com/~webcom/html/tutor/forms/

Description: This document, maintained by Web Communications, provides an overview of HTML forms, how to create them, and how to process the data from them.

Title: HTML Form-Testing Home Page

URL: http://www.research.digital.com/nsl/formtest/home.html

Description: This document, maintained by Glenn Trewitt, provides access to a form-testing program that you can use to validate your forms.

Title: Instantaneous Introduction to HTML Forms

URL: http://kuhttp.cc.ukans.edu/info/forms/forms-intro.html

Description: This document, written by Michael Grobe, provides a comprehensive overview of how HTML forms work.

Using multimedia in your document

Title: Yahoo's List of Multimedia Resources

URL: http://www.yahoo.com/Computers_and_Internet/Multimedia/

Description: This document provides links to information, programs, and companies associated with multimedia.

Title: MPEG Technical Information

URL: http://www.eit.com/techinfo/mpeg/mpeg.html

Description: This document describes how to create MPEGs (video clip file format) for Macintosh and UNIX platforms.

Title: MPEG Moving Picture Expert Group FAQ

URL: http://www.crs4.it/HTML/LUIGI/MPEG/mpegfaq.html

Description: This document, maintained by Luigi Filippini, provides answers to the most frequently asked questions.

Testing your HTML document

Title: Testing Your Online Hypertext

URL: http://www.w3.org/hypertext/WWW/Provider/Style/Testing.html

Description: This document, written by Tim Berners-Lee, provides instructions and recommendations for testing your HTML document.

Title: Weblint

URL: http://www.unipress.com/web-lint/

Description: This document describes and provides access to a program called Weblint that checks the HTML coding of a document.

Web site administration

This section lists resources that contain information about how to set up and maintain a Web site.

HTTP reference documents

Title: Overview of HTTP

URL: http://www.w3.org/hypertext/WWW/Protocols/Overview.html

Description: This document, maintained by the W3 Consortium, provides an overview of HTTP, including its history and its future.

Title: HTTP: A Protocol for Networked Information

URL: http://www.w3.org/hypertext/WWW/Protocols/HTTP/HTTP2.html

Description: This document, maintained by the W3 Consortium, is a hypertext version of the Internet Draft that describes the specifications of HTTP version 2.0.

Web servers

Title: CERN HTTP Server Status

URL: http://www.w3.org/hypertext/WWW/Daemon/Status.html

Description: This document provides the current status of the CERN server as well as links to other useful documents, such as the current known problems (or bugs).

Title: CERN Server User Guide

URL: http://www.w3.org/hypertext/WWW/Daemon/User/Guide.html

Description: This document describes how to install and maintain the CERN server (http daemon) version 3.0.

Title: NCSA HTTPd Overview

URL: http://hoohoo.ncsa.uiuc.edu/docs/Overview.html

Description: This document describes how to install and maintain the NCSA server (http daemon).

Title: Yahoo's List of Web Servers

URL: http://www.yahoo.com/Computers/World_Wide_Web/HTTP/Servers/

Description: This document provides links to information about more than 50 Web servers.

Common Gateway Interface (CGI)

Title: The Common Gateway Interface

URL: http://hoohoo.ncsa.uiuc.edu/cgi/

Description: This document provides an overview of the Common Gateway Interface (CGI) and examples of how CGI programs work.

Title: World-Wide Web Gateway Software

URL: http://www.w3.org/hypertext/WWW/Gateways.html

Description: This document, maintained by Tim Berners-Lee, provides access to numerous gateway programs.

Title: Yahoo's Information on the Common Gateway Interface

URL: http://www.yahoo.com/Computers/World_Wide_Web/
CGI_Common_Gateway_Interface/

Description: This document provides links to a dozen gateway scripts, as well as information on how to write your own.

Security recommendations

Title: Security and the World Wide Web

URL: http://www.tis.com/Home/NetworkSecurity/WWW/Article.html

Description: This document, written by David Dalva, discusses the need for security on the Web.

Title: Access Authorization in WWW

URL: http://www.w3.org/hypertext/WWW/AccessAuthorization/
Overview.html

Description: This document provides instructions for using the Access Authorization protocol, which conforms to the Basic Protection Scheme. It also contains links to information on the Public Key Protection Scheme and the proposed RIPEM-based HTTP authorization scheme.

Title: Rutgers WWW-Security Index page

URL: http://www-ns.rutgers.edu/www-security/

Description: This document, maintained by the Rutgers University Network Services WWW security team, provides links to numerous documents that discuss security on the Web.

Title: CERN Server Protection Setup Manual

URL: http://www.w3.org/hypertext/WWW/AccessAuthorization/
CERNServer.html

Description: This document, written by Ari Luotonen, describes the files that
control access authorization in the CERN server, and how to modify them.

Title: The Secure HyperText Transfer Protocol

URL: http://www.eit.com/projects/s-http/index.html

Description: This document, written by Chini Krishnan, provides an overview of
Secure HTTP and links to several reference documents, including an FAQ on
Secure HTTP.

Title: The SSL Protocol

URL: http://www.netscape.com/info/SSL.html

Description: This document, written by Kipp Hickman, is the Internet Draft that
describes the specifications for the Secure Sockets Layer protocol.

Title: Shen: A Security Scheme for the World Wide Web

URL: http://www.w3.org/hypertext/WWW/Shen/ref/shen.html

Description: This document, written by Phillip Hallam-Baker, describes the
proposed Shen security scheme.

Related information

This section lists resources that contain other information related to establishing a
presence on the Web.

Web browsers

Title: Yahoo's List of Web Browsers

URL: http://www.yahoo.com/Computers/World_Wide_Web/Browsers/

Description: This document provides links to more than 50 Web browsers available for numerous operating systems.

Title: WWW Client Software products

URL: http://www.w3.org/hypertext/WWW/Clients.html

Description: This document, maintained by the W3 Consortium, provides links to more than 30 Web browsers available for numerous operating systems including line-mode browsers for mainframes.

Making your document available on the Web

Title: Publishing a Home Page

URL: http://nearnet.gnn.com/gnn/news/feature/netizens/publish.html

Description: This document provides tips and recommendations for making your document available on the Web.

Advertising your new Web server

Title: What's New with NCSA Mosaic

URL: http://www.ncsa.uiuc.edu/SDG/Software/Mosaic/Docs/whats-new.html

Description: The "What's New" page advertises new Web servers. This document includes instructions for submitting a request for your Web server to be advertised.

Renting space on someone else's server

Title: Yahoo's List of Internet Presence Providers

URL: http://www.yahoo.com/Business/Corporations/Internet_Presence_Providers/

Description: This document provides links to information about Internet Presence Providers, from whom you can rent server space for your HTML documents.

Other items of interest

Title: Newsgroups Relevant to the World Wide Web Project

URL: http://www.w3.org/hypertext/WWW/Newsgroups.html

Description: This document, maintained by the W3 Consortium, provides links to forums that discuss the World Wide Web and related topics.

Title: World Wide Web Virtual Library: Subject Catalogue

URL: http://www.w3.org/hypertext/DataSources/bySubject/Overview.html

Description: This document, maintained by the W3 Consortium, provides links, categorized by subject, to information on the Web.

Title: World Wide Web Robots, Wanderers, and Spiders

URL: http://web.nexor.co.uk/mak/doc/robots/robots.html

Description: This document, maintained by Martijn Koster, provides links to information about programs that systematically roam the Web, gathering data about the information stored on the servers they encounter.

Title: World Wide Web Conferences

URL: http://www.w3.org/hypertext/Conferences/Overview-WWW.html

Description: This document, maintained by the W3 Consortium, provides links to information about past, current, and upcoming World Wide Web conferences.

Title: Conferences on Hypertext

URL: http://www.w3.org/hypertext/Conferences/Overview.html

Description: This document, maintained by the W3 Consortium, provides links to information about past, current, and upcoming conferences that focus on on-line information, specifically hypertext.

Appendix D

Samples

his appendix illustrates sample HTML documents and sample CGI programs designed to help you get your Web site "up and running" quickly. The source files for these documents and programs are included on the CD in the back of this book. Feel free to use these samples to create your own documents and CGI programs. The samples are supplied without any expressed or implied warranty.

Appendix D. Samples

HTML document samples

To assist you in creating your HTML documents, this section illustrates some sample HTML documents. The source files for these documents are included on the CD in the back of this book.

Sample home page

This is a sample home page. This sample is also included with the IBM Internet Connection Servers. The source file for this sample is called **homepage.htm**.

```
<!--------------------Start Document-------------------->
<!doctype html public "html2.0">
<html>
<head>
<!----------------document identification---------------->
<title>Document title goes here - used by web search tools
to identify this document.</title>
<meta name="abstract"  content="Describe your document here">
<meta name="keywords"  content="Enter searchable keywords
here separated by spaces">
<meta name="owner"  content="Put your e-mail address here">
<meta name="review"  content="Put a date YYYYMMDD here for
when this document should be reviewed">
<meta name="security" content="public">
<!---------------------begin body---------------------->
<!--------------------begin heading--------------------->
</head>
<body>
<!--In the next line, replace "sampmast.gif" with the name
of your own image file and replace "Sample Home Page" with a
text  message that will appear if the user's viewer can't
display images.-->
<img src="/Admin/sampmast.gif" alt="Sample Home Page">
<h1>Document title (This is a size 1 header)</h1>
<!--Next line shows how to insert a separator line-->
<HR>
<!----------------------end heading--------------------->
```

```
<H2>Document Body (This is a size 2 header)</H2>
This is an example of a simple Home Page.  This is the first
paragraph. To see the HTML source that generates this document, use
your browser's command to view HTML source.  You can save this
document in HTML source format and then modify it to create your
own document.<p>
<hr>
<H3>Links (This is a size 3 header)</H3>
This paragraph shows a text link to another document. This
is a link that will take you back to the
<A HREF="/admin-bin/cfgin/initial">Configuration Page</A>.
<P>
This paragraph shows an image link to another document. To
go back to the configuration page, click on this image:
<A HREF="/admin-bin/cfgin/initial">
<IMG SRC="/Admin/skycfg.gif" alt="Image Link"></A>.<P>

<! —To make a link within the same document work, you must
also insert a "name=anchorname" attribute in the definition
of the link you are jumping to.  For an example, see the
"Administration Page" anchor in the footer of this
document. —>
This paragraph shows a text link to another point within
this document - the footer at the bottom of this page. This
is a link that will scroll the page down to the
<A HREF="#Footer">Footer</A>.  <P>
<hr>
<H3>Text (This is a size 3 header)</H3>
Here is an example of a word in <I>italics</I>.  Here is an
example of a word in <B>bold</B>.<P>
This is an example of an in-line (in a text line) GIF image:
<IMG SRC="/Admin/graphic4.gif" alt="Sample Inline Image">.   It
is not a link, it is just an illustration
that is embedded inside a text paragraph. <P>
Sometimes you need text to align vertically. You can use
fixed width fonts. Here is an example:<P>
<PRE>
   Row one: column1 column2 column3
   Row two: column1 column2 column3
</PRE><p>
```

```
This is an unordered list with three items:<P>
<UL>
<LI> item one
<LI> item two
<LI> item three
</UL>
This is a numbered list:<P>
<OL>
<LI> item one
<LI> item two
<LI> item three
</OL>
<!--------------------begin footer-------------------->
<hr>
<H3>Footers  (This is a size 3 header)</H3>
Below is an example of a footer that can be placed at the
bottom of your document. It contains examples of links you
might want to include in a footer.
<hr>
<a href="/Frntpage.html" name="Footer">
<img src="/Admin/go2first.gif" alt="Front Page |"></a>
<a href="/admin-bin/cfgin/initial">
<img src="/Admin/skycfg.gif" alt="Configuration and
Administration Page |"></a>
<img src="/Admin/greyhome.gif" alt="Sample Home Page |">
<a href="/wwres.html"><img src="/Admin/skyres.gif"
alt="WebMaster Resource List |"></a>
<a href="/Docs/doj10mst.html">
<img src="/Admin/skydoc.gif" alt=" Documentation"></a>
<!-----------------------end body----------------------->
</body>
<!--------------------End of Document------------------->
</html>
```

Sample catalogue

This is a sample of an initial catalogue page. The source file for this sample is called **catalog.htm**.

```
<html>
<head>
<title>Insert your title here</title>
<meta name="abstract" content="Describe your document here">
<meta name="keywords" content="Enter searchable keywords here
separated by spaces">
<meta name="owner"    content="Put your e-mail address here">
<meta name="review"   content="Put a date YYYYMMDD here for when
this document should be reviewed">
<meta name="security" content="public">
</head>
<body>
<!—In the next line, replace "sampmast.gif" with the name
of your own image file and replace "Sample Catalogue" with
a text message that will appear if the user's viewer can't
display images.—>
<img src="/Admin/sampmast.gif" alt="Sample Catalogue">
<H1>Sample Catalogue</H1>
<! Replace news.gif with the name of your news graphic.
Replace "news.html" with the name of your news document -!>
<p>
<img src=/images/news.gif align=middle>
<a href="news.html">News: What's new with Your Company</a>
<br>
<! Replace products.gif with the name of your product graphic.
Replace "products.html" with the name of the document that lists
your products --!>
<img src=/images/products.gif align=middle>
<a href="products.html">Products: Your Company's products</a>
<br>
```

```
<! Replace services.gif with the name of your services graphic.
Replace "services.html" with the name of the document that
lists your services --!>
<img src=/images/services.gif align=middle>
<a href="services.html">Services: Technical services and
customer support</a>
<hr>
<! Replace survey.html with the name of your survey form. -!>
Take a minute to <a href="survey.html">tell us what you think
</a> of our products and services.
<hr>
<! Replace mail.gif with the name of your mail graphic.  Replace
"webmaster@your.company.com" with the e-mail address of the
person who should receive comments --!>
<img src=/images/mail.gif align=bottom>
Please send comments and suggestions to
<a href="mailto:webmaster@your.company.com">
webmaster@your.company.com</a>.
<hr>
<! The following can be used in place of a button bar.
Replace the URLs as appropriate. Remove any anchors you do not
need.  -!>
<b>
[
<a href="http://your.company.com/">Your home page</a> |
<a href="http://your.company.com/orders/">Place an order</a> |
<a href="http://your.company.com/search/">Search</a> |
<a href="http://your.company.com/Assist/">Contact us</a> |
<a href="http://your.company.com/copyright.html">(C)</a> |
<a href="http://your.company.com/trademarks.html">(TM)</a>
]
</b>
</body>
</html>
```

Sample survey

This is a sample of a survey. The source file for this sample is called **survey.htm**.

```
<HTML>
<Head>
<Title>Insert your title here</Title>
<meta name="abstract" content="Describe your document here">
<meta name="keywords" content="Enter searchable keywords here
separated by spaces">
<meta name="owner"    content="Put your e-mail address here">
<meta name="review"   content="Put a date YYYYMMDD here for when
this document should be reviewed">
<meta name="security" content="public">
</Head>
<Body>
<! Replace "/cgi-bin/survey.pl" with the name and location of your
survey processing CGI program -!>
<H1>Survey</H1>
<FORM METHOD=POST ACTION="/cgi-bin/survey.pl">
Please complete this survey so that we may better improve our
service.<P>
Name: <INPUT TYPE="text" NAME="name" SIZE=45 MAXLENGTH=50
VALUE="Enter your name here"><P>
Address: <TEXTAREA NAME='address' COLS=40 ROWS=3>
Enter your address here.
</TEXTAREA><P>
Account ID: <INPUT TYPE="text" NAME="acctID" SIZE=30><P>
Password: <INPUT TYPE="password" NAME="password" SIZE=10><P>
Which products do you use?<P>
<INPUT TYPE="checkbox" NAME="prods" VALUE="P1"> Product 1
<INPUT TYPE="checkbox" NAME="prods" VALUE="P2"> Product 2
<INPUT TYPE="checkbox" NAME="prods" VALUE="P3"> Product 3
<INPUT TYPE="checkbox" NAME="prods" VALUE="P4"> Product 4
<INPUT TYPE="checkbox" NAME="prods" VALUE="P5"> Product 5
<INPUT TYPE="checkbox" NAME="prods" VALUE="P6"> Product 6<P>
```

```
How would you rate your overall satisfaction with our products?<P>
<INPUT TYPE="radio" NAME="rating" VALUE="VS" CHECKED> Very satis-
fied
<INPUT TYPE="radio" NAME="rating" VALUE="S"> Satisfied
<INPUT TYPE="radio" NAME="rating" VALUE="N"> Neutral
<INPUT TYPE="radio" NAME="rating" VALUE="D"> Dissatisfied
<INPUT TYPE="radio" NAME="rating" VALUE="VD"> Very dissatisfied<P>
What type of information would you like to see on our home page?
<Select MULTIPLE NAME="info" SIZE=1>
<Option>Product announcements</Option>
<Option>Upgrade information</Option>
<Option>Frequently asked questions</Option>
<Option>Tips and techniques</Option>
<Option>Related information</Option>
</select><p>
Reset fields: <INPUT TYPE="reset"><P>
Select to submit your responses: <INPUT TYPE="submit" Value="SEND">
</FORM>
</Body>
</HTML>
```

Sample comment form

This is a sample of a comment form. The source file for this sample is called
comment.htm.

Note: This form is designed to work with the sample mail processing program
shown later in "Sample e-mail program."

```
<html>
<head>
<title>Sample Comment Form</title>
<meta name="abstract" content="Describe your document here">
<meta name="keywords" content="Enter searchable keywords here
separated by spaces">
<meta name="owner"    content="Put your e-mail address here">
```

```
<meta name="review"    content="Put a date YYYYMMDD here for when
this document should be reviewed">
<meta name="security" content="public">
</head>
<body>
<! Replace "images/mail.gif" with the name of your mailbox image -
!>
<br><img src="/images/mail.gif" align=middle>
<b>Comments, Questions, Compliments? Let us hear from you.</b>
<form action="/cgi-bin/sendmail.pl" method=POST>
<! Replace "e-mail_addr@your.company.com" with the e-mail address
of the
intended recipient -!>
<input type="hidden" name="to" value="e-mail_addr@your.company.com"
size=40>
<pre>
<b>Your  name</b>: <input type="text" name="name" size=40>
<b>Your EMAIL</b>: <input type="text" name="email" size=40>
</pre>
<textarea name="data" rows=6 cols=60>
Your message......
</textarea><br>
<input type="submit" value="Send It">
<input type="reset" value="Forget It">
Thanks for taking the time!
</form>
</body>
</html>
```

CGI program samples

To assist you in using the Common Gateway Interface, this section illustrates some sample CGI programs. Some of the programs are written in Perl, a portable scripting language that is often used for CGI programs, or scripts. Others are written in REXX, a simple scripting language available for VM, OS/2, and AIX systems. The source files for these programs are included on the CD in the back of this book.

Sample e-mail program

The following is a sample e-mail program written in Perl by Steven Brenner (and modified by Paul Chamberlain). It takes the content of a form and forwards the information via e-mail to a specified recipient. It assumes that the destination e-mail address has been specified using the forms HIDDEN attribute. The source file for this program is **sendmail.pl**.

Note: This program is designed to work with the sample comment form shown earlier in "Sample comment form."

```
#!/bin/perl — -*- C -*-

# Perl Routines to Manipulate CGI input
#
# Copyright 1993 Steven E. Brenner
# Unpublished work.
# Permission granted to use and modify this library so long
# as the copyright above is maintained, modifications are
# documented, and credit is given for any use of the library.
# ReadParse
# Reads in GET or POST data, converts it to unescaped text,
# and puts one key=value in each member of the list "@in"
# Also creates key/value pairs in %in, using '\0' to
# separate multiple selections
# If a variable-glob parameter (e.g., *cgi_input) is passed
# to ReadParse, information is stored there, rather than in
# $in, @in, and %in.

sub ReadParse {
  if (@_) {
    local (*in) = @_;
  }

  local ($i, $loc, $key, $val);

  # Read in text
  if ($ENV{'REQUEST_METHOD'} eq "GET") {
    $in = $ENV{'QUERY_STRING'};
  } elsif ($ENV{'REQUEST_METHOD'} eq "POST") {
```

```perl
      for ($i = 0; $i < $ENV{'CONTENT_LENGTH'}; $i++) {
        $in .= getc;
      }
    }

  @in = split(/&/,$in);

  foreach $i (0 .. $#in) {
    # Convert plus's to spaces
    $in[$i] =~ s/\+/ /g;

    # Convert %XX from hex numbers to alphanumeric
    $in[$i] =~ s/%(..)/pack("c",hex($1))/ge;

    # Split into key and value.
    $loc = index($in[$i],"=");
    $key = substr($in[$i],0,$loc);
    $val = substr($in[$i],$loc+1);
    $in{$key} .= '\0' if (defined($in{$key})); # \0 is the multiple
separator
    $in{$key} .= $val;
  }

  return 1; # just for fun
}


# PrintHeader
# Returns the magic line which tells WWW that we're an HTML
# document

sub PrintHeader {
  return "HTTP/1.0 200 Virtual Document follows\nContent-type:
text/html\n\n<TITLE>E-mail Transmission Status</TITLE>";
}

sub preventEscape {
  if ( $_[0] =~ /([~]|%3D)/ ) {
    print "
```

```
<HEAD><TITLE>400 Bad Request</TITLE></HEAD>
<BODY><H1>400 Bad Request</H1>
Your request had bad syntax or was inherently impossible to sat-
isfy.
<p>
$_[1] $1
</BODY> \n";
    exit 99;                      # security threat!
  }
}


# This part was written by Paul Chamberlain, IBM
# This is an e-mail gateway.  It expects to be
# called from a form which has the following fields:
# to           Intended recipient
# email        E-mail address of the sender
# name         Full name of the sender
# data         The actual message content
#

print &PrintHeader;
print "<h1>E-mail transmission status</h1>\n";
&ReadParse,

$server = $ENV{"SERVER_NAME"};
$host = $ENV{"REMOTE_HOST"};
$to = $in{"to"};
$email = $in{"email"};
$name = $in{"name"};
$subject = $in{"subject"};
if (!$subject) {
      $subject = "Via WWW-Mail gateway at $server";
}
$to =~ s/[||!~'"']//g;
$subject =~ s/[||!~'"']//g;

&preventEscape($in{data},"sendmail: a mail message may not contain
a ");
```

```
# Really should make sure $to doesn't have any quotes
open(MAIL, "|/usr/sbin/sendmail -F\"$name\" -f \"$email\"
\"$to\"");
print MAIL "Subject: $subject\n";
print MAIL "Reply-To: $email\n";
print MAIL "Remote host: $host (name determined by IBM
software)\n";
print MAIL "Sender: $email\n";
print MAIL "Full name: $name\n\n";
print MAIL $in{"data"};
print MAIL "\n--\n";
print MAIL "Please doublecheck the \'Reply-To:\' address in this
message.\n";
print MAIL "It was entered by the sender, and may be invalid.\n\n";
print MAIL "This mail is delivered courtesy of the IBM WWW Server
on $server\n";
$rc = close(MAIL);

if ($rc == 0 || $rc == 1) {
# print "The mail command returned $rc when mailing to: $to\n";
# print "Normally it returns 1\n";
#} elsif ($rc == 1) {
    print "Your message was successfully mailed to: $to\n";
} else {
    print "The mail command returned $rc when mailing to: $to\n";
    print "<p>This probably means it failed.\n";
}

exit 0; #return true
```

Sample counter program

The following is a sample counter program written in Perl. Have you seen the
HTML documents that display something similar to "You are visitor number **09364**
to our home page"? Now you can do the same using this program. The program

keeps a running total of the number of requests the server has received. As a new request is received, the program increments the running total and creates an image of the incremented value (in XBM format) that can be displayed in an HTML document. The source file for this program is **counter.pl**.

```perl
#!/bin/perl
# $Id: counter.pl,v 1.1 94/10/07 10:41:06 nrstools Exp $
#
# counter - increment a counter for WWW
#
# To install add the following lines to the files specified
#    1. Place this script into your cgi-bin directory.
#    2. Update "counterfile" to indicate a writable location
#        for storing the count.
#    3. Imbed into a HTML page as:
#
#       To date, there have been
#            <a href="/counter.html">
#            <img src="/cgi-bin/counter.pl"
#             alt="[NOT AVAILABLE WITH YOUR WEB CLIENT]">
#            </a> connections to this page.
#
# Written 3/8/94 by Dan Rich (drich@corp.sgi.com)
#     Based on C code written by Frans van Hoesel
(hoesel@chem.rug.nl)
#

sub usage {
    print STDERR "usage: $0 [-i]\n";
    exit 1;
}

# $counterfile = "/projects/wwwidd/counts/counter.txt";

if ($#ARGV > $[) {
        print "Content-type: text/plain\n\n";
        print "Too many args: @ARGV\n";
        print "<br>Try passing no args\n";
        exit 0;
```

```perl
} elsif ($#ARGV == $[) {
        $counterfile = "/projects/wwwidd/counts/$ARGV[$[]";
}

require('getopts.pl') || die "can\'t do getopts.pl: $@";
#require('sys/file.ph') || die "can\'t do sys/file.ph: $@";

if ( ! &Getopts('i') ) {
    &usage();
}
# $inv = $opt_i;
$inv = 1;
# bitmap for each digit
@invdigits = (0xff,0xff,0xff,0xc3,0x99,0x99,0x99,0x99,
             0x99,0x99,0x99,0x99,0xc3,0xff,0xff,0xff,
             0xff,0xff,0xff,0xcf,0xc7,0xcf,0xcf,0xcf,
             0xcf,0xcf,0xcf,0xcf,0xcf,0xff,0xff,0xff,
             0xff,0xff,0xff,0xc3,0x99,0x9f,0x9f,0xcf,
             0xe7,0xf3,0xf9,0xf9,0x81,0xff,0xff,0xff,
             0xff,0xff,0xff,0xc3,0x99,0x9f,0x9f,0xc7,
             0x9f,0x9f,0x9f,0x99,0xc3,0xff,0xff,0xff,
             0xff,0xff,0xff,0xcf,0xcf,0xc7,0xc7,0xcb,
             0xcb,0xcd,0x81,0xcf,0x87,0xff,0xff,0xff,
             0xff,0xff,0xff,0x81,0xf9,0xf9,0xf9,0xc1,
             0x9f,0x9f,0x9f,0x99,0xc3,0xff,0xff,0xff,
             0xff,0xff,0xff,0xc7,0xf3,0xf9,0xf9,0xc1,
             0x99,0x99,0x99,0x99,0xc3,0xff,0xff,0xff,
             0xff,0xff,0xff,0x81,0x99,0x9f,0x9f,0xcf,
             0xcf,0xe7,0xe7,0xf3,0xf3,0xff,0xff,0xff,
             0xff,0xff,0xff,0xc3,0x99,0x99,0x99,0xc3,
             0x99,0x99,0x99,0x99,0xc3,0xff,0xff,0xff,
             0xff,0xff,0xff,0xc3,0x99,0x99,0x99,0x99,
             0x83,0x9f,0x9f,0xcf,0xe3,0xff,0xff,0xff
             );
@digits = (0x00,0x00,0x00,0x3c,0x66,0x66,0x66,0x66,
          0x66,0x66,0x66,0x66,0x3c,0x00,0x00,0x00,
          0x00,0x00,0x00,0x30,0x38,0x30,0x30,0x30,
          0x30,0x30,0x30,0x30,0x30,0x00,0x00,0x00,
          0x00,0x00,0x00,0x3c,0x66,0x60,0x60,0x30,
```

```
            0x18,0x0c,0x06,0x06,0x7e,0x00,0x00,0x00,
            0x00,0x00,0x00,0x3c,0x66,0x60,0x60,0x38,
            0x60,0x60,0x60,0x66,0x3c,0x00,0x00,0x00,
            0x00,0x00,0x00,0x30,0x30,0x38,0x38,0x34,
            0x34,0x32,0x7e,0x30,0x78,0x00,0x00,0x00,
            0x00,0x00,0x00,0x7e,0x06,0x06,0x06,0x3e,
            0x60,0x60,0x60,0x66,0x3c,0x00,0x00,0x00,
            0x00,0x00,0x00,0x38,0x0c,0x06,0x06,0x3e,
            0x66,0x66,0x66,0x66,0x3c,0x00,0x00,0x00,
            0x00,0x00,0x00,0x7e,0x66,0x60,0x60,0x30,
            0x30,0x18,0x18,0x0c,0x0c,0x00,0x00,0x00,
            0x00,0x00,0x00,0x3c,0x66,0x66,0x66,0x3c,
            0x66,0x66,0x66,0x66,0x3c,0x00,0x00,0x00,
            0x00,0x00,0x00,0x3c,0x66,0x66,0x66,0x66,
            0x7c,0x60,0x60,0x30,0x1c,0x00,0x00,0x00
            );

$hex = "0123456789abcdef";

# Read and increment the counter file
while (-f "$counterfile.lock") { sleep 1 }
open(LOCK,">$counterfile.lock");
open(COUNTERFILE,"<$counterfile") || die "can\'t open $counterfile:
$!\n";
#flock(COUNTERFILE,&LOCK_EX) || die "can\'t lock $counterfile:
$!\n";
$text = <COUNTERFILE>;
close(COUNTERFILE);
$text++;
$len = length($text) > 7 ? length($text) : 7;
open(COUNTERFILE,">$counterfile") || die "can\'t open $counterfile:
$!\n";
printf COUNTERFILE "%0${len}u\n",$text;
$text = sprintf("%0${len}u",$text);
#flock(COUNTERFILE,&LOCK_UN);
close(COUNTERFILE);
unlink("$counterfile.lock");

# Generate an X11 bitmap on STDOUT
```

```
printf STDOUT "Content-type: image/x-xbitmap\n\n";
printf STDOUT "#define count_width %d\n#define count_height 16\n",
$len*8;
printf STDOUT "static char count_bits[] = {\n";
for ($y=0; $y < 16; $y++) {
    for ($x=0; $x < $len; $x++) {
        $d = substr($text,$x,1) - '0';
        print STDOUT '0x';
        if ($inv) {                   # $inv = 1 for inverted text
           printf STDOUT "%1x",($invdigits[($d * 16) + $y] >>
                           4) & 0xf;
           printf STDOUT "%1x",$invdigits[($d * 16) + $y] & 0xf;
        } else {
           printf STDOUT "%1x",($digits[($d * 16) + $y] >> 4) & 0xf;
           printf STDOUT "%1x",$digits[($d * 16) + $y] & 0xf;
        }
        if ($x < $len-1) {
            print STDOUT ',';
        }
    }
    if ($y==15) {
        print STDOUT '};';
    } else {
        print STDOUT ',';
    }
    print STDOUT "\n";
}
```

Sample parsing program

The following is a sample generic parsing program written in REXX. The program does not need to know anything about the data being passed; it simply breaks the input string at the ampersands and converts any ASCII hexadecimal characters it encounters. The source file for this program is **frmparse.rex**.

Note: An HTML document, called **testform.htm**, which can be used to test this program, has been included on the CD in the back of this book.

```
#!/usr/bin/rexx
/***********************************************************
*                                                         *
*   FRMPARSE.REXX is a Rexx/6000 program for use with the *
*   WWW CGI interface.                                    *
*   FRMPARSE is a generic CGI parsing routine that can be *
*   used to *  parse input from any HTML form.            *
*   For example, to use FRMPARSE.REXX to handle your HTML *
*   form, you would: add your code below (look for comment)*
*   store in CGI-BIN directory on your WWW server make it *
*   executable in your HTML, code the following:          *
*                                                         *
*   <form method=POST action="/cgi-bin/frmparse.rexx">    *
*   .                                                     *
*   <form tags for input fields, etc. >                   *
*   .                                                     *
*   <input type="reset" value="Clear Form">               *
*   <input type="submit" value="Submit">                  *
*   </form>                                               *
*                                                         *
*   Date:   01/18/1995                                    *
*   Author: Terry Foster                                  *
*           Work e-mail:   str8aro@vnet.ibm.com           *
*                                                         *
***********************************************************/

/***********************************************************
* Handle input arguments (there aren't any)               *
***********************************************************/
Parse Arg Argv
Argc = 0
If Argv = ''
 Then Argv = 'blank'
 Else Argc = Words(Argv)

/***********************************************************
* Set up a response to the client (optional)              *
***********************************************************/
```

```
Say 'Content-type: text/html'
Say ''
Say '<html><head>'
Say '<title>WWW CGI Forms Support with Rexx/6000</title>'
Say '</head>'
Say '<body>'

/************************************************************
* Get a few environment variables                          *
************************************************************/
env = 'ENVIRONMENT'
method = Value('REQUEST_METHOD',,env)
len    = Value('CONTENT_LENGTH',,env)
server = Value('SERVER_NAME',,env)

/************************************************************
* Get data from form                                       *
************************************************************/
If (method = 'POST') & (len > 0)
 Then Do                 /* Use POST method to pass parameters */
        count = 0
        Do While 1
         post_string = LineIn()
         If post_string <> ""
           Then Do
                   count = count + Length(post_string);
                   If count >= len
                    Then Leave
                End
           Else Leave
        End
      End

/************************************************************
* Figure out how many variables there are.                 *
************************************************************/
vars = 1
start = 1
```

```
Do Forever
 ph = Pos('26'x,post_string,start)
 If ph=0
  Then Leave
 vars = vars+1
 start = ph+1
End


/************************************************************
 *  Convert URL encoded + to space                         *
 ************************************************************/
post_string = Translate(post_string,' ','+')


/************************************************************
 *  Split into key and value                               *
 ************************************************************/
Do j = 1 to vars While post_string <> ''
 Parse Var post_string first '26'x rest
 Parse Var first var_name.j '=' var_value.j
 Call Do_hex
 Call Value var_name.j, var_value.j
 post_string = rest
End


/************************************************************
 *  At this point variables defined in the form HTML are   *
 *  usable by name                                         *
 ************************************************************/
/* Your code to process input data goes here.
   Refer to your variables by name, they will contain input
   entered by the user.
   For example, if you coded:
   <input type="text" name="test" size=40>

   then you can use the variable named TEST from here on,
   etc. For example you could use the following code here:

   Say 'Variable named TEST contains:' test
```

```
   See TESTFORM HTML for an example.
*/
   Say 'Variable named TEST contains:' test
/*************************************************************
*  Finish the response to the client                       *
*************************************************************/
Say '</body>'
Say '</html>'

Exit

Do_hex:
/*************************************************************
*  Convert URL encoded hex (%XX) to character              *
*  Beware of the lone, valid '25'x '%'                     *
*************************************************************/
strt = 1
Do While Pos('25'x,var_value.j,strt) <> 0
 pp = Pos('25'x,var_value.j,strt)
 left = Substr(var_value.j,1,pp-1)
 right = Substr(var_value.j,pp+1)
 If Datatype(Substr(right,1,2),'X') = 1
  Then Do
        char = x2c(Substr(right,1,2))
        right = Substr(right,3)
        var_value.j = left||char||right
        If char = '25'x
         Then strt = Pos('25'x,var_value.j)+1
       End
  Else Do
        var_value.j = left||'25'x||right
        strt = Pos('25'x,var_value.j)+1
       End
End

Return
```

Glossary

This glossary defines terms used in this book.

absolute URL

A complete URL that contains the protocol, server name, and location (directory and file name) of a document. See also *relative URL*.

access control

A means of limiting access to data. Access control is usually based on a set of rules that define who has access to which data.

address, IP

See *internet address*.

Advanced Interactive Executive (AIX)

IBM's implementation of the UNIX operating system.

American National Standards Institute (ANSI)

An organization consisting of producers, consumers, and general interest groups that establishes the procedures by which accredited organizations create and maintain voluntary industry standards in the United States.

American National Standard Code for Information Interchange (ASCII)

The standard code used for information interchange among data processing systems, data communication systems, and associated equipment. The ASCII set consists of control characters and graphic characters. ASCII is the default file transfer type for FTP, used to transfer files that contain ASCII text characters.

animation

A file that contains a series of images joined (or sequenced) in such a way that the objects in the images appear to move or have life.

annotation

Comments regarding a document, which are saved separately. The annotation function provided with NCSA Mosaic allows you to save comments about a document.

application

A program or collection of software components used to perform specific types of user-oriented work on a computer.

Archie

A standard Internet search tool that searches through known anonymous FTP servers for files with names that match the specified criteria.

argument

Any value of an independent variable; for example, a search key.

attribute

A characteristic or property of a file, directory, window, or object; for example, the color of a line, or the length of a data field. In HTML, a characteristic of an element specified as part of an HTML tag, such as the NAME associated with a link.

audio clip

A file that contains a segment of recorded or created sounds.

authentication

A means of verifying the identity of a server or browser.

authorization

The right granted to a user or group of users to communicate with, or to make use of, a computer system, network, database, or service.

backbone

A set of nodes and their interconnecting links providing the primary data path across a network. In a local area network multiple-bridge configuration, a backbone is a high-speed link to which the rings are connected by means of bridges or routers. A backbone may be configured as a bus or a ring. In a wide area network, a backbone is a high-speed link to which nodes or data switching exchanges (DSEs) are connected.

binary

A file mode assigned to files that consist of binary digits (1s and 0s). Examples of binary files are: programs, Microsoft Word .doc files, images (such as bitmaps), and sound files.

bitmap (BMP)

An image format created by Microsoft. It is designed to store raster images, particularly screen captures.

bridge

A device that connects two or more networks and forwards packets among them. Bridges do not make any decisions about the route that information should take.

button

A mechanism on a pointing device, such as a mouse, or an area on the computer screen, used to request or initiate an action.

button bar

A type of image map that appears to contain push buttons.

cache

Special-purpose buffer storage, smaller and faster than main storage, used to hold a copy of data that may be frequently accessed. Use of a cache reduces access time, but may increase memory requirements.

caching

The act of holding previously accessed documents and images in cache for faster future access. See also *persistent caching*.

case-sensitive

A condition in which entries for a field must conform to a specific lower-case, upper-case, or mixed-case format in order to be valid.

certificate

A digital document used in authentication that binds an encryption key to the identity of the certificate owner.

CGI program

A program, written in any language supported by the operating system, that interacts with a Web server through the Common Gateway Interface.

CGI script

A CGI program written in a scripting language, such as Perl or REXX.

check box

A square box with associated text that represents a choice. When selected, a check mark appears in the square box. In HTML, a form element that produces a selectable square box associated with a choice. See also *radio button*.

chunking

In writing, the practice of grouping information into discrete parts, based on content.

client

A computer system or process that requests a service of another computer system or process. For example, a workstation or personal computer requesting mail from a mail server is a client of the mail server. See also *server*.

client/server technology

A computer technology in which the functions of a program are divided into two or more separate processes that are distributed between the client and the server. See also *client* and *server*.

clipboard

An area of memory that temporarily holds data being passed from one program to another.

cloning

The act of spawning duplicate windows or processes. With NCSA Mosaic, the cloning function allows you to open another browser window.

command

A statement used to request a function of the system. A command consists of the command name abbreviation, which identifies the requested function, and its parameters.

command line input

A mechanism used to pass information to a program, such as a CGI program. The command line is used to pass data from an ISINDEX document to a CGI program. Other mechanisms for passing information to a CGI program are *environment variables* and *standard input*.

command prompt

A displayed symbol that indicates where you enter commands.

Common Gateway Interface (CGI)

A standard for the exchange of information between a Web server and an external program. The external program can be written in any language supported by the operating system. See also *CGI script* and *gateway program*.

Computer Graphics Metafile (CGM)

An image format developed by the American National Standard for Information Systems. It is best suited for vector images, but can also be used for raster images.

configuration file

A file that describes options and parameters to be used by a program.

connection

A communication link from a local device to a shared resource on a server.

database

A collection of interrelated data organized according to a database scheme to serve one or more applications.

default

A value, attribute, or option that is assumed when none is explicitly specified.

Defense Advanced Research Projects Agency (DARPA)

The United States Department of Defense agency responsible for creating ARPANET. This agency was formerly called the Advanced Research Projects Agency (ARPA).

destination Internet (IP) address

The unique 32-bit address assigned to the device that receives your request for connection.

directory

A named grouping of files in a file system.

document streaming

A technology used by many Web browsers that allows you to scroll through a document even before the entire document is received and displayed.

domain

In an Internet, a part of the naming hierarchy. A domain name consists of a sequence of names (labels) separated by periods (dots).

domain name

A name of a host system in a network. A domain name consists of a sequence of names (labels) separated by a periods (dots).

domain name server

A server program that supplies name-to-address translation by mapping domain names to Internet addresses. Use of a domain name server allows users to request services of another computer using a symbolic name, which is easier to remember than an Internet address.

dotted-decimal notation

The syntactical representation for a 32-bit integer that consists of four 8-bit numbers, written in base 10 and separated by periods (dots). It is used to represent IP addresses.

drag

To use a pointing device to move an object; for example, selecting an icon and dragging it out of its folder to the desktop.

drive

The device used to read and write data on disks or diskettes.

drop

To fix the position of the object being moved by releasing the pointing device.

dynamic document

A temporary HTML document created on-the-fly to satisfy a particular request, such as a search request. Dynamic documents are generally produced by CGI programs. See also *static document*.

e-mail

On the Internet, the means of exchanging messages through files, or mail, sent electronically.

encryption

A means of scrambling data to prevent the data from being read by anyone other than the intended recipient.

entry field

A panel element, usually highlighted in some manner and usually with its boundaries indicated, where you type in information.

environment variable

A mechanism used to pass information to a program, such as a CGI program. Using environment variables, information is passed to a program as a value assigned to a parameter. Other mechanisms for passing information to a CGI program are *command line input* and *standard input*.

explicit highlighting

Tags that instruct the browser to display the surrounded text in a specific manner, such as bold or italic. See also *interpreted highlighting*.

file transfer protocol (FTP)

An application protocol used for transferring files to and from host computers. FTP requires a user ID and sometimes a password to allow access to files on a remote host system.

firewall

A computer that connects a private network, such as a business, to a public network, such as the Internet. It contains programs that limit the access between two networks. See also *proxy*.

font

A family of characters of a given size and style; for example, 9-point Helvetica.

freeware

Programs on the Internet that users are allowed to copy, use, and distribute at no cost. However, freeware cannot be modified or sold without written permission from the author of the program.

Frequently Asked Questions (FAQ)

A compilation of often asked questions (and the answers) on a specific topic.

gateway

A functional unit that connects a local data network with another network having different protocols. See also *proxy*.

gateway program

A CGI program written in a programming language, such as C and C++.

Gopher

The protocol, developed at the University of Minnesota, that provides a menu-driven interface for accessing files and information on other computers.

Graphic Interchange Format (GIF)

An image format developed by CompuServe that uses a compression method, called LZW, patented by Unisys.

graphic streaming

See *image streaming*.

history list

A document or list that contains hypertext links to all the documents, files, and resources that you have visited since you started your browser.

host

A computer, connected to a network, that provides an access point to that network. A host can be a client, a server, or a client and server simultaneously. See also *local host* and *remote host*.

host name

The symbolic name assigned to a host on the Internet. Host names are resolved to IP addresses through a domain name server.

home page

The initial HTML document that is displayed when a Web site is accessed, typically the default page of the server. Also called a *welcome page*.

hot list

A document or list that contains hypertext links to user-defined documents, files, or other Web resources. Also called a *quicklist*.

htimage

The program associated with CERN servers that processes information passed from image maps. See also *image map*.

hypermedia

Text, images, and other elements, such as video and audio clips, that are linked together through hypertext links.

hypertext

The concept (and practice) of linking nodes of related on-line information. The origin of the concept of hypertext is attributed to Vannevar Bush. The first use of the term, hypertext, is attributed to Ted Nelson.

Hypertext Markup Language (HTML)

The language used to create hypertext documents. Hypertext documents include links to other documents that contain additional information about the highlighted term or subject.

Hypertext Transfer Protocol (HTTP)

The protocol used to transfer and display hypertext documents.

Hypertext Transfer Protocol daemon (HTTPD)

The basis for a program that runs on a Web server and enables the server to respond to HTTP requests.

icon

A graphical representation of an object (a file or program), consisting of an image, image background, and label.

image map

An image that contains defined areas that link to different documents. Imagemap is also the name of the program associated with NCSA servers that processes information passed from such images.

image streaming

A technology used by many Web browsers that allows you to scroll through a document even before all of the images are received and displayed.

interactive

Pertaining to a program or a system that alternately accepts input and then responds. An interactive system is conversational; that is, a continuous dialog exists between user and system.

interlaced image

An image stored in a format that allows the image to be sent and displayed in a series of layers, improving performance and resulting in a fade-in effect at the browser.

International Organization for Standardization (ISO)

An organization of national standards bodies from various countries established to promote development of standards to facilitate international exchange of goods and services, and develop cooperation in intellectual, scientific, technological, and economic activity.

Internet

A wide area network connecting thousands of disparate networks in industry, education, government, and research. The Internet network uses TCP/IP as the standard for transmitting information.

internet address

The unique 32-bit address identifying each device or workstation in the Internet. Also known as IP address.

Internet Architecture Board (IAB)

The technical committee that oversees the development of the Internet suite of protocols that are known as TCP/IP.

Internet Protocol (IP)

A connectionless protocol that routes data through a network or interconnected networks. IP acts as an intermediary between the higher protocol layers and the physical network.

interpreted highlighting

Tags that allow the browser to determine how the surrounded text should be displayed, such as emphasis (EM) or variable (VAR).

Joint Photographic Experts Group (JPEG)

An image format developed by the ISO Joint Photographic Experts Group. It is best suited to true color images, such as scanned photographs.

kiosk mode

SPRY's name for presentation mode. See *presentation mode*.

local area network (LAN)

A network in which communications usually cover a moderate-sized geographic area, such as a single office building, warehouse, or campus, and that does not extend across public rights-of-way.

local host

The computer you are using to access the Internet. See also *remote host*.

logical network

The abstract organization overlaid on one or more physical networks. The Internet is an example of a logical network.

mail server

A computer on the Internet that is a repository for electronic mail. Mail is stored here until the intended user has received it.

mailto

A protocol used on the Web to send electronic mail.

map file

The file associated with an image that contains definitions of selectable areas and the URL associated with each area. See also *image map*.

mapping

The process of relating Internet (IP) addresses to physical addresses in the network. Mapping is also the process of relating symbolic names to Internet resources.

mark

A method of highlighting text or graphics that you want to perform clipboard actions on (cut, copy, paste, or delete).

markup language

A set of tags, or codes, included in a document that indicate how a document is to be formatted.

menu bar

The highlighted area at the top of the panel that contains the choices currently available in the application program that you are running.

MiniWeb

With NaviPress, a utility that allows you to see the relationships of your linked documents. In a MiniWeb, documents and images are represented as icons, and the relationships, or links, between them are represented by arrows.

modem (modulator/demodulator)

A device that converts digital data from a computer to an analog signal that can be transmitted on a telecommunications line, and converts the analog signal received to data for the computer.

morph

An image that transforms into another image.

mouse

A device that is used to move a pointer on the screen and select items.

multimedia

The combination of two or more communications media, such as text and animation.

Multiple Virtual Storage (MVS)

The operating system that manages System/390 computers.

Multipurpose Internet Mail Extensions (MIME)

A protocol that defines how information, such as binary files and multimedia, can be included in electronic mail.

Musical Instrument Digital Interface (MIDI)

A protocol that allows musical instruments to communicate with one another. MIDI has also been adapted to allow computers to record the output from musical instruments.

name server

A host that provides name resolution for a network. Name servers translate symbolic names assigned to networks and hosts into the Internet (IP) addresses used by machines.

National Science Foundation Network (NFSNET)

A collection of local, regional, and midlevel networks in the United States that are connected by a high-speed backbone. NFSNET provides scientists access to a number of computers across the country.

National Information Center (NIC)

In Internet communications, the local, regional, and national groups throughout the world who provide assistance, documentation, training, and other services for the Internet.

network

A configuration of data processing devices (computers, printers, routers, etc.) connected for the purpose of sharing resources and for information exchange. See also *physical network* and *logical network*.

network news transfer protocol (NNTP)

The protocol used to access, open, and post information maintained on news servers.

news

A protocol used on the Web to access newsgroups.

newsgroup

A collection of articles in the USENet that fall under a certain topic. For example, there are newsgroups about baking, computing, law, sports, and so forth.

news server

A computer on the Internet that is a repository for the news database.

node

In writing, the discrete chunks of information, which, when linked together, form a hypertext document.

Operating System/2 (OS/2)

An IBM licensed program that can be used as the operating system for personal computers. OS/2 can perform multiple tasks at the same time.

OpenGL

A standard API used in the development of 3D image applications. OpenGL is licensed by Silicon Graphics and controlled by the OpenGL Architecture Review Board.

packet

A unit or block of data for one transaction between a client and a server. Packets are the exchange medium used on the Internet to send and receive data.

parameter

A variable used in conjunction with a command to affect its result.

parse

To analyze the operands entered with a command and create a parameter list in the command processor from the information.

path

A statement that indicates where a file is stored on a particular drive. The path consists of all the directories that must be opened to get to a particular file. The directory names are separated by the backslash (\).

persistent caching

The act of holding documents and images in cache during and between browser sessions.

physical network

The hardware (computers, printers, routers, etc.) that makes up a network.

port

An end point for communication between applications, generally referring to a logical connection. A port provides queues for sending and receiving data. Each port has a port number for identification. When the port number is combined with an Internet address, it is called a socket address.

PostScript

A standard specified by Adobe Systems, Inc., that defines how text and graphics are presented on printers.

presence provider

A company or organization with access to the Internet who, for a fee, will allow you to store HTML documents on their server for the purpose of establishing a presence on the Web or Internet.

Presentation Manager (PM)

A component of OS/2 that provides a complete graphics-based user interface, with pull-down windows, menu bars, and layered menus.

presentation mode

In Web browsers, a mode that provides the maximum viewing space. The window frame, including the title bar, menu bar, and tool bar, are hidden.

process

A function that can be performed; any operation or combination of operations performed on data.

protocol

The set of rules governing the operation of functional units of a communication system if communication is to take place. Protocols can determine low-level details of machine-to-machine interfaces, such as the order in which bits from a byte are sent; they can also determine high-level exchanges between application programs, such as file transfer.

proxy

A server that forwards requests and responses on behalf of the client. Typically, a proxy server enables communication between clients located on an internal protected network and servers located on an external network, such as the Internet. See also *firewall*.

public domain

An abstract region of the Internet that contains documents and programs available for public use without charge. Files stored on the Internet that are available freely for others to use are said to be part of the public domain.

push button

A rectangle labeled with text or graphics or both. Push buttons are used in windows for actions that occur immediately when the push button is selected.

quicklist

See *hot list*.

radio button

A circle with associated text that represents a choice. Radio buttons are mutually exclusive; you can select only one in a set. When you select a radio button, the center becomes filled. In HTML, a form element that produces a selectable circle associated with a choice. See also *check box*.

raster

In images, a file format in which the image is stored as a collection of dots or pixels. See also *vector*.

README file

A file containing information and instructions for using the associated program or programs. Most freeware and shareware come with a README file.

relative URL

A partial URL that contains only the location (directory and file name) of a document in relation to the location of the current document. See also *absolute URL*.

remote host

Any host on the Internet other than the (local) host you are using. See also *local host*.

Request For Comments (RFCs)

In Internet communications, the document series that describes the Internet suite of protocols.

resource mapping rules

Statements contained in a server's configuration file that associates the real path to a document or resource with an alias. Resource mapping is useful for maintaining a virtual hierarchy of Web documents and resources that is independent of the physical structure of the server.

root URL

The protocol and server portion of the URL of a document. For example, in http://www.ibm.com/Overview.html, http://www.ibm.com/ is the root URL.

router

A device that connects two or more networks having the same protocols and determines the path of network traffic based on the most efficient route available.

server

A computer that provides shared services to other computers over a network; for example, a file server, a print server, or a mail server.

service provider

A company or organization with access to the Internet who, for a fee, will allow you to connect to their network to access the Internet.

simple mail transfer protocol (SMTP)

An application protocol used to transfer mail among users of the Internet.

shareware

Programs on the Internet that users can download and try for free. After a specified "trial period," users are expected to register with the author of the program and usually pay a small fee for continued use of the program.

standard input (stdin)

A mechanism used to pass information to a program, such as a CGI program. Standard input is used to send information from forms that use the PUT method to CGI programs. Other mechanisms for passing information to a CGI program are *environment variables* and *command line input*.

standard output (stdout)

A mechanism for passing information from a program. Standard output is used to pass information from a CGI program to a Web server.

stateless

In client/server technology, a category of protocols that maintain the connection between the client and server only as long as is necessary to process a request. Once the request is processed, the connection is ended. Subsequent requests require a new connection to be established.

static document

An HTML document for which the source is stored on a Web server. See also *dynamic document*.

subdirectory

A directory contained within another directory in a file system hierarchy.

Tag Image File Format (TIFF)

An image format developed by Aldus Corporation. It is designed to store raster images, such as screen captures and scanned images.

telnet

The terminal emulation protocol, a TCP/IP application protocol for remote connection service. Telnet allows a user at one site to gain access to a remote host as if the user's workstation were connected directly to that remote host.

template

An object or file that you can use as a model to create additional objects or files.

terminal emulator

A program that allows a device such as a microcomputer or personal computer to operate as if it were a particular type of terminal linked to a processing unit and to access data.

time stamp

The identification of the day and time when a file was created.

Transmission Control Protocol (TCP)

A communications protocol used in the Internet. TCP provides reliable host-to-host exchange of information. It uses IP as the underlying protocol.

Transmission Control Protocol/Internet Protocol (TCP/IP)

A suite of protocols designed to allow communication between networks regardless of the communication technologies used in each network.

transparent image

An image, typically a GIF, in which the background takes on the background color of the browser.

uniform resource locator (URL)

A statement that indicates the location of an item on the Web. It includes the protocol followed by the fully-qualified host name, and can include the path and file name.

URL-encoded

The format used to pass information between a client (browser) and a server as part of a URL string. Used primarily to pass information to Web servers for processing by a CGI program.

User Network (USENet)

The network of newsgroups maintained on news servers around the world.

vector

In images, a file format in which the image is stored as a collection of complete objects, such as lines and circles, rather than as dots or pixels. See also *raster*.

video clip

A file that contains segments of recorded visual information.

virtual reality

An interactive simulation of a concept or situation. Virtual reality usually includes animation, video, and audio.

Virtual Reality Modeling Language (VRML)

A specification, developed by Tony Parisi and Gavin Bell, for the development of virtual reality on the Web.

Virtual Machine (VM)

A virtual data processing system that appears to be at the exclusive disposal of a particular user, but whose functions are accomplished by sharing the resources of a real data processing system.

welcome page

See *home page*.

wide area network (WAN)

A data communications network designed to serve an area of hundreds or thousands of miles.

window

An area of the screen with visible boundaries within which information is displayed. A window can be smaller than or the same size as the screen. Windows can appear to overlap on the screen.

working directory

The directory in which an application program is found. The working directory becomes the current directory when the application is started.

World Wide Web

The network of Web servers that contain programs and files, many of them hypertext documents that contain links to other documents on Web servers.

Bibliography

Barrett, Edward. *Text ConText and Hypertext: Writing with and for the Computer* (Cambridge, Mass.: The MIT Press, 1988).

Barrett, Edward. *The Society of Text: Hypertext, Hypermedia, and the Social Construction of Information* (Cambridge, Mass.: The MIT Press, 1989).

Bolter, Jay David. *Writing Space: The Computer, Hypertext, and the History of Writing* (Hillsdale, N.J.: Lawrence Erlbaum Associates, Inc., 1991).

Hodges, Matthew E. and Russell M. Sasnett. *Multimedia Computing: Case Studies from MIT Project Athena* (Reading, Mass.: Addison Wesley Publishing Company, 1993).

Nielsen, Jakob. *Multimedia and Hypertext: the Internet and Beyond* (Boston, Mass.: AP Professional, 1995).

Nyce, James M. and Paul Kahn. *From Memex to Hypertext: Vannevar Bush and the Mind's Machine* (Boston, Mass.: Harcourt Brace Jovanovich, Publishers, 1991).

Acronyms

API

Application Programming Interface

ACL

Access Control List

AIX

Advanced Interactive Executive

ARPA

Advanced Research Projects Agency

ASCII

American National Standard Code for Information Interchange

CERN

Conseil Europeen pour la Recherche Nucleaire (European Laboratory for Particle Physics)

CGI

Common Gateway Interface

CGM

Computer Graphics Metafile

CMS

Conversational Monitoring System

DEC

Digital Equipment Corporation

DOD

Department of Defense

FAQ

frequently asked questions

FTP

File Transfer Protocol

GIF

Graphic Interchange Format

HMD

head-mounted display

HTML

Hypertext Markup Language

HTTP

Hypertext Transfer Protocol

IAB

Internet Architecture Board

IBM

International Business Machines

ISO

International Standards Organization

JPEG

Joint Photographic Experts Group

LZW

Lempel-Zev-Welch

MIDI

Musical Instrument Digital Interface

MIME

Multipurpose Internet Mail Extensions

MPEG

Moving Picture Experts Group

MVS

Multiple Virtual Storage

NCSA

National Center for Supercomputing Applications

PRPQ

Programming Request for Price Quotation

QBIC

Query By Image Content

RFC

Request for Comments

RGB

red green blue

SGI

Silicon Graphics Incorporated

SGML

Standard Generalized Markup Language

S-HTTP

Secure Hypertext Transfer Protocol

SMTP

Simple Mail Transfer Protocol

SQL

Structured Query Language

SSL

Secure Sockets Layer

TCP/IP

Transmission Control Protocol/Internet Protocol

TIFF

Tag Image File Format

TSO

Time Sharing Option

URI

Universal Resource Identifier

URL

Uniform Resource Locator

VM

Virtual Machine

VRML

Virtual Reality Modeling Language

WIT

WWW Interactive Talk

WWW

World Wide Web

Index

IDG BOOKS WORLDWIDE LICENSE AGREEMENT

Important — read carefully before opening the software packet. This is a legal agreement between you (either an individual or an entity) and IDG Books Worldwide, Inc. (IDG). By opening the accompanying sealed packet containing the software disc, you acknowledge that you have read and accept the following IDG License Agreement. If you do not agree and do not want to be bound by the terms of this Agreement, promptly return the book and the unopened software packet(s) to the place you obtained them for a full refund.

1. License. This License Agreement (Agreement) permits you to use one copy of the enclosed Software program(s) on a single computer. The Software is in "use" on a computer when it is loaded into temporary memory (i.e., RAM) or installed into permanent memory (e.g., hard disk, CD-ROM, or other storage device) of that computer.

2. Copyright. The entire contents of this disc and the compilation of the Software are copyrighted and protected by both United States copyright laws and international treaty provisions. You may only (a) make one copy of the Software for backup or archival purposes, or (b) transfer the Software to a single hard disk, provided that you keep the original for backup or archival purposes. The individual programs on the disc are copyrighted by the authors of each program respectively. Each program has its own use permissions and limitations. To use each program, you must follow the individual requirements and restrictions detailed for each in Appendix B of this Book. Do not use a program if you do not want to follow its Licensing Agreement. None of the material on this disc or listed in this Book may ever be distributed, in original or modified form, for commercial purposes.

3. Other Restrictions. You may not rent or lease the Software. You may transfer the Software and user documentation on a permanent basis provided you retain no copies and the recipient agrees to the terms of this Agreement. You may not reverse engineer, decompile, or disassemble the Software except to the extent that the foregoing restriction is expressly prohibited by applicable law. If the Software is an update or has been updated, any transfer must include the most recent update and all prior versions. Each shareware program has its own use permissions and limitations. These limitations are contained in the individual license agreements that are on the software disc. The restrictions include a requirement that after using the program for a period of time specified in its text, the user must pay a registration fee or discontinue use. By opening the package which contains the software disc, you will be agreeing to abide by the licenses and restrictions for these programs. Do not open the software package unless you agree to be bound by the license agreements.

4. Limited Warranty. IDG warrants that the Software and disc are free from defects in materials and workmanship for a period of sixty (60) days from the date of purchase of this Book. If IDG receives notification within the warranty period of defects in material or workmanship, IDG will replace the defective disc. IDG's entire liability and your exclusive remedy shall be limited to replacement of the Software, which is returned to IDG with a copy of your receipt. This Limited Warranty is void if failure of the Software has resulted from accident, abuse, or misapplication. Any replacement Software will be warranted for the remainder of the original warranty period or thirty (30) days, whichever is longer.

5. No Other Warranties. To the maximum extent permitted by applicable law, IDG and the author disclaim all other warranties, express or implied, including but not limited to implied warranties of merchantability and fitness for a particular purpose, with respect to the Software, the programs, the source code contained therein and/or the techniques described in this Book. This limited warranty gives you specific legal rights. You may have others which vary from state/jurisdiction to state/jurisdiction.

6. No Liability For Consequential Damages. To the extent permitted by applicable law, in no event shall IDG or the author be liable for any damages whatsoever (including without limitation, damages for loss of business profits, business interruption, loss of business information, or any other pecuniary loss) arising out of the use of or inability to use the Book or the Software, even if IDG has been advised of the possibility of such damages. Because some states/jurisdictions do not allow the exclusion or limitation of liability for consequential or incidental damages, the above limitation may not apply to you.

7. U.S.Government Restricted Rights. Use, duplication, or disclosure of the Software by the U.S. Government is subject to restrictions stated in paragraph (c) (1) (ii) of the Rights in Technical Data and Computer Software clause of DFARS 252.227-7013, and in subparagraphs (a) through (d) of the Commercial Computer—Restricted Rights clause at FAR 52.227-19, and in similar clauses in the NASA FAR supplement, when applicable.

Replacement Discs. If a replacement CD-ROM is needed, please write to the following address: IDG Books Disc Fulfillment Center, ATTN: *IBM's Official Guide to Building a Better Web Site*, IDG Books Worldwide, 7260 Shadeland Station, Indianapolis, IN 46256, or call 800-762-2974.

Installation Instructions

This CD contains the following:

Sample CGI programs

The \SAMPLES\ subdirectory contains five sample CGI programs (some in Perl, some in REXX). These programs are described in Appendix D, "Samples."

HTML templates

The \SAMPLES\ subdirectory also contains five HTML documents that you can use as templates to create your own HTML documents. These HTML templates are described in Appendix D, "Samples."

A Web resource list

The \SAMPLES\ subdirectory contains an HTML document that provides links to more than 60 HTML documents that contain information about writing for the Web and establishing a Web site.

To access this list from your Web browser, specify the following URL:
`file:///f:/samples/wwwres.htm`
where f is your CD-ROM drive.

An HTML version of "IBM's Official Guide to Building a Better Web Site"

The \BOOK\ subdirectory contains an HTML version of this book, complete with graphics and links to all the programs, products, and services mentioned in the book.

To access this document from your Web browser, specify the following URL:
`file:///f:/book/wwwtoc.htm`
where f is your CD-ROM drive.

A multimedia demo of the IBM Internet Connection Servers

To install this demo from the Windows Run command type:
`f:\demo\setup.exe`
where f is your CD-ROM drive.

IDG BOOKS WORLDWIDE REGISTRATION CARD

RETURN THIS REGISTRATION CARD FOR FREE CATALOG

Title of this book: IBM's Official Guide To Building A Better Web Site

My overall rating of this book: ❏ Very good [1] ❏ Good [2] ❏ Satisfactory [3] ❏ Fair [4] ❏ Poor [5]

How I first heard about this book:

❏ Found in bookstore; name: [6]

❏ Advertisement: [8]

❏ Word of mouth; heard about book from friend, co-worker, etc.: [10]

❏ Book review: [7]

❏ Catalog: [9]

❏ Other: [11]

What I liked most about this book:

What I would change, add, delete, etc., in future editions of this book:

Other comments:

Number of computer books I purchase in a year: ❏ 1 [12] ❏ 2-5 [13] ❏ 6-10 [14] ❏ More than 10 [15]

I would characterize my computer skills as: ❏ Beginner [16] ❏ Intermediate [17] ❏ Advanced [18] ❏ Professional [19]

I use ❏ DOS [20] ❏ Windows [21] ❏ OS/2 [22] ❏ Unix [23] ❏ Macintosh [24] ❏ Other: [25]_____
(please specify)

I would be interested in new books on the following subjects:
(please check all that apply, and use the spaces provided to identify specific software)

❏ Word processing: [26]

❏ Data bases: [28]

❏ File Utilities: [30]

❏ Networking: [32]

❏ Other: [34]

❏ Spreadsheets: [27]

❏ Desktop publishing: [29]

❏ Money management: [31]

❏ Programming languages: [33]

I use a PC at (please check all that apply): ❏ home [35] ❏ work [36] ❏ school [37] ❏ other: [38] _____

The disks I prefer to use are ❏ 5.25 [39] ❏ 3.5 [40] ❏ other: [41]_____

I have a CD ROM: ❏ yes [42] ❏ no [43]

I plan to buy or upgrade computer hardware this year: ❏ yes [44] ❏ no [45]

I plan to buy or upgrade computer software this year: ❏ yes [46] ❏ no [47]

Name: _____ Business title: [48] _____ Type of Business: [49]

Address (❏ home [50] ❏ work [51]/Company name: _____)

Street/Suite# _____

City [52]/State [53]/Zipcode [54]: _____ Country [55] _____

❏ **I liked this book!** You may quote me by name in future
IDG Books Worldwide promotional materials.

My daytime phone number is _____

IDG BOOKS

THE WORLD OF COMPUTER KNOWLEDGE

❏ YES!

Please keep me informed about IDG's World of Computer Knowledge.
Send me the latest IDG Books catalog.